DATE DUE

| | | | |
|---|---|---|---|
| Mar 31 '71 | | | |
| Apr 20 '71 | | | |
| May 4 '71 | | | |
| Nov 29 '82 | | | |
| | | | |
| | | | |
| | | | |
| | | | |
| | | | |
| | | | |
| | | | |
| GAYLORD M-2 | | | PRINTED IN U.S.A. |

# The Unrepentant Pilgrim

*A Study of the Development of Bernard Shaw*

# The Unrepentant Pilgrim

*A Study of the Development of Bernard Shaw*

J. Percy Smith

Houghton Mifflin Company · Boston
The Riverside Press · Cambridge
1965

W

*First Printing*


*Library of Congress Catalog Card Number: 65–16950*

*Printed in the United States of America*

For: Kevin
Rhonda
Valerie
Sylvia

"*. . . and though with great difficulty I am got hither, yet now I do not repent me of all the trouble I have been at to arrive where I am.*"

Pilgrim's Progress

# *Acknowledgments*

It is not possible to thank individually each person who helps in the writing of a book: as Shaw's most famous heroine observes, "God does not allow the whole truth to be told." I hope therefore that those whom I have failed to name in what follows will understand and forgive.

My first thanks must go to two splendid teachers who more than anyone initiated and fostered my first interest in Shaw, many years ago: Professors (now, alas, Dean and Professor Emeritus respectively) Carlyle King, of the University of Saskatchewan, and Benjamin H. Lehman, of the University of California, Berkeley. To the former especially I owe a debt of gratitude for his mercifully ruthless reading of the first draft, and for countless perceptive suggestions made in conversations through our years as colleagues. I should like to thank Professors D. R. Cherry, of the University of Saskatchewan; R. D. Chambers, of Trent University; Josephine Miles, of the University of California, Berkeley; and Mr. Ralph Arnold and Mr. Lovat Dickson, of London; all for help most generously provided. I thank the Canada Council, which awarded me a senior fellowship that enabled me to spend a year in England working on the Shaw papers; and the staff of the Manuscript Room of the British Museum, and Mr. Allen, of the library of the London School of Economics, who were most efficiently cooperative. To Mrs. Carole McGinley I owe a debt of gratitude for typing the manuscript. Parts of Chapters 8 and 9 have already appeared in print in an earlier form, and I thank the editors of the *Yale Review* and *The Tamarack Review*, and Messrs. W. J. Gage, Limited, for their generous permission to use here material that has already been published by them. I thank also Random House, Inc., for permission to use a brief quotation from Robinson Jeffers's poem "Meditation on Saviors," in *The Selected Poetry of Robinson Jeffers* (New York, 1937).

Finally, I should like especially to thank those connected with the Shaw Estate for their great helpfulness in allowing me to quote abundantly from both published and unpublished writings by Shaw. Details as to individual works are made throughout the book. But to the Public Trustee and the Society of Authors, and particularly to Miss Philippa MacLiesh, I here tender my grateful thanks.

J.P.S.

# *Contents*

# The Unrepentant Pilgrim

*A Study of the Development of Bernard Shaw*

# I

# *A Shabby Genteel Boyhood*

As we move further away from the lifetime of George Bernard Shaw, it is evident that the image of him which remains in the public mind is the one caught by Max Beerbohm's famous cartoon: the Mephistophelian one. Even in late photographs of him, the direct, sharp, impudently questioning eyes, the fierce white beard and shaggy upturned eyebrows, the mocking, arrogant mouth, the lithe, erect frame, with head tilted slightly back, all somehow combine to convey an impression of simultaneous vanity and otherworldliness. The otherworldiness might suggest the saint; but saints are not allowed the luxury of vanity; and so we plump instead for the devil. To do so increases Shaw's entertainment value; and it has the additional merit of giving us the soundest possible reason for ignoring anything serious that he may say.

There is no doubt that Shaw is partly responsible for fixing the image. He would, it is true, sometimes make fun of his own appearance, as when, in an essay in which he spoke of the magnificent beard and apostolic presence of H. M. Hyndman, he observed:

> My own beard is so like a tuft of blanched grass that pet animals have nibbled at it.[1]

[1] *Pen Portraits and Reviews*, p. 131. All references to Shaw's published works are to the Standard Edition (London: Constable and Company Limited) unless otherwise stated.

But his love of being photographed suggests no such modesty. One might guess that if only one copy of each photograph taken of him could be secured, there would be enough to paper that Shavian shrine, the Reading Room of the British Museum. Augustus John tells in his autobiography about driving through the Irish countryside in the company of Shaw, who talked brilliantly most of the time. But whenever he saw that they were approaching a village he would suddenly cease, and sit up and adjust his clothing in the full expectation of being asked for his snapshot. Bertrand Russell, who at the beginning of this century was Shaw's companion on many a Socialist occasion, commented recently:

> Shaw felt nothing but vanity. That was the whole of him. There was nothing more.[2]

We may admit the vanity, then. But Shaw is responsible for the image in another way. One object of the Shavian mission was to challenge vigorously, by every means in his power, traditional dogma and accepted morality. Since assaults on the sacred citadels of society must logically be inspired by the official Enemy, Shaw candidly declared himself on the Devil's side; and so invited the diabolist interpretation. The device had its advantages, it is true; but its drawbacks become clearer each year. It is all too easy — as the manufacturers of movies and "musicals" have discovered — to accept the fun that his crackling wit and unfailing high spirits provide, then cheatingly to shrug off, distort, or even excise the core of meaning without which the fun would not have existed.

The truth — which the Mephistophelian image too readily

[2] *Speaking Personally*, a record released by Nonesuch Records. Reported by Mordecai Richler in "Bertrand Russell Cuts a Disc," *MacLean's* (Dec. 16, 1961).

obscures — is that Shaw was concerned not with the destruction of religion but with its affirmation. It is strange that although he did his Shavian best to make this fact clear, his critics — with few exceptions — are not much disposed to take it seriously, and his biographers, embarrassed by it, tread round it nervously and with astonishing condescension. Even those writers who give it serious consideration see it almost exclusively in relation to *Man and Superman* and *Back to Methuselah*. When in the course of a letter to G. K. Chesterton in 1908 Shaw called himself a mystic, Chesterton accepted the description, and in his book on Shaw he used it, prefixing it with the adjective "pagan" to show that his own orthodoxy was intact. But even the Chestertonians seem not to have understood the point. Maisie Ward in her biography makes the astonishing assertion that Shaw was joyless, and goes on:

> Here comes the great parting of the two men's thought. G.K. believed in God and joy.[3]

Nor is much note taken of Shaw's comment that if he had to choose just one of the countless books and articles about him to be remembered by, it would be a brief essay in which are drawn the parallels between his thought and that of William Blake.[4]

I do not think that we can hope to understand Shaw or do him justice — whatever justice may be — until we first understand his religious belief, and recognize that it had the profoundest implications for him and that it underlay everything he wrote, at least from *Candida* onward — though it was taking shape much earlier. Successive writers, from W. B. Yeats

[3] Maisie Ward: *Gilbert Keith Chesterton* (New York: Sheed and Ward, 1943), p. 232.

[4] Irving Fiske: *Bernard Shaw's Debt to William Blake* ("Shavian Tract No. 2," published by The Shaw Society, London).

to J. B. Priestley, have commented on the apparent suddenness with which, in his late thirties, he burst on the literary and dramatic scene. Yeats sets the date as the opening night of *Arms and the Man* (1894):

> On the first night the whole pit and gallery, except certain members of the Fabian Society, started to laugh at the author, and then, discovering that they themselves were being laughed at, sat there not converted — their hatred was too bitter for that — but dumbfounded, while the rest of the house cheered and laughed. In the silence that greeted the author after the cry for a speech one man did indeed get his courage and boo loudly. "I assure the gentleman in the gallery," was Shaw's answer, "that he and I are of exactly the same opinion, but what can we do against a whole house who are of the contrary opinion?" And from that moment Bernard Shaw became the most formidable man of modern letters, and even the most drunken of medical students knew it.[5]

Shaw himself liked to encourage the impression that when opportunity at last presented itself he "rose like a rocket," and indeed there is no denying the speed of the ascent.

Yet the phenomenon cannot be explained in simple terms of slow maturation or lack of earlier opportunities, long though Shaw's apprenticeship undoubtedly was. It is clear that in a period of several years — perhaps almost a decade — before the moment mentioned by Yeats, he experienced what was in effect a slow religious conversion. There was nothing dramatic about it: the habit of searching analysis that he adopted in boyhood must have led him to contest every step. Moreover, the process was complicated by the fact that his social-

[5] W. B. Yeats: *Autobiographies* (London: Macmillan, 1955), p. 231.

ism was a part of it; probably for a time it seemed the most important part.

If we are to understand Shaw the mature playwright, the artist-philosopher, it is essential that we look carefully at his earlier life and try to see the nature of the change that took place in him. The release of his notebooks, diaries, manuscripts, letters, and other papers, to the British Museum and the London School of Economics, coupled with the results of Mr. Dan H. Laurence's somewhat frantic collecting activities, makes it possible to do so more closely than the various biographies did. I propose therefore, on the basis of these materials, to consider Shaw's early life and background, his apprenticeship to letters, and his work as a socialist; then to examine the course of his religious belief and the creed at which he arrived; and to show how that faith affected his writing and brought him to drama. The study will help not only to modify the Mephistophelian image, but to throw light on the troubled question of the relation between the man Bernard Shaw and the role of G.B.S. that he played on the stage of the world. For the question inevitably occurs, whether what Shaw arrived at was not a kind of made-to-measure religion, whether he was not engaged unconsciously in creating God in his own image. This is not to question his integrity — but certainly it raises questions about his claim to mysticism. He himself seems sometimes to have thought of his religion as one especially designed to suit his own needs and make him complete. Looking back on his first years in London, he wrote:

> I had the intellectual habit; and my natural combination of critical faculty with literary resource needed only a clear comprehension of life in the light of an intelligible theory: in short, a religion, to set it in triumphant operation. It was the

lack of this last qualification that lamed me in those early days . . .[6]

The general facts of Shaw's early life are familiar. His half-jocular claim to descent from the Macduff who figured in Shakespeare may be ignored, though unquestionably some of the truths about his relatives are a good deal stranger than that fiction. In the 1880's he used from time to time to regale William Morris's wife with stories of them, including one about a great-uncle who committed suicide by the novel device of shutting his head in a carpet-bag. Obviously the vein of eccentricity in the family ran deep. What is perhaps more important is that both Shaw's parents came from families of what Hardy called "decayed gentility." Like his contemporary Yeats, he was born in the aristocratic tradition in Ireland; though by the time he arrived, there was about the Shaws — to use the expression he coined — a good deal of the "downstart." Nevertheless the tradition exercised its influence of bigoted, inverted provinciality:

> This society was not only violent and odd. It was also exclusive. At a time when its English counterpart was opening up to anyone who had sufficient money to oil the lock, it still maintained a strong contempt for trade. My own grandmother . . . was disowned by her family for marrying an Englishman, the head of a respectable firm of chemists, while Yeats himself rejoiced that he inherited "blood that has not passed through any huckster's loins,"

writes C. Day Lewis.[7]

[6] *Immaturity*, Preface, p. xliv.

[7] C. Day Lewis: "A Note on W. B. Yeats and the Aristocratic Tradition," in *Scattering Branches*, ed. Stephen Gwynn (New York: Macmillan, 1940), p. 162.

Shaw's father, George Carr Shaw, was one of many children of a businessman who, in one disastrous moment, fell from affluence to bankruptcy. George, an amiable young man with no training of any sort, was interceded for by an influential (and solvent) relative and given a pension. This he capitalized promptly, investing the sum realized in a partnership in a wholesale firm; then, since neither he nor his partner had any capacity for business, they proceeded slowly down the long road towards bankruptcy, their progress being undoubtedly aided by George's drinking habits.

Shaw's mother, Lucinda Elizabeth, had been brought up by her grand-aunt, who had determined that she should be "unquestionably ladylike," and from whose intransigent policies Lucinda fled at the first opportunity. She was, as she herself said bitterly long afterward, "educated within an inch of my life," and trained to be a concert pianist without anyone's having the humanity to tell her that she lacked sufficient talent for such a career. Ladylike and educated, but entirely ignorant of everyday practicalities, she hastily accepted marriage with a man many years her senior, about whom she knew almost nothing except that he was the second cousin of a baronet, and superficially pleasant — and that his name was George Carr Shaw. Marriage with him soon turned out to mean in fact "shabby-genteel poverty with a drunken husband," with all the shame and torment of uncertainty and disgust that the phrase implies. It is not surprising that, remembering her own bitter childhood, she found what refuge she could in music and the company of musicians, and left the upbringing of her three children very largely in the hands of the illiterate servants whom the Shaws' gentility required even when their poverty could not afford them.

For it must be remembered that Shaw's childhood was by

no means a slum childhood, nor was his Dublin the Dublin of Sean O'Casey, with its hunger and disease, quick fears and slow deaths. The poverty was present, and it was increasing; but its cries were not those of starvation and crime. They resembled more the whispers that echoed in the house of the boy on the rocking horse, in D. H. Lawrence's story: "There must be more money! There must be more money!" The Shaw children, who in fact were never uncertain about their next meal, were not allowed to forget that the family background and connections were of the upper class. When they were small — before their father's drunken habits had made him a completely unreliable guest — they were taken on brief visits to Bushy Park, the seat of a more securely aristocratic branch of the family. And Shaw never forgot how his father lectured him on the distinction between people like themselves, who as wholesalers were of the gentry, and those who, as retailers — "in trade" — or artisans, were firmly beneath their notice.

There were other pretensions besides those of gentility, though allied to them: the pretensions of an "Established" but minority Protestantism in an overwhelmingly Roman Catholic country.

> Irish Protestantism was not then a religion: it was a side in political faction, a class prejudice, a conviction that Roman Catholics are socially inferior persons who will go to hell when they die and leave Heaven in the exclusive possession of Protestant ladies and gentlemen. In my childhood I was sent every Sunday to a Sunday-school where genteel little children repeated texts, and were rewarded with cards inscribed with them. After an hour of this we were marched into the adjoining church . . . to sit around the altar-rails and fidget there until our neighbors must have wished the

service over as heartily as we did. I suffered this, not for my salvation, but because my father's respectability demanded it.[8]

So Shaw wrote in 1898.

Decaying gentility, religious bigotry, growing poverty—these three strands stand out in the background pattern of Shaw's childhood. In the foreground, one sees a household in which the father is an amiable and ineffectual eccentric, so given to self-delusion that he believes himself a teetotaller with a horror of alcohol even though he is constantly more or less drunk; the mother is a woman brought up in a refinement that she recognizes to have been fraudulent, and bitterly disillusioned by her marriage; and any love that may have existed has turned to detestation on her part and easygoing indifference on his. Towards the three children the father's attitude is one of amiable regard, but little or no responsibility; while the mother preserves a kind of tolerant unconcern. There is little wonder that Mrs. Shaw, finding that marriage gave her more reason than leisure to repent, should have had little affection for her offspring. The surprising thing, as her son once remarked, is not that she endured her husband and tolerated her children for so many years, but that she did not hate them all. Instead, she sought refuge in the one place available, the world of music; and into its joyous sanctuary she carried with her her eldest daughter, Lucy, a bright and vivacious child. The second child, Agnes, was a sickly girl, whose role in the family is shadowy. The son, named after his father and a drunkard uncle who late in life substituted religious fanaticism for alcohol, was left in his early childhood to the doubtful ministrations of servants and the even more erratic ones of his

[8] *Sixteen Self-Sketches*, p. 45.

father; and later, to the unhelpful hands of a series of humdrum Dublin schoolteachers.

What force held together this family circle — so much more an irregular polygon than a circle — one may well wonder. But there was in fact something more vital than mere gravitation: there was music. One of the most important influences in the family therefore was a curious, eccentric "professor" of music, with a good deal of charlatanism in his makeup, who seems to have arrived on the scene like Prospero's musicians, out of the air; for no one has been able to trace his origins. Shaw's accounts of this man are probably inaccurate in some important respects, as H. G. Farmer has shown;[9] they nonetheless give an impression of his peculiar qualities and of his influence on the Shaws. His name was George John Lee — though subsequently, doubtless in the interest of polyphony as well as prestige, he transmuted this to G. J. Vandaleur Lee.

In one of his accounts[10] Shaw tells us of Lee's quarrel with the orthodox teachers of music, who had told him that there was a voice in the head, another in the chest, and a third in the throat. Thereupon Lee

> dissected birds, and with the connivance of medical friends, human subjects, in his search for these organs. He then told the teachers authoritatively that the three voices were fabulous, and that the voice was produced by a single instrument called the larynx. They replied that musical art had nothing to do with anatomy . . .

and so left Lee and his eccentricity with the best of the argument. Lee devised a method of singing based on his "discov-

[9] In *Bernard Shaw's Sister and her Friends* (Leiden: E. J. Brill, 1959).

[10] *London Music in 1888–89 as Heard by Corno Di Bassetto*, Preface, pp. 10–16.

ery," and apparently enjoyed some success in Dublin — though Shaw's account probably exaggerates this. For a time he lived in the next street to the Shaws; and Mrs. Shaw, from being one of his pupils, became his "musical factotum," for she was a skilled arranger and copyist. On the death of a brother with whom he had been living, Lee moved into the Shaws' house — or else, as is just possible, they moved in with him. He had, Shaw tells us, a "meteoric impact"

> with his music, his method, his impetuous enterprise and his magnetism, upon the little Shaw household where a thoroughly disgusted and disillusioned woman was suffering from a hopelessly disappointing husband and three uninteresting children . . . to say nothing of the humiliating inadequacy of my father's income. We never felt any affection for Lee; for he was too excessively unlike us, too completely a phenomenon, to rouse any primitive human feeling in us.

Lee's success was nevertheless such that he was able to buy a cottage overlooking the sea at Dalkey, which he presented to Mrs. Shaw — thereby providing her son with some intervals of supreme childhood happiness. Shaw denies that there was ever even a suggestion of impropriety in the relationship between Lee and Mrs. Shaw:

> Although he supplanted my father as the dominant factor in the household, and appropriated all the activity and interest of my mother, he was so completely absorbed in his musical affairs that there was no friction and hardly any intimate personal contact between the two men: certainly no unpleasantness.

A household in which there is music is likely to be one in which there are books. Whether the Shaw establishment was book-filled or the young George (he did not become Bernard until he reached mature manhood) began as a child his practice of haunting libraries we do not know. When he was middle-aged he could not remember a time when he did not read everything that came his way, with the exception of children's books; these — he recorded —

> from the accursed "Swiss Family Robinson" onwards, I always loathed and despised for their dishonesty, their hypocrisy, their sickly immorality, and their damnable dulness.[11]

His lifelong fondness for *Pilgrim's Progress* began when he was very young. It was one of the two "literary sensations" of his childhood, the other being the *Arabian Nights*. He was to recall that as a boy he knew all the characters of Shakespeare's plays, from Hamlet to Abhorson, much better than he knew the people about him. He told Chesterton of his early intimate knowledge of the world of Dickens. And in 1944 he recalled that in his teens he had "almost venerated" *Middlemarch*. There is nothing to suggest that his reading was in the least degree systematic; like most readers, no doubt, he forgot much more than he remembered. But reading and music were providing light and warmth in an environment that had much bitter bleakness in it.

It is difficult to say precisely what Shaw's relationship was to this strange household. He grew into a tall, thin youth, auburn-haired and rather pale, overshadowed in the family by his sister Lucy, ashamed of his father and ignored by his mother. Too intelligent and sensitive to be unaware of the real facts and equivocations of his family's position, he could not accept the institutionalized dishonesties, as he saw them, of school and church; and before he reached his teens he rebelled against them. His rebellion would perhaps have been a good

[11] "The Books of My Childhood," *T.P.'s Weekly* (Dec. 19, 1902).

deal more explosive than it was, but for the fact that the Shaws had given up churchgoing and assumed an attitude of indifference to the beliefs and opinions of their children, at least where religion was concerned; so that if there was little stability in the family, there was little repression of ideas. Moreover, the boy himself was full of the irrepressible, high-spirited energy not merely of youth but of genius — of Irish genius, quick to perceive the ludicrous, to seize it, and to inflate it through sheer delight until all other feelings were lost in laughter. This trait was heightened even more by his father's sense of anticlimax, which led the latter to roar with merriment — while his partner wept — over the discovery of staggering financial losses to their firm. It was heightened also by the "exhilarating exuberance" of the "Rabelaisian" Dr. Walter Gurley, Mrs. Shaw's brother, who visited the family between his voyages as a ship's doctor. In later years in London Shaw could not endure his Uncle Walter's company, and used to go into another room or slip out of the house to avoid meeting him, if possible; but as a youngster he found him an exciting companion.

Some of the best glimpses we have of Shaw in this period are provided by Edward Matthew McNulty, who was his boyhood friend. McNulty, who became a banker and a novelist, published in 1901 an article called "George Bernard Shaw as a Boy." [12] Among the incidents it relates is that of a cricket-match in the course of which McNulty sent a ball through a stained glass window in the nearby Roman Catholic chapel. For a moment awe-struck silence descended on the playground. Then

> suddenly came an unearthly scream of laughter, and we saw Shaw rolling on the ground in hysterics of delight.

[12] In *The Candid Friend* (July 6, 1901), p. 384.

McNulty tells also that when in their country walks he and Shaw came upon one of the many signs announcing that trespassers would be prosecuted, they invariably proceeded to cross the forbidden ground

> not from a spirit of bravado, but because of our conviction that though men might use land, they should not own it. The establishment of the Fabian Society was simply Shaw's roundabout way of reviving, in the minds of people, the elemental instinct for universal ownership.

Whether or not the boys in fact philosophized to this extent, the incidents reveal the comic response to anticlimax (which found solemnity irresistibly funny) and the methodical disrespect for self-constituted authority (which made mere conventionality impossible) that were to characterize the adult Shaw. W. B. Yeats, reflecting on this impish irreverence in Shaw's personality, found it characteristic of the Irish mind under certain environmental conditions:

> . . . Our minds, being sufficient to themselves, do not wish for victory but are content to elaborate our extravagance, if fortune aid, into wit or lyric beauty, and as for the rest 'There are nights when a king like Conchobar would spit upon his arm-ring and queens will stick out their tongues at the rising moon.' This habit of the mind has made Oscar Wilde and Mr. Bernard Shaw the most celebrated makers of comedy to our time, and if it has sounded plainer still in the conversation of the one, and in some few speeches of the other, that is but because they have not been able to turn out of their plays an alien trick of zeal picked up in struggling youth.[13]

[13] W. B. Yeats: *Synge and the Ireland of his Time* (Churchtown: Cuala Press, 1911), p. 34.

It is clear then that the young Shaw was finding a good deal of pleasure in activity and companionship; indeed, his friendship with McNulty was a very intimate one that lasted far into their adult life. There were other pleasures too: the music that surrounded him; the books that he devoured, unhampered by parental guidance; the pictures in the National Gallery of Ireland, which he and McNulty haunted; so that while he was still very young he had an astonishingly wide-ranging knowledge of literature and the arts. Yet he was going daily to one or another school where uninspired teachers attempted to funnel facts into his resisting brain, and his fellow pupils dealt, in typical schoolboy fashion — as he recalled much later — in evasiveness, tyranny, and smut. And he was living in a home where, though there was no outright unkindness or physical want, there was also no affection and little responsibility; where he felt himself continually overlooked; where the shadow of shameful defeat and poverty grew slowly darker.

It is not surprising that many decades later, when he looked back at this period, his comment was the bitter one that he made to Ellen Terry:

> Oh, a devil of a childhood, Ellen, rich only in dreams, frightful and loveless in realities.[14]

Interestingly, however, his comments are not consistent, for on another occasion he wrote:

> My family, though kindly, might be called loveless; but what did that matter to a child who could sing *A te O cara* and *Suone la tromba intrepida* before he was perfect in the

[14] *Ellen Terry and Bernard Shaw. A Correspondence* (London: Reinhardt and Evans, 1949), p. 196.

> Church Catechism. In these there was sentiment and chivalry enough for any child.[15]

But this is Shaw exercising a species of hindsight that was frequently called in to support the G.B.S. myth; and the argument will not hold. The worlds of art and of everyday life are not one and the same, as he himself often said. In a similar vein is his description of the distress he suffered as a result of the walks through the Dublin slums on which, as a small boy, he was taken by the servants. He explained the distress by saying that his "artist nature," which had required "beauty and refinement," was offended. Yet, as he was also to argue, the artist nature is not necessarily much concerned with beauty and refinement; and it is difficult not to conclude that the snobbish class-consciousness that had been drilled into him from the beginning of his life had a good deal more to do with his discomfort.

For Shaw could no more escape the effects of the forces of his childhood environment than other men can. Though he rebelled against some of them, and professed to be quite objective about them, they extended their influence over his life — as they do over all men's — in ways of which he was unaware. Thus his class-consciousness was expressed not only by snobbishness. In later years, he quite frankly admitted that he and his fellow Fabians were snobs, that he hated the poor, and that unlike his friend William Morris he could not be at ease among laborers who worked with their hands. It is equally significant that though he claimed that like Hamlet he lacked ambition, and though certainly no one has attacked the inequities and iniquities of capitalist society with more devastating vigor, he was nonetheless a success-worshiper. His he-

[15] *Sixteen Self-Sketches*. p. 69.

roes are the Undershafts and the Caesars, and the Colonel Lawrences and the Lenins; nor would Joan have been his heroine had she not succeeded before she was destroyed. He never had the slightest respect for the cheap success that is more often than not merely the result of luck or unscrupulousness — or of both; but success in the achievement or exercise of power, against hazards and difficulties — this he could not resist. That shrewd observer Augustus John tells of an occasion in 1945 when he was painting a portrait of Field Marshal Montgomery. The latter expressed some interest in meeting his fellow Irishman, whom John had also painted, and the artist offered to bring about an introduction. Shaw was then nearing ninety, but an invitation to come to one of Montgomery's sittings was extended in perfect confidence; and the painter tells us:

> Shaw consented to meet the General, for he admired success more than anything. Any man who knew his job could be sure of Shaw's approval.[16]

It is true that Shaw's deference to what William James called the bitch goddess was probably in part the effect of a reaction against his father's failure and ineffectuality. Clearly, as he passed from his early childhood and began to recognize his father for what he was, his feeling about him was one of increasing shame and disgust. One can only wonder how much unconscious resentment against him was expressed in his long effort to have the "George" in his name—by which he was called throughout his early life — superseded.

If we consider the more general effect of his unusual home environment, two or three points are at once clear. The child of a family in which there is neither conjugal nor parental

16 Augustus John: *Chiaroscuro* (London: Jonathan Cape, 1952), p. 274.

affection, and the ordinary conventionalities are largely disregarded, is bound to be a child of inexperience, the inexperience being reflected in his attitude towards those things. It may range from one of superstitious veneration for what he does not know, to denial that it has any value at all — since unfamiliarity sometimes breeds contempt. With Shaw it was the latter development that occurred. He was far too intelligent to be unaware of the facts of his family's situation, far too sensitive not to respond passionately. On the surface, his response took the form of endless scornful attacks on convention and on anything resembling sentiment, which he saw as mere devices by which men disguise the truth from each other and themselves, and nothing more. He himself dated the development from what — significantly — he called his "first moral lesson":

> The first moral lesson I can remember as a tiny child was the lesson of teetotalism, instilled by my father, a futile person you would have thought him. One night, when I was still about as tall as his boots, he took me out for a walk. In the course of it I conceived a monstrous suspicion. When I got home I stole to my mother and in an awestruck whisper said to her, "Mamma, I think Papa's drunk." She turned away with impatient disgust and said "When is he ever anything else?" I have never believed in anything since: then the scoffer began . . .[17]

But the development involved something else besides disillusionment, something equally profound: the two deepest passions — perhaps the only fully realized passions — of his nature, the passion for truth and the passion for freedom. Throughout his life he felt impelled to get to the bottom of

[17] *Ellen Terry and Bernard Shaw*, p. 196.

every idea that presented itself to him — a quality that those who worked with him commented on again and again. Beatrice Webb, who was not fond of Shaw, remarked of him:

> I have never known a man use his pen in such a workmanlike fashion, or acquire such a thoroughly technical knowledge upon any subject on which he gives an opinion.[18]

His passion for freedom was equally deep. He never lost his hatred of enforced restraint, whether of men or animals, and imprisonment seemed to him the supreme cruelty, far worse than death. In *Saint Joan*, it is the threat of solitary confinement that settles the Maid's mind for martyrdom.

There is another aspect of the matter that is no less important to one's understanding of Shaw. As we have seen, there were in the Shaw home — except perhaps in the boy's very early relationship with his father — no deep personal feelings of any kind, either of love or hate. Mrs. Shaw's response to her bitter disappointment in her marriage was not anger or hatred, but withdrawal into music. The escape may in itself have been admirable. One effect of the situation for her son, however, was that his inexperience of convention was matched by inexperience of the emotional give-and-take that is commonly provided by the family environment, and is perhaps its chief educative function to supply. The paradoxical upshot was that, though he was to devote a great deal of his life to attacks on "illusions" of all kinds, and to affirmations about "objective" reality, he grew up without ever coming to terms with the passional side of human nature, and indeed knew a good deal more about the warmth and passion of music than about the tides of life. These he mistrusted always.

[18] Beatrice Webb: *Our Partnership* (London: Longmans, Green, 1948), p. 38.

One of his most revealing sentences is one in which he comments on his mother's attitude to him in childhood:

> Her almost complete neglect of me had the advantage that I could idolize her to the utmost pitch of my imagination and had no sordid or disillusioning contacts with her.[19]

For Shaw, immediate contacts — physical contacts — between people always had something about them of the "sordid and disillusioning," because he never learned to accept the facts of the flesh. His rejection of them is expressed in his shuddering dislike of the world's Falstaffs; his scorn for the "tasteless vulgarity" of Freud; his strange indifference to, even denial of, grief — other people's or his own; his dream of an evolutionary Utopia inhabited by beings of pure intelligence. He did not altogether deny the demands of the flesh, but he was embarrassed and irritated by them. In 1898 in a letter to the woman with whom he was presently to form a marriage that was probably never consummated he wrote:

> Curse this cycling and country air; it revives my brute strength and brings unrest. I want a woman and a sound sleep. I am never happy except when I am worked to desperation in London and can eat only a little. I may be frantic, desperate, piteous with arrears and burdens; but I am never unhappy. What people call health — appetite, weight, beefiness — is a mistake. *Fragility is the only endurable condition.*[20]

The only truly satisfactory love affair, he was to argue, is one carried on by mail.

[19] *London Music in 1888–89*, Preface, p. 13.
[20] British Museum, Add. Mss. 46505, No. 91 (Italics mine).

In the early 1870's — probably 1872 — Mrs. Shaw and her two daughters left Dublin. The immediate reason was the illness of the second daughter, Agnes, who was suffering from tuberculosis and was taken to the Isle of Wight in the hope that her condition might improve. Very probably a second reason was that without the dynamic presence of Vandaleur Lee, who had moved to London, Mrs. Shaw found her husband — though he had suddenly turned teetotaller in fact as well as fancy — unendurable. For when Agnes died at Ventnor she made no effort to return to Dublin, but went with Lucy to live in London. There for a time they joined musical forces with Lee.

They left behind them in Dublin Mr. Shaw — moving slowly closer to bankruptcy — and his son, now working as a clerk in the office of a "highly genteel" firm of estate agents. He had entered it when he was sixteen, and soon seemed on the high road to success; but advancement in the business world was meaningless to him, and though he very quickly became chief cashier (a responsible post for a lad in his teens) he found no satisfaction there for the needs of his nature. These expressed themselves better through the lessons in operatic performance that he gave to the rest of the staff when the proprietor was absent; the arguments that arose with his fellow clerks through his attacks on religion, until they had to be forbidden; and the countless, laborious hours of piano lessons that he gave to himself after his mother's departure. In an office job he was a misfit — not because he lacked ambition, but because he had more of it than any amount of success in a world so alien could satisfy. On March 31, 1876, the day of the death of Agnes and a month after he had handed in his resignation, he left the firm and went to live with his mother and Lucy in London.

# 2
# *Decade of Discontent*

THE MOTIVES that sent Shaw to London were probably confused: restless dissatisfaction with the life he was leading, its scope too narrow for his needs; longing for the music that had filled his earlier years; dismay and disgust at the continuing decline of his father, who — so far as his effectiveness in the world was concerned — might as well have kept on drinking. There must also have been more positive forces. The passionate love of freedom that he had had since early childhood and the passion for truth that had led him to rebel against the empty formulas of church and school must have made the restraints and the shams of the business world equally abhorrent. His soul could not be fettered to an office stool, and for him there were no golden rules. The lies and monotony of commerce, the stuffy conventionalities of middle-class Dublin, were prison walls. London and music meant escape.

It was not money that drew him. Though in later years he drove many a hard bargain with publishers and theatrical producers, Shaw was never avaricious. He wanted money, for it was a symbol of success and a means to freedom; but he wanted it only on his own terms, and until they were fulfilled he was quite prepared to remain poor. Beatrice Webb described him as

> a fellow with a crank for not making money, except he can make it exactly as he chooses.[1]

[1] *Our Partnership*, p. 38.

He seems to have understood from the first the truth of Rousseau's observation that "it is too difficult to think nobly when we think for a livelihood." H. M. Hyndman, who tried to give Shaw a leg-up in journalism by introducing him to the editor of the *St. James's Gazette*, testified that

> nothing would induce Shaw to write below the high literary level he had set up for himself . . . I suppose if a man will persist in tearing up articles which were quite good enough, because he felt he could make them better . . . his literary conscience becomes a very hard taskmaster from the pecuniary point of view.[2]

When Shaw left Dublin he no doubt believed that his mother, who had a small income from some family property and a bequest of £4000, would be able to help him until a career worthy of his talents was opened to him; but it is grossly unfair to conclude, as a recent writer does, that

> it seems transparent that Shaw left the Liffey's banks so as to take the fullest advantage of his share — the three children had an equal interest — in the Whitcroft bequest.[3]

Our knowledge about his first eight years in London seems at first glance sketchy. Yet he kept to the end of his days a considerable number of letters from friends and associates, sometimes with draft copies of his replies, through which it is possible to learn a good deal about his life and personality in this period. In 1885 the record suddenly becomes much clearer, for at the opening of that year he began to keep a

[2] H. M. Hyndman: *Further Reminiscences* (London: Macmillan, 1912), p. 202.

[3] H. G. Farmer: *Bernard Shaw's Sister and her Friends* (Leiden: E. J. Brill, 1959), p. 33.

diary; and he continued to do so until the beginning of 1894, when it became a mere engagement book. He wrote it in shorthand, recording briefly the day-by-day events of his life — meetings with friends, lectures attended or given (or missed), meals eaten, hours of sleeping and waking. He did not write in it daily, often letting it go for a week or more and then bringing it up to date — with the result that he sometimes forgot what a day's activities had been. But his keeping it up at all was a remarkable achievement for a young man of his irregular habits.

The record provided by letters and diaries contains some interesting surprises for the reader who approaches it with the familiar G.B.S. image in mind, or with that of the young Shaw which he himself in his later years liked to conjure up. There is little to suggest the impoverished but self-sufficient and singleminded recluse, turning his back on society and working his way daily along the shelves of the British Museum reading room and nightly through his five novels, pausing only to attend a debate, give a lecture, or discuss Ibsen with William Archer. What the record reveals is less impressive, but more human: a young man of unusual ability and great charm who simply does not know what to do with himself — though he partly knows what not to do. Throughout this period one sees him to be a person with an almost hypochondriacal concern for his health, eccentric in his diet and irregular in his habits, subject to endless colds, neuralgia, headaches, toothaches, and general depression. Like other such people — one thinks of Samuel Johnson — he carries on an interminable battle against physical laziness, with the aid of alarm clocks old and new, a watch that he frequently sets wrongly, and an engagement book that he forgets to consult. Paradoxically, he combines with his hatred of getting out of bed a physical restlessness that — once he is up — sends him on walks about London which may last from two to seven hours and bring him home at any time of night. Eccentric though his habits are, he has an almost neurotic dependence on society — especially the company of women, for whom he has a particular attraction. He responds to society with a lighthearted gaiety and brilliance of conversation that not only makes him a delightful companion but enables him to forget his aimless discontent and depression. After spending an afternoon and evening in visiting three or four women friends one after another, he is only too likely to sit down after midnight and write letters to them all — in an obvious effort to prolong the state of mind which their company has induced. Through a large part of the period he is without any clear purpose in life, and the Shavian student who assumes that his intention was to become a man of letters comes with a shock on a note in the diary for 1885 to the effect that the writing Shaw is doing is obstructing his real mission!

It was of course the company of individual friends and acquaintances to which Shaw responded. His inexperience of social formalities together with his native rebelliousness made him thoroughly uncomfortable in the stiffer atmosphere of "polite" society. The effect was sometimes to make him a difficult guest:

> I owe you a debt of gratitude for some very agreeable visits [wrote one of his hostesses], only [sic]when you talk about religion, so please don't do it again.[4]

More often it was he himself who suffered — from pangs of diffidence and the fear of being thought a mere parvenu.

[4] British Museum, Shaw Papers for 1878.

Early in 1880 he met the Lawsons, a family prominent in London artistic and musical circles to whom he was greatly attracted. In the following January he received a letter from Mrs. Lawson inviting him to a dancing party at her house. The reply that he drafted after much painful rephrasing and editing not only conveys the diffidence he felt, but suggests its real source:

> I am certainly the most unfortunate of men, for I shall be engaged on Tuesday evening in a sordid matter of business, which will not be put off. What is worse, even if I were free, I should be afraid to accept your invitation, as I do not know how to dance, and am a more dispiriting object in a drawing-room than I am — as you know — at a supper table; because I could unquestionably eat if I liked, whereas I could not accomplish a waltz for the sake of the most attractive partner you could offer me, and this, for one who has the privilege of knowing the resources you have at hand, is saying everything. I should be an envious and gloomy wallflower, and in your house an unhappy guest would be an anomaly.[5]

The self-disparagement that he expressed here suggests the real source of his feeling of social inadequacy: it was not only his inexperience, which could soon have been remedied, or his rebelliousness, which would have expressed itself in other terms. Rather it was a deep need of reassurance, which had its origin, one may guess, in the circumstances of his early childhood. Later in his life this quality hardened into vanity and expressed itself in his love of the limelight; but in his young manhood he profoundly needed to be told that he mattered. Just as his later philanderings were the expression of his longing to be loved rather than his need to love, so his apologies

[5] British Museum, Shaw Papers for 1881.

for boorishness expressed not so much his regret as his desire for reassurance. Five years after the letter to Mrs. Lawson, William Morris's daughter May tried in a teasing note to exorcise the demon that seemed to be tormenting him:

> I remember your informing me of your innate vulgarity . . . I was amused then and am amused now and still unconvinced . . . I never knew a vulgar man however clever who did not betray himself sooner or later. Will you kindly betray your vulgarity at your earliest possible convenience and oblige,
>
> Yours expectantly,
>
> M. MORRIS.[6]

Whatever his diffidence in society, and the causes of it, there is no doubt that in a relaxed and congenial group, or with individual friends, Shaw was a thoroughly engaging companion. His later accounts of this period, in which he states that he cut himself off from society, are misleading. He had a large circle of friends, and he received — and accepted — innumerable invitations to dinners, musical evenings, and so on. In 1879 he met a well-known doctor named Kingston Barton, and at his house he was a weekly visitor for many years. In March of that year he met James Lecky, a civil servant whose leisure interests Shaw shared, and in whose home he was often a guest. He was an occasional visitor at the home of Lady Wilde, and at one of her musical at-homes had his first, uncomfortable meeting with her son Oscar. There were also such families as the Bells — relatives of the inventor of the telephone — with whose daughter he carried on one of his earliest flirtations; there were the Lawsons; and many others. About these friends of his early London years — many of whom were helpful to him in a variety of ways — Shaw was

[6] British Museum, Shaw Papers for 1885.

strangely reticent in later times. They formed part of a picture that he preferred to forget — or at least to alter.

In the same way, much of what he had to say about his family is not altogether trustworthy — at least as it touches his mother and sister. His picture of the Shaws as a "remarkably unsentimental family" with "even an indifference for one another's deaths" was in the main true of their Dublin period, and remained true of Shaw. Yet between his mother and Lucy a very close affection had grown; indeed, Lucy seems to have extended this not only to her brother but to her father, for she was a warmhearted young woman. I have already discussed the causes of Shaw's lack of sentiment, finding them in the family milieu itself. Still, it is ironical that the man who directed some of his most withering attacks at conventional ideas about "home" and "duty" should nevertheless have done exactly and only his "duty" by his sister in the long illness that ended in her death in 1920; for though she admired and loved him, and longed for him to come to her, he "visited her only at very long intervals when he had some business to discuss," refusing to believe that Lucy's regard for him was any warmer than his for her. It is still more ironical that his fraternal duty, which mainly consisted in seeing that she did not lack money, included also a step that must have seemed strange for the author of *The Doctor's Dilemma*, with its scathing attack on vaccination, to take.

> My lung has been galloping away [Lucy wrote in a letter to a friend] and a halt had to be called if I did not want to follow Mama, which I certainly did. So my brother has put me into the hands of a very clever chest specialist who has cured himself and several others of consumption. He says he is going to make a good job of me, but I have my doubts; I think I

> have let it go too far. Anyhow, he sent me promptly to bed . . . I am having vaccine treatment which is to go on for a year.[7]

In his early years in London it was of course Shaw who was dependent on his mother and her bequest — and perhaps in part on Lucy's earnings, for she soon became a professional actress in light opera. Despite the dependence and his own rejection of sentiment, he probably enjoyed for a time a family companionship with these two which he had not experienced before. Once away from his father he seems scarcely to have given him a thought, until it occurred to him that the old man might be interested in the novel he had written. The father, sending off to his wife a weekly remittance of thirty shillings, which became less regular as he neared outright bankruptcy, wondered why his son did not write occasionally:

> You are a miserable cur [he observed with Shavian candor] that you would not once in a way, say 6 to 12 months, drop me a few lines, no matter whether you have anything to say or not . . . Tell the Mrs. I got her letter yesterday.[8]

He wondered also whether his son ever intended to begin contributing to the family budget. In 1884, just a few months before his death, he sent him fifteen shillings for "the Mar" — perhaps his last remittance to his wife — and wrote:

> I have not time to write now as I intended doing to explain to you the necessity of making some money. The fact is I am coming to grief myself, if I have not come to it already.[9]

[7] H. G. Farmer: *op. cit.* p. 189.
[8] British Museum, Shaw Papers for 1881.
[9] British Museum, Shaw Papers for 1884.

Certainly by this time the family fortunes needed mending. Though Mrs. Shaw earned a small amount as a teacher of singing, and Lucy probably contributed something, they found it impossible to keep the semi-detached villa in Chelsea where they had first settled, and in December 1880 they moved to cheaper and much less pleasant quarters on the first floor of a house on Fitzroy Street in St. Pancras. Two years later they had to move again, this time to second-floor quarters in Osnaburgh Street; and in 1887 — when their fortunes were just perceptibly beginning to improve — they moved to Fitzroy Square.

Shaw's contributions to the household budget had been most unimpressive, and his father might well wonder whether he understood the necessity of money. Aside from a few months of work for the Edison Telephone Company, from which he escaped when the firm was taken over by another one, he had no regular employment, though he had declined several possible openings and been declined for others.

People who wanted to help him to find work were apt to encounter special difficulties.

> Dear Mrs. Shaw [wrote a family friend in 1878]. Will you please direct your son to call on . . . the manager of the Imperial Bank South Kensington . . . tomorrow. The salary is £60 per annum but your son must *not* talk about religion or give his views thereon and he must make up his mind to work and do what he is told if not there is no use in his calling . . .[10]

Through the years from 1876 to 1884 the jobs that came in sight ranged from tutoring a backward youth to serving as

[10] British Museum, Shaw Papers for 1878.

secretary to the Committee on the Thames Subway.[11] At one point he studied for a few weeks for the Excise Branch of the Civil Service. At another, he considered emigrating to Canada; for in 1881 his friends the Bells left for North America. They kept in touch with him, the father employing him to send books and pamphlets that he needed ("and for God's sake don't put two n's in Manitoba") and the daughter responding to a flirtation by mail.

It was only in the world of arts and letters that he seemed capable of any persistent effort — and even here he floundered almost hopelessly for years. The removal to London had of course meant the return of music — certainly the art about which he knew most. On arriving there, he resumed his work at the pianoforte and in addition asked his mother to teach him to sing. She did so, and he worked with sufficient energy and purpose that before long he was joining her and Lucy in helping along some of the activities of Vandaleur Lee — producing operas, arranging concerts, directing rehearsals. In addition, he spent some time in studying musical theory and counterpoint, in which his friend Lecky was especially interested. In a surprisingly short period he found his services in demand not only for informal musical evenings, but as an accompanist and — on occasion — even a soloist. It is tempting to speculate that he may have dreamed of a career in music; though he probably reached his zenith as a performer on a night in November 1884. Among the letters and papers of that year which he kept was a program for a "Grand Entertainment" to be given under the auspices of the Social-Democratic Federation (Paddington and Bayswater Branch) in Perseverance Hall in the Edgware Road. Included on the program, together with comic songs, selections on the mouth or-

[11] British Museum, Shaw Papers for 1882.

gan, and a reading by Shaw's Marxist acquaintance E. B. Aveling, were two piano solos by Shaw: the Egmont Overture and the War March from *Athalie*. Perhaps as he swung into the Mendelssohn piece he remembered the opening scene of his second novel, still unpublished. A young electrical engineer of Irish descent who is an amateur musician is dressing for a concert at the Wandsworth Town Hall. His sister, a professional singer in light opera, preparing for her own evening's work, reads his program and comments:

> "Tickets will be distributed to the families of working men by the Rev. George Lind . . . Part I. Symphony in F: Haydn. Arranged for four English concertinas by Julius Baker . . ." Good Lord! "Song: Rose softly blooming: Spohr. Miss Marian Lind." I wonder whether she can sing! "Polonaise in A flat major: Chopin"—what rot! As if working people cared about Chopin! . . .

Shaw also tried his hand at composing, with even less distinguished results. From time to time he made a note in his diary that he "sat and composed a little music in the morning," or "produced some bars of a very amateurish minuet," but there is nothing to suggest that he took himself at all seriously as a budding composer. His versifying friends nevertheless were happy to make use of his talents. In 1884 Mrs. Caroline Radford, at whose home he was a frequent visitor, sent him some verses she had written, with the suggestion that he set some of them to music.[12] Shaw did so — apparently one beginning

> Why am I singing all alone
> Outside your window here?
> Because the roses are all blown
> And all the sky is clear.

[12] British Museum, Shaw Papers for 1884.

Mrs. Radford was more than pleased:

> We are all delighted with the song; and want you, if you will, to come and play and sing it please.

There is nothing to indicate whether he went; if he did, perhaps Mrs. Radford had him also sing Tosti's "Good-bye."

There remained the profession of letters; Shaw's apprenticeship to it must be the subject of a separate chapter. Yet even here, though he struggled on with the most dogged persistence, he had no clear idea of the direction in which he wished the struggle to take him. He wanted success; he did not know *what* success.

His apparent inability to follow a steady course in any direction — or even to find a course to steer — was matched by the irregularities and eccentricities of his daily life. The most famous of the latter is doubtless the vegetarianism which he began to practise in 1881 and — after an early and brief relapse — maintained throughout his life. The notes in the first volume of his diary (1885) mention others, and reveal some of his problems:

> When I lay too late in the mornings (which was most often the case) I did not go to the museum until after dinner, which I took at 14 or 15 o'clock. [2 or 3 P.M.]

> Took an active part in the Fabian Society. Wrote 2 pamphlets for it and worked on the Executive . . . Gave my first provincial lecture at Leicester on 22nd November. Continued a member of the Bedford, Browning, & Dialectical Societies, and attended the meetings of the New Shakespeare Society pretty regularly.

*Fads*, etc. — Continued vegetarianism. Took to the woollen clothing system and gave up using sheets in bed. Acting — made an attempt to act in a third-rate comedy at Notting Hill with the Avelings, on the 30th January.

*Family Circumstances* — My father's death in April put a stop to the 30/-a week he had been sending us, but we got nearly £100 by a policy of insurance on his life. With this we could do little more than pay off our debts and replace our worn-out clothes. Lucy was at work on the stage in the provinces all the year. My mother suddenly struck a new vein of work as the teacher of singing in the High Schools towards the end of the year. I also slipped into paid journalism; but this put a stop to my life work.

*Studies* — Almost nil. Towards the end of the year I began to read German with Sidney Webb once a week, but I pursued it in a very desultory manner. I lost much time by my laziness in the matter of getting up in the morning. I had no time to read much in economics, but I attended a circle at Hampstead formed for the study of Marx and Proudhon; and in November I began to go to the house of Beeton, a stockbroker in 42 Belsize Square where Foxwell, Wicksteed, Edgeworth and others met fortnightly to discuss economic questions. My practical interest in music was revived by my duties as critic of the Dramatic Review.

About the *Dramatic Review* he had already noted:

At first I contributed only signed articles, and later in the year I wrote a set of paragraphs every week for the musical column. The paper ceased to pay in the autumn, and I am now keeping up the paragraphs without any hope of getting paid for them.

Shaw's much-discussed vegetarianism was doubtless prompted by various motives — humanitarian, aesthetic, and financial. But his eating habits were further complicated, as he said in his diary, by his habit of lying late in bed. This tended to run his breakfast into his lunch; and since he not infrequently overlooked a meal entirely when absorbed in an article or a lecture, and moreover firmly believed that to eat or drink anything in the evening caused nightmares, it is not surprising that he presented a very fragile appearance, or that his friends tried periodically to persuade him to change his ways.

> I shall preserve your letters [Emma Brooke wrote him in 1885]. For when your biography is published after your death (which I shortly expect) they will throw much light on your character.[13]

She went on to predict that he would soon die of undernourishment, and concluded:

> I consider that you are keeping yourself alive out of pure contrariness.

In the year or so just preceding his father's death, the family fortunes must have been at their lowest ebb. Yet — though he continued to accept his mother's support — he refused all other offers of help with a pride which in anyone else he would have labelled *bourgeois*. When his aunt sent him money for clothes, he returned it at once, causing her to exclaim, "What a stupid boy you are!" Indeed, though Shaw himself testifies to the shabbiness of his attire in this period, Belfort Bax, who knew him intimately, could not remember him "ever at any time showing the usual signs of impecunios-

[13] British Museum, Shaw Papers for 1885.

ity" and on one occasion twitted Shaw for his "pedantic scrupulosity" in returning by postal order a half-crown borrowed for cab fare.[14]

By this time — the mid-1880's — Shaw was nearly thirty and had been in London for almost a decade. Except for his reputation in certain debating circles as a ready and fluent speaker and his new interest in economics, there was little to suggest the G.B.S. who was to appear in the next few years. There was only an impoverished, lean, restless young man of irregular and eccentric ways; profoundly hungry for companionship and an audience, yet diffident and self-conscious about manners; apparently incapable of steady effort in any capacity unless that of a completely unsuccessful novelist — yet consumed with a desire for success on some terms of his own, even though he himself did not know what they were; brilliant in intellect and imagination, yet snobbish and not a little vain; outwardly good-humoured, companionable and fun-loving — yet inwardly tormented by the sense of failure, futility, and purposelessness.

What happened in the next few years to make it possible for this unlikely material to emerge as "the most formidable man of modern letters"? Before going on to that question, we must consider his long apprenticeship in the craft of writing.

[14] E. Belfort Bax: *Reminiscences and Reflections* (London: George Allen & Unwin, 1918), p. 114.

# 3
# *A History of Failure*

SHAW'S APPRENTICESHIP to the craft of letters must have been one of the longest in history. In the decade after his arrival in London he tried one literary form after another — novels, short stories, poetry, essays, drama — with a most impressive uniformity of failure. Yet a history of failure can be instructive and revealing, as Shaw's is. In it we can follow his discovery of his own capacities and limitations, and come to recognize the extent of his courage and determination; and, in part at least, see what it was that for him made the difference between failure and success.

Shaw began the first of his five novels in March 1879 and ended the last of them in December 1883. The first of them he called — "with merciless fitness," as he said later — *Immaturity*. It is probable that, in an accession of youthful vanity and diffidence, he did not press for its publication with any great energy, and in fact he authorized one publisher to burn it. Subsequently at least three others turned it down, one offering to bring it out on payment of a hundred pounds and the promise of a quarter of any profits. By the end of 1880, when he finished the second, he was ready to adopt a more vigorous sales policy; *The Irrational Knot* passed through the hands of six publishers in 1881 and was rejected by them all. In the following year, *Love among the Artists* had an equally extensive career, as did *Cashel Byron's Profession* in 1883 and *An Unsocial Socialist* in 1884 — all with similar results.

The young writer's doggedness in working on in the face of this monotony of failure may be attributed partly to the encouragement of certain of his friends who read the manuscripts — Dr. Kingston Barton, for example, and one discerning person with an illegible signature, who wrote to ask Shaw whether he had considered writing plays. More fundamental, of course, was Shaw's determination to achieve success. As I have said, the success must be on his own terms, not a result of his pandering to public taste. That allowed for, he was prepared to venture into various subjects in his efforts to find a market.

> I must admit the justice of your hint that my style is not congenial [he wrote to the publisher Bentley on the latter's rejection of *The Irrational Knot*]; it has been confirmed by my most candid friends. Nevertheless, as you cannot be unaware of the difference between what the public like and what they will read (and the latter is the only consideration that influences me when writing) I fear the book has graver faults, of which you have spared me a recital . . .[1]

Two years later he wrote to the same publisher, asking him why it had taken him so long to decide against *Cashel Byron's Profession*, and commenting with the same disarming modesty:

> You are quite right as to the horrible blackguardism of the book, but pray remember that I have tried science and the finer arts as subjects in vain, and that the lower I go, the better I seem to please.[2]

[1] British Museum, Shaw Papers for 1881.
[2] British Museum, Shaw Papers for 1883.

When the novels did at last begin to see printer's ink, it was in two struggling and rather obscure socialist journals with little of the gloss of success and less of money about them. Even then there were editorial reservations.

> I was sure of two things [J. L. Joynes wrote Shaw, after persuading Belfort Bax to publish *An Unsocial Socialist* in *Today*, in 1884,] that we could not get another story so able without having to pay for it . . . and . . . in any case we could not get another story so much to the socialistic point, for nobody else would make his hero discourse on surplus value to his lady love with real knowledge of what he was talking about it [sic].[3]

J. M. Robertson agreed with Annie Besant that *The Irrational Knot* might be published in *Our Corner*, but he was whimsically irritated by the title:

> "Irrational Knot" is irrational; it is knot in the knature of knots to be rational or irrational.[4]

He had little liking for the plot—

> one of those impossibilities which are understood to be reserved for the stage—

and one of Shaw's devices of dialogue annoyed him:

> If you stick to those seven hundred "Humph"s, your blood be on your own head.

[3] British Museum, Shaw Papers for 1884.
[4] British Museum, Shaw Papers for 1885.

Two of the novels did in fact appear in book form in the late 1880's; the other three had to wait until after the turn of the century, when their author was famous on other grounds.

The title of *Immaturity* is, as Shaw suggested, a sufficient comment on the book. It is an attempt to express through the medium of narrative a whole range of conflicting ideas and impulses that were troubling the mind of the young writer — snobbish class-consciousness coupled with diffidence and poverty; deep desire for a serious and coherent view of life coupled with contemptuous distaste for conventional religion; youthful loneliness and inexperience coupled with mistrust of human intimacy. The ideas are confused, and they remain confused; they are not brought under the perspective of a controlling purpose or view of life. The novel is the work of a writer who does not know what he thinks — only what he does not think: the last action of its hero is "to shake his head negatively and go home."

There is no doubt that that hero, Robert Smith, is "a younger version of the author," as Dr. C. T. Bissell has remarked.[5] He is opinionated, sententious, vain, even priggish; but he is also determined to find his own course in life, not to conform to the ways of the business world in which he is at first employed. He is saved from being insufferable only by the grace of humour with which he is sometimes touched, especially as the novelist describes his hero's dealings with women. There is the foreshadowing of more than one Shavian scene in an episode near the end of the novel. Smith finds himself in difficulties with the romantic-minded daughter of his employer, as a result of his showing her some love poems which he has written and which she mistakenly supposes to

[5] C. T. Bissell: "The Novels of Bernard Shaw" *University of Toronto Quarterly*, Vol. XVII (October 1947), pp. 38-51.

have been addressed to her. In order to escape an awkward situation without offending her, he finds himself obliged to participate in a sentimental scene in which he must struggle to conceal his nonexistent disappointment by agreeing to be "content to be her friend."

> "Let us shake hands on our bargain" said Isabella, in an indescribable voice, losing all control over the roguish caprice of her eyes. Smith, hopelessly confused, could remember nothing but the gallant convention that a man who loses the chance of kissing a pretty woman is a fool. He took her hand: threw his left arm round her; kissed her twice; and ran out of the room. As he passed through the hall, he was in such a hurry to escape, that after clapping on his hat, he snatched his overcoat and goloshes, and fled into the night without waiting to put them on, slamming the door behind him . . .
>
> When he was seated in dry clothes before his fire in Danvers Street, the recollection of his interview with Miss Woodward humiliated him. Yet it made him laugh and behave ridiculously. He pulled his slight moustache; went to the mirror; and gazed at the face which had won a woman's admiration. He tried to imagine himself married. Isabella in a decorated apartment, with her pretty costumes and expressive eyes, was an attractive figure; but Isabella always, Isabella everywhere, inevitable, the first face to be seen in the morning, the last at night, Isabella in sickness or trouble, in a bad temper, in curl papers, at meals, Isabella old and decaying, Isabella a mother or housekeeper, dragging the chain of union even more wearily than her husband! Smith shook his head.
>
> "And yet I do not feel safe from her" he said to himself. "The least worthy women are the least consistent; and she

might take it into her head to achieve a triumph of constancy to her present lowly lover that nothing but a honeymoon could explode. I wish I had burnt those accursed poems. I have acted like a scoundrel, or, what is the same thing, a fool. Well, what is done cannot be undone. With which sententious remark, I, Don Juan Lothario Smith, will to bed, to bed." [6]

Shaw's second novel, *The Irrational Knot,* is better than *Immaturity* for several reasons, not the least of them being that it is shorter. It has a fairly clearly defined subject and a firm narrative line. It comprises a study of two "marriages," both of which cut across class barriers, and both of which fail. They fail because each involves a rational person in opposing his rationality in one way or another to the irrationalities of class distinction, convention, and feeling. The first marriage involves a talented actress, of lower-class origins, and a spoiled though not unlikable young man of the minor aristocracy. They are in love, but their union remains an illicit one, Susannah Conolly refusing Marmaduke Lind's proposal on the ground that

> ". . . I wont let you put a collar round *my* neck. Matrimony is all very fine for women who have no better way of supporting themselves, but it wouldn't suit me."

They live together, and Susannah has a child. But the disparity between them — Susannah's talent and devotion to her art, against Marmaduke's good-natured sloth and willingness to live on her earnings — soon becomes destructive. Susannah takes the way of alcoholism to a sordid death.

The second marriage, which is studied more fully, is that

[6] *Immaturity,* pp. 410–411.

between Susannah's brother and Marmaduke's cousin. Ned Conolly is an electrician and a successful inventor, with a variety of talents and a liberal mind. A thorough rationalist, when he achieves spectacular financial success he concludes that marriage with a beautiful and cultivated heiress is appropriate. Marian Lind, attracted by his reasonableness and candour and even more by his effectiveness in the world, which contrasts strongly with the uselessness of the lives of most of her acquaintances, accepts him in the most detached and academic betrothal scene in English fiction. Marian, however, is a thoroughly conventional and sentimental young lady. Before long her husband's complete rationalism and constant concern with efficiency lead him to offend her sensibilities again and again. She leaves him at last for the arms of an old admirer of hers, an aristocratic idler. When, having become pregnant by him, she turns penitently back to Conolly, the latter insists that they must part, with — so far as he is concerned — nothing so irrational as a single regret:

> "One folly more," he said, taking her in his arms and kissing her. She made no resistance. "If such a moment could be eternal, we should never say goodbye," he added. "As it is, we are wise not to tempt Fortune by asking for such another."
>
> "You are too wise, Ned," she said, suffering him to replace her gently in the chair.
>
> "It is impossible to be too wise, dearest," he said, and unhesitatingly turned and left her.

So the novel ends.

It is far from being a great novel. Yet in its essential structure — two lines of narrative, dealing in distinctive yet parallel ways with the same subject, and linked by characters common to both — it is undeniably strong. Moreover, it embodies Shaw's first concerted attack on a group of Victorian conventions which in later years he was to assault again and again: conventions dealing with the relationship between parents and children, the position of women in society, and marriage. In *The Irrational Knot* the attack often finds its sharpest expression through the words of a young woman who has maintained a high degree of somewhat embittered independence of spirit, against a background of parental bullying. It is she who argues explicitly that amiability is too often merely a euphemism for lying cowardice, that a lower-class woman who earns her own living and keeps her independence is far superior to the "respectable nonentities" of the upper classes, that marriage as practised by the upper classes is only socially approved prostitution.

*The Irrational Knot* was followed by the most unreadable of the novels, *Love Among the Artists*, and it in turn by the most readable, *Cashel Byron's Profession*. The former is a shapeless effort at exploring the lives and minds of artists and pseudo artists and their patrons, with much comment on marriage, class distinctions, manners, religion, and the ways and tastes of "polite" society as Shaw understood them. *Cashel Byron's Profession*, by contrast, is a crisp and lively account of the rise of an illiterate young pugilist who becomes "champion of Australia, the United States, and England" and falls incongruously in love with a beautiful, cultivated, unapproachably rich orphan. Like the Conollys of the second novel, Lydia Carew is a rationalist. Unlike them, she becomes suspicious of her rationalism and decides to marry Cashel Byron after an interview with his trainer's wife, who has been almost a mother to him:

> . . . Just before they parted, Lydia, suddenly recurring to their former subject [i.e. Byron], said,
>
> "Does Mr. Byron ever think?"
>
> "Think!" said Mrs. Skene emphatically. "Never. There isn't a more cheerful lad in existence, miss."

Mrs. Skene's response seems to have settled the matter. That evening in her library Lydia came upon a passage in a book of poems of her father's:

> What would I give for a heart of flesh to warm me through
> Instead of this heart of stone ice-cold whatever I do!
> Hard and cold and small, of all hearts the worst of all.

> Lydia hastily stepped down from the ladder, and recoiled until she reached a chair, where she sat and read and reread these lines. The failing light roused her to action. She replaced the book on the shelf, and said, as she went to the writing-table, "If such a doubt as that haunted my father, it will haunt me, unless I settle what is to be my heart's business now and for ever. If it be possible for a child of mine to escape this curse, it must inherit its immunity from its father, and not from me — from the man of impulse who never thinks, and not from the rationalizing woman, who cannot help thinking. Be it so."

Unlike the Conolly marriages, this one does not fail, perhaps because of Lydia's refusal — announced with great reasonableness — to "drift back again into mere rationalism"; but undoubtedly also because Byron turns out to be the sole heir to the estates of "one of the oldest county families in England," gives up his profession, and enters Parliament as a Conservative — though shortly afterward he turns independent. We are not told whether the children of the marriage escape the taint of their mother's habit of cerebration.

*An Unsocial Socialist* is a much weaker novel. Its narrative is thin and uncertain, and much of it comprises long harangues about class structure, art, education, marriage — the subjects that Shaw has knocked about in the preceding novels. It has some of the comic delight in incongruity of character and situation that appears from time to time in them and is strong in *Cashel Byron's Profession;* but it has none of that novel's deftness of action or clarity of form. It has, nevertheless, two important aspects. One I shall discuss at a later stage of this book. The other is the fact that *An Unsocial Socialist,* as its title might suggest, reflects the first effects of Shaw's early socialism on his writings. The hero, Sidney Trefusis, is a Socialist, actively engaged in propagating his ideas. If these are in fact not very clearly defined, they simply reflect the author's own notions on the subject, which were none too secure as yet. For it was only in the year before he wrote this novel that Henry George had opened Shaw's eyes to the economic facts that underlay the inequities which he had been attacking in the earlier works; it was in the year in which he wrote it that he first read *Das Kapital,* and about the time when he finished it that he joined a discussion group where his ideas about economics began to be threshed out — a process that took two years at the very least.

No one but a fairly zealous Shavian is likely to turn to these novels, with the possible exception of *Cashel Byron's Profession,* and it is tempting to comment that their principal achievement was that of showing the author that he was no novelist. Yet in fact they did much more. The determination that enabled him to press on with his writing of them in the face of a steady series of rejections provided him also with an invaluable training, revealed where his strengths and weaknesses lay, and went a long way towards giving him the mastery which he eventually achieved of athletic, lucid prose. In lengthy description of scene or incident he would rarely shine; but in dialogue — especially the dialogue of discussion — and in the shaping of witty, incongruous situations, he would be unsurpassed. The novels did not by any means bring him to mastery of these things. As Professor D. R. Cherry has remarked in a perceptive essay:

> The characters who speak for [Shaw] in the novels about love and marriage, art and socialism, are permitted to do so at length, and their arguments are either not answered at all or are answered by obvious fools. There is no real conflict of ideas or of personalities; there is little room for excitement, suspense, or surprise.[7]

Yet in their development the novels were pointing the way towards the plays.

Whether Shaw ever really thought of himself as a novelist is doubtful; he did, however, as Professor Cherry has pointed out, frequently refer to himself as a journalist. While he was likely to use the term to include all his writing, it is profitable to consider his career in the field to which it is commonly applied: writing for journals. Here, more clearly even than in the novels, one can see him making false starts, mistaking his proper direction, modestly accepting (or rejecting) advice, and at last finding a purpose — and with it a style.

The career began rather unpromisingly a few months after he reached London, when Vandaleur Lee was invited to become music critic for a small weekly magazine called *The*

[7] D. R. Cherry: "Shaw's Novels," *Dalhousie Review,* Vol. 42, No. 4 (Winter 1962–63), p. 470.

*Hornet.* Lee, who wanted prestige but had no talent for writing, saw an opportunity to do both himself and Shaw a favour, and it was agreed that the latter should write the criticisms and receive the money, while Lee received the credit. The arrangement seems to have been more or less satisfactory while it lasted — for ten months. Whether the editor ever discovered its existence is open to question. It is worth noting that Lee — with whom Mrs. Shaw eventually broke because he became, in her opinion, a mere charlatan — continued to use Shaw, getting him to write squibs for his productions, transpose arrangements, and so on. In return he did his best to introduce the young man to people who he thought might be helpful to him; and in August 1886, only three months before his death, he invited Shaw to join him in a holiday in Scotland.

Shaw might have a degree of success under Lee's name; he was less successful under his own. When he submitted to Novello & Co. a piece about conducting, it was firmly rejected. Perhaps it was ironical reflection on the pains of ghost-writing, added to some lingering feeling against his father — whose first name he bore — that led Shaw to write his first successful article. It was called "Christian Names," and there was nothing in it to suggest that a future master of the comic was at work. The author insists that his subject had better be taken seriously, and criticizes other writers on it for being flippant:

> Unfortunately the attraction of the whimsical element which the subject contains has so diverted these writers from its practical and universally applicable side, that their dissertations, entertaining as many of them are, have actually done harm, by placing a matter of serious importance in the reason-repelling regions of the ludicrous.[8]

[8] *One and All* (October 11, 1879).

An apt description of a technique that Shaw himself was to master! He goes on to admonish parents to be sensible in their choice of names for their children, and objects especially to the practice of calling a child after its parent. Moreover:

> Speciously disguised polysyllables, such as "George," which is in reality a trisyllable, are quite inadmissible.

When in the summer of 1879 Shaw received from the editor of *One and All* a note of acceptance of his article which did not mention payment, he wrote a prompt reply:

> I am much gratified by your acceptance of my article "Christian Names." At the same time, as I am not an amateur, may I ask whether, in the event of my sending you any further contributions it will be worth your while to remunerate me for them? [9]

The editor was equally prompt and to the point:

> All articles appearing in "One and All" are paid for on publication at the rate of 10s/a column. There are no amateurs on the staff.

Confirmed in his professionalism, Shaw now turned his hand to writing a short story called "The Brand of Cain." It was rejected by various editors, one of whom, however, made some helpful suggestions and offered to reread the manuscript. This led Shaw to reread it himself, and to acknowledge gloomily that "the failure of the story is more radical than you suppose."

In May 1880 John Morley, who as Macmillan's reader had read Shaw's first novel (*Immaturity*) and concluded that the

[9] British Museum, Shaw Papers for 1879.

author had some talent, invited him to submit an article or two for possible publication in the *Pall Mall Gazette*, of which Morley was editor. Shaw responded with an essay called "Exhausted Arts" and a review of *The Merchant of Venice*, then playing at the Lyceum with Ellen Terry as Portia. In a letter to Morley enclosing the articles, he referred to his expectation of being offered an appointment that would leave him less time for writing (an appointment that probably belongs with the corpus of Shavian fiction) and asked whether he should take it. Morley's advice as he returned the articles was blunt: Give up journalism.

> It is a precarious, dependent, and unsatisfactory profession, excepting for a very few who happen to have the knack, or manage to persuade people that they have it.[10]

Shaw's reply must have astonished his adviser:

> Thank you very much for your attempt to befriend me. I am sorry for having baffled it; but I fear I am incorrigible. Instead of cultivating that unfortunate knack, I laboriously rub all signs of it out. I wonder whether the public really does like it.
>
> Should you ever require anything particularly unpleasant written about anybody, pray remember,
>
> Yours faithfully, etc.

The matter did not end there. Shaw took the *Merchant of Venice* piece to his civil service friend James Lecky and asked his advice on it. Lecky wrote him a long letter which included some forthright and salutary criticism, of the sort that Shaw needed and had the good sense to profit by. What

[10] British Museum, Shaw Papers for 1880.

Lecky demanded especially was firm, coherent organization based on clearly recognized principles:

> Deal with Shakespeare's Portia before mentioning Ellen Terry, so that you may give the reader a definite idea of what the actress ought to have done before you criticize what she really does.
>
> . . . Don't talk to me about your principles, there are no principles in this article of yours, no art theory, no construction whatsoever. It is all pell-mell and harum-scarum . . .
>
> . . . It is only fair to tell you in conclusion that however freely I criticize your article, I should be quite unable to invent half the ideas in it. I admire it and want it to succeed.[11]

Years later, when Shaw returned to writing theatre criticism, Lecky's advice — whether or not he was conscious of the fact — served him well. Meanwhile, he ignored Morley's and went on with his efforts at novel-writing and journalism. He made occasional contacts with editors, and from time to time an article was accepted. In January 1883 the editor of *Colburn's New Monthly Magazine*, a trade journal, invited him to write an article on Messrs. E. H. Bennett & Co., for a series on prominent London firms. Shaw did so — and for this prostitution of his talents was duly punished; though his earnings were almost nonexistent, he had to write the editor three times during the ensuing months to ask for his payment, and it is not clear that he ever received it.

It is obvious that although his determination to succeed along his own lines was unshaken, he had not yet found his journalistic métier; and in the following year he again did violence to his proper nature — if almost total inaction can be called violence — though in a very different way. An anti-

[11] *Ibid.*

quarian organization in Glasgow called the Hunterian Society had undertaken to bring out a complete scholarly edition of the works of the sixteenth-century writer Thomas Lodge. For this they wished to have an adequate glossarial index; and at the suggestion of F. J. Furnivall, scholar and chairman of the New Shakspere Society, they invited Shaw to do the job. In a misguided moment he agreed — and so took on a burden that was to torment him like the shirt of Nessus. Though he began the assignment, he simply could not bring himself to complete it; nor could he bring himself to tell the Hunterians so; nor could he — quite — forget it. The unhappy Glaswegians sent him letter after letter in the next year and a half, protesting that their printer, who had been waiting for months, was going to be forced to "disturb" his type and so put them to double expense; pleading with their glossarist to save the publishing committee from disgrace with the general membership; and finally — when Shaw sent the proofs that he had completed — becoming wrathful:

> What then of the unglossed words? Have you a list of them? For it seems to me that a glossary to Lodge with the hard words left out is like the play minus Hamlet.[12]

So wrote the secretary. In July 1885 Dr. Furnivall sent a note to Shaw asking him to show the job to the Shakespeare scholar Thomas Tyler and see if he would undertake it, adding:

> I think that six hours work will set the whole thing right enough for the printer.

Tyler agreed to take over the task — and Shaw suggested that

[12] British Museum, Shaw Papers for 1884–85.

he himself should not be paid; but the Hunterians were men of principle:

> If in Dr. Furnivall's view you have done work for the money —the money you shall have, and something additional must go to the new hand.

By the time this curious episode had ended, Shaw's interest in social problems had been aroused. But though he proceeded to struggle through the discipline of economic theory and thought, he never again undertook a piece of sheer academic drudgery.

Despite his failure with "The Brand of Cain," he continued to work sporadically at short stories. In 1881 he wrote one called "The Serenade," which concerns the rivalry of a baritone singer and a very amateur French horn player for the love of a young lady whose only real passion is for Schubert's "Serenade." It was published, unsigned, in the *Magazine of Music* for November 1885. In that year also *Time* published "The Miraculous Revenge." This is the tale of an erratic and somewhat disreputable young man who is sent by his uncle, a Cardinal of the Church, to investigate a reported miracle at Four Mile Water. There a cemetery has been mysteriously transported across a river on the night of the arrival in it of Brimstone Billy, a "dirty, drunken, blasphemous blackguard." In the general migration of the cemetery, Brimstone Billy was of course left behind. The Cardinal's nephew, arriving at Four Mile Water, finds that indeed the miracle has occurred; falls in love with the local priest's niece; and is scorned by her and knocked down by her rustic sweetheart. Whereupon he avenges himself on them all by going at night and digging up the offensive B.B.'s coffin, and transporting it across the river

— thus causing the rest of the cemetery to return to its former site, discrediting the reported miracle, and putting to shame the local priest, his niece, and all his flock for ever having claimed it had happened.

Beyond their humorous situations and a pleasing economy of narrative technique, these stories have little to recommend them; but they do reveal, as the greater part of Shaw's early writing does not, that the love of anticlimax and of the ludicrous in general that had made the impact of a cricket ball on a stained-glass window excruciatingly funny to him as a boy had not vanished. Perhaps Yeats, when he included "The Miraculous Revenge" in the first number of his Irish miscellany *The Shanachie* (1903), felt that it exhibited this Shavian quality in its pure form.

In 1885 Shaw "slipped into paid journalism" — though the word "paid" was not always appropriate. This meant that he began doing journalistic hackwork: book reviews; notes on plays, concerts and picture exhibitions; and, occasionally, reports on events of the moment. The art criticism is revealing in its own way, and the accounts of music and theatre became famous; I shall return to them presently. As for the book reviews, they were as undistinguished as the books reviewed — second-rate Victorian fiction for the most part. Just occasionally something exciting turned up, such as Samuel Butler's *Luck, or Cunning?* And just occasionally the reader who is injudicious enough to go back to these pieces may come on a sentence reminding him that the reviewer is Shaw after all. In August 1884, for example, as L. O. Streeter — one of several pseudonyms he used in this period — he wrote a review of recent poetry for *Today*, beginning in this promising fashion:

> I have often wondered why Milton wrote *Paradise Lost.* Perhaps he could not help it. In that case there is nothing

> more to be said on the subject. Perhaps he thought that it would gratify his fellow-creatures. If so, I think he was wrong . . .

As the review proceeds, Shaw expresses his desire

> to suggest . . . to all enthusiasts for liberty and progress that the claims of collective Socialism to be the somehow, and of the ranks of the Democratic Federation to be the somewhere, are worthy of consideration in view of the paucity of results from the publication of fervid verse.

This was the most Shavian journalistic piece that had yet appeared. The writer has begun to find a purpose that goes beyond the review itself — and with it has found gaiety.

That purpose was socialism. I shall examine Shaw's socialist activities in a later chapter; but it is essential to recognize here the effect that his espousal of the cause in 1884 had on his journalism. It did not solve all his problems: the art criticism that I am about to consider reveals some of his limitations very clearly. Nevertheless his socialism served to order his energies and give them purpose such as they had never had. His writing — whatever form it took — was brought under the control of a central aim; and because of this, it became at the same time more powerful and more relaxed.

Years later he was to comment that

> for art's sake alone I would not be at the trouble of writing a single sentence.

The truth is that for art's sake alone he *could* not write. It was psychologically necessary for him to have a purpose outside himself toward which he could direct his creative energies. When he looked into his own soul and wrote, he was only awkward and embarrassed: he tripped, as it were, over his own psyche. It was socialism that first delivered him from himself.

The change did not occur overnight. Shaw had still to go on fighting his private battles against physical laziness, disorderliness, hypochondria, and a dozen other foes. Through the years 1885–1890 he was still an impoverished and rather obscure journalist. Yet he gradually won his personal battles; and in his journalistic pieces, especially those that are directly political, there is a zest, a gaiety, that is new. His adoption of a religious faith was a slower and more profound process; and his plays would never have existed without it. But the beginning of the change was his adoption of socialism.

Before turning to the art criticism, it is instructive to look briefly at the last false start that he made in journalism. It came as late as 1889, by which time he was a writer of considerable experience, and well known as a lecturer and debater on socialist economics and politics. It is surprising to find him agreeing to provide for the editor of the *Penny Illustrated Paper* a weekly column of comment on miscellaneous topics of special interest to Londoners. The column was called "Asides," and bore the initials "N.G.," which were explained in the opening paragraph:

> I need not introduce myself. Since I am 'No Gentleman,' you do not desire my acquaintance . . .

It was a sour note to begin with—and the column, which needed the sweetening influence of laughter, never recovered. Perhaps Shaw had momentarily thought that he could preach socialism by way of weekly gossip. He commented self-consciously on the behavior of the police in a Saturday crowd;

the convention of requiring men to wear evening dress in order to sit in the stalls at Covent Garden; the state of the medical profession; and a variety of other subjects. It is all uncomfortable; and when the editor returned the third contribution (in which Shaw had devoted some space to vindicating a burglar) and terminated the column, "N.G." seized his pencil and wrote across the envelope with obvious relief, "Can't stand any more of it." [13]

John Morley's advice of a decade before would have been right for almost anyone else; perhaps it would have been right for Shaw in any other decade. Yet by 1890, though he had by no means solved all his personal problems — or his financial ones — he had unquestionably begun to make his mark. He had found a great practical mission and made himself a sufficient authority on socialist economics to have elicited an invitation to lecture to the Economic Section of the British Association — and to have commanded a respectful hearing from its members.[14] Whether he had rubbed out all signs of the "unfortunate" knack for journalism, as he told Morley he was doing, is a matter of opinion. He did feel experienced enough to write one of the earliest of those letters of advice and admonition which were to become almost habitual in later years. This one, with its revelation of his thoughts about writing and the writer, and its modest conclusion, deserves to be famous. It was addressed to a young author who had sent Shaw, as "a writer of fame and influence," a sample of his work and asked for his comments. Shaw replied: [15]

[13] British Museum, Shaw Papers for 1889.

[14] With one exception. Professor Henry Sidgwick, having heard Shaw argue for nationalization of the land, angrily announced that he would not even discuss such a criminal proposal — and, according to one account, stamped out of the meeting.

[15] British Museum, Shaw Papers for 1890.

29 Fitzroy Square W.,
11th February 1890

Dear Sir,

I have now read your pamphlet. You have got unusual literary power; but you lack skill, intellectual training, and discretion. Your sentences are often ambiguous, awkwardly punctuated, and even ungrammatical; and you have actually had stereoed 26 pages in which I have spotted nearly three dozen misprints offhand. It is only by scrutinizing every letter and weighing every word and stop anxiously that you will ever become a workmanlike writer and get a style of your own. Not, you understand, by aiming at "style," but by laboriously seeking until you find the exact expression of your own thought. If you examine the cautious, formal, but conscientious wording of Carlyle's early writings, you will see with what hard work he attained to the freedom and directness as well as the force of his mature style. Now, you have tried to jump head over heels into *his* style (not your own) at once; and although you have not made such a desperate bungle of it as your cheek deserved, yet you have done nothing but say at second hand what he said at first hand — and said so well, that there is not the least occasion for you to come forward and finish the job, especially as things, bad as they are, are better in your time than they were in his. The world does not now want to be told that society is rotten; it wants to know how it came to be rotten and what it should do to get sound. There is no use in telling it that the sparrows are all fed and that you are for Christianity and Democracy and so forth. It knows better. Doubtless if you were a great poet, or a great prose writer with a style of your own, it would accept you as microcosmically all that you declare yourself, for the sake of reading your books. But at present it will see at a glance that you are simply a young man made very sensitive by privations of all sorts racking a hungry talent; that you are fresh from discovering that the majority of your "brothers," as you call them, are fools (you haven't as yet half sounded their incapacity for your ideals); and that you have become excited over Carlyle's books and are lashing out into a clever imitation of his pamphlets. This will not interest it in the least: it is accustomed to it and a little impatient of it. Until you can amuse it, interest it, fascinate it by your artistic skill and the novelty of your originality, it will concern itself no more about your impulses and sufferings than if you were a tramway horse.

If you can starve it out, keep from drink, and hammer away, you may find yourself a coolheaded skilled writer or preacher some of these days. To begin with, I advise you to drop exhortation and cultivate information and accuracy. But if you depend on other people's advice, you will do little good. A man of your sort is, and must remain, alone in the world. I worked at literature for nine years without earning a pound; and at present I can do little more than scrape along as a bachelor, vegetarian, teetotaller, non smoker, etc. My "fame and influence" are quite illusory, from the publisher's point of view.

Yrs. truly,
G. BERNARD SHAW

# 4
## *Evolution of a Critic*

"My 'fame and influence' are quite illusory, from the publisher's point of view." It was a simple statement of fact; for though Shaw was now well known in circles interested in economics and socialism, he was still not much more than a nonentity outside them. In the world at large his first real success came neither as novelist, short story writer, nor playwright, but as critic of the arts. In that capacity he had in effect two successes, one partial and in a sense spurious, and one full and genuine; and it is instructive to look at the spurious one — which came first — as well as at the other. For it occurred while Shaw's socialism was still fresh and his religious beliefs were only taking shape. It had to do with his criticism of painting and played its curious minor part in the G.B.S. legend.

Shaw's writings about painting and sculpture are not voluminous; the only substantial group of them was produced just when "G.B.S." was beginning to emerge as a distinct character — and in fact they were among the very first pieces to bear these initials. This phase of his journalistic career opened when William Archer — with whom Shaw had formed a close friendship after meeting him in the British Museum in 1884 — invited him to review pictures for the *World*. The invitation came in December 1885, Archer having been told by Edmund Yates, the *World's* famous editor, that he was to take up the duties of art critic. Already established as drama critic for the paper, Archer did not want the added burden, especially since he felt he had no aptitude for it. He therefore persuaded Shaw to assist him in it, and then (probably with a little more difficulty) persuaded Yates to give Shaw the sole responsibility. Yates conveyed his decision to Archer in February 1886:

> Your friend — I have most idiotically forgotten his name — seems to understand his business, and I shall be glad, as you wish it, to transfer the art criticism to him.[1]

Archer was pleased, although his hopes for the new critic cannot have been buoyant. Shaw, he commented later —

> didn't know much more about painting than I, but he thought he did, and that was the main point.[2]

He warned Shaw, too, not to expect great critical longevity; and when Yates published Shaw's first offering complete with a blunder that made Archer wince, the latter sent his protégé a postcard:

> Yates has apparently a stronger sense of humor than I credited him with — or else a more vivid appreciation of your critical genius. I am very glad, even at the cost of my reputation as a prophet; but don't, for heaven's sake, presume too much on this initial triumph.[3]

Shaw's estimate of himself was more optimistic. At one time in his boyhood he had been ambitious to become an art-

[1] British Museum, Shaw Papers for 1886.
[2] Lieutenant Colonel C. Archer: *William Archer. Life, Work and Friendships* (London: George Allen & Unwin Limited, 1931), p. 135.
[3] British Museum, Shaw Papers for 1886.

ist, and had taken some lessons and assiduously practised sketching. He had spent many hours in the National Gallery of Ireland ("I believe I am the only Irishman who has ever been in it, except the officials," he once wrote) and had conceived there a particular admiration for Michelangelo. He had read with great attention Vasari's *Lives of the Painters* and Duchesne's *Outlines of Old Masters.* Moreover, for seven months in 1885 he had conducted an "Art Corner" for a little magazine called *Our Corner*, which was then being published by Annie Besant. True, only one of the seven pieces he had written had been about painting, and the magazine itself was not long for this world; all the same, Shaw was its art critic.

His first full review for the *World* appeared on March 24, 1886; his second on April 21; and in the ensuing three and a half years he did twenty-five articles and a considerable number of paragraphs and snippets. All the articles are reviews of exhibitions in various London galleries. All follow much the same pattern, beginning with a general comment on the exhibition under review, with some reference to the state of British painting. Then comes a series of terse remarks about the individual artists who have been lucky (or, more often, unlucky) enough to draw the critic's special attention.

The first article differs from the others in that it deals with the work of only one painter and also in that it treats him with respect — not unqualified, it is true. Yet it contains so much that is characteristic of what Shaw was to write as art critic that it is worth quoting at some length. The painter in question was the Pre-Raphaelite Holman Hunt, whose familiar "The Light of the World" had been hung beside "The Shadow of the Cross," a picture showing Jesus as a workman in the carpenter's shop, in the act of straightening his back and stretching his arms as he pauses in his task — and unwittingly casting on the wall behind him a shadow as of a man in the agony of crucifixion. Shaw unhesitatingly refers to both as masterpieces, and goes on:

> Before "The Light of the World" I am a child again. In my nonage, when my Evangelical parents and pastors told me, in Scriptural metaphor, of the light and the entering in, I used to think vaguely of the stable-lantern and the garden-door. Behold my childish conception realised — the man in the white garment; the stable-lantern (a madly expensive one, but a stable-lantern still); the garden door; and the still night; with everybody in bed! It is astonishing that a grown-up man — contemporary of Spencer, Comte, and Darwin — should have painted that; but there it is; and whilst England is Evangelical and children are children, it must remain a treasure of English art, faithfully copied from a picture that every English child makes for itself and never quite forgets. As an antidote to the sentiment it inspires, I turn to "The Shadow of the Cross," a picture reflecting no imagination of any human being, young or old; a destructive collision of realism with crude symbolism: a lean Syrian carpenter throwing the shadow of a god; an old Jewish housewife ransacking the regalia of the Queen of Heaven . . . How is one, without dislocation of every fibre, to preserve the normal attitude, with its insistent associations and prepossessions, in the face of all this? Better take refuge at once before the secular masterpiece, "Isabella and her Basil Pot."

"The ardency of Isabella's nature," says the catalogue, "seems to be expressed in the whole and single expression of her grief, and in the abandonment of her action" — seems to be expressed in the expression of her expression, in short. But what the normal spectator sees is a magnificently vigorous woman clasping in ecstasy a generously moulded vase, from which springs exuberantly a flourishing vegetable, its thick stalks strong with much sap. The joyousness of her abounding strength and the "abandonment of her action" almost make you dodge, lest she should give vent to her energy by throwing the vase at your head in irrepressible animal spirits. Grief, quotha? Nonsense! . . . There is only one pathetic picture in the room, and that is the poor scapegoat sinking, famished and weary, into the Dead Sea quicksand, and blinking at the setting sun with a goatishly vague prescience of his end . . .

The facial expression of Mr. Holman Hunt's men and women is not so intelligible as that of his goats and sheep . . . In the "Scene from *Measure for Measure*," Ferdinand undeniably looks bothered; but the tame little nun beside him is not the terrible Isabella of Shakespeare. As Ferdinand's cell has such a pretty look-out, and as he is allowed to keep a dainty mandoline . . . he is presumably a first-class misdemeanant. Yet great stress is laid on the unclean condition of his thick hair. To allow a prisoner a mandoline, and deny him a wash, seems inconsistent enough to justify the introduction, in the painter's favourite vein of symbolism, of a bundle of red tape.

The prodigious value imparted to all these pictures by sheer labour is acknowledged not less in the seriousness with which they are challenged by some than in the enthusiasm with which they are accepted by others. Most of them are elaborated beyond the point at which elaboration ceases to be improvement in the eyes of the normal Londoner; but even he must admit the apparent solidity, the convincing power, and the vital glow of these pictures . . . Mr. Holman Hunt, the catalogue tells us . . . painted "The Hireling Shepherd" "in rebuke of the sectarian vanities and vital negligences of the nation." The seriousness of the painter's aim probably did not bring a single Sandemanian into the fold of the Established Church, or induce one woman to give up tight-lacing (the most familiar form of "vital negligence"): but it is the secret of the perseverance and conscientiousness which has made this small picture one of the most extraordinary units of a collection that does not contain one square inch of commonplace handiwork.

The most un-Shavianly inaccurate reference to Ferdinand elicited a pained postcard from Archer. What is significant, however, is the revelation of Shaw's sympathy with the Pre-Raphaelites, touched with jocularity though it may be. Never much interested in landscape, he shared their belief in the importance of incident — what William Morris called the "epical quality" — in subject matter, and of naturalism in treatment. He wanted (as they did) painting to be didactic, and it was Holman Hunt's moral earnestness that especially appealed to him. In general he took the Pre-Raphaelite view — which he was to state repeatedly in later years — that after Michael Angelo (to use the spelling that Shaw preferred) painting in Western Europe had become sentimental and conventional, and increasingly academic. On the other hand, he stopped short of Morris's belief that romance — in terms of remoteness of time and place — was necessary. Ruskin had warned the Pre-Raphaelites against mediaevalism; and when Morris began turning out mediaeval poems at the Kelmscott Press, Shaw scoffed at him.

Now there was nothing new about pre-Raphaelism when Shaw began writing his reviews. The movement was in fact well past its zenith, some of its most famous members having been elected to the Academy against which, twenty years earlier, they had revolted. They in turn were faced with what seemed like a new revolt, with a name — "Impressionism" — even vaguer than pre-Raphaelism, but instigated by a man who was not vague at all: J. A. McN. Whistler. Whistler's famous libel suit against Ruskin had been fought in 1878, and the pre-Raphaelites had supported Ruskin. By the time Shaw began writing for the *World*, Whistler and his followers were sufficiently numerous and well established to have organized the New English Art Club, for the purpose of holding their own exhibitions.

The point to note is that Shaw began with pre-Raphaelite sympathies, and, despite the notoriety attendant on the Ruskin case, he seems to have known little about what Whistler was doing. As I have said, he was interested in paintings that depict incident, and he wanted them naturalistic. In his second review he says:

> The President of the Institute exhibits some of his irreproachable studies of knighthood and maidenhood. His picture of Romeo exclaiming as he dies, "O true apothecary!" misses the intended pathos, because Romeo's gesture, though it may be that of a poisoned man, is also that with which one prepares to receive a ponderous object descending from above. Romeo, therefore, suggests a Rawdon Crawley of the Renascence tossing up his infant son, and just realizing that its head is about to hit the ceiling and wake mamma.

Again, in a later piece:

> Mr. Goodall's "Misery and Mercy" (Christ and the adulterous woman) is too big to be passed in silence. The chief figure is posing with sham impressiveness at the spectator, and not paying the least heed to the woman, who is unexpressive and uninteresting.

He is repelled by the sentimental and the hackneyed.

> In spite of occasional novelty in choice of treatment of subject, painters of the British school display hardly enough invention per thousand to furnish a single shilling dreadful —

he writes, eyeing an exhibition of 1066 water colours; and again, more specific and more devastating:

> Mr. Orchardson gives "Master Baby," whose prevalence at our exhibitions makes us feel that there is much to be said in extenuation of the policy of Herod.
>
> Mr. Henry Stock's [exhibit], with his "Immortality's Sunrise," rather reminds one of the man in Ibsen's play, who . . . persistently held aloft the banner of the ideal with results favourable to the popularity of realism. "Disaster" is the title given by Mr. Walter Lanley to his scene in a Cornish fishing-village; and, on the whole, I agree.

One is of course struck by the fact that these comments — valid in themselves though they may be — are not really criticism of painting at all: they belong, if anywhere, in the category that Whistler dismissed as "literary." Only occasionally does Shaw turn from discussing subject matter to remark on an artist's draughtsmanship or use of light; and his most developed observations do not go much beyond this sort of thing:

> [James Orrock's] touch with a full brush is often wonderfully happy; witness the "Solway from Burgh Marsh," which you can hardly look at without forgetting that you are in 133 Bond Street; and in his composition and his treatment of the play of sunlight and cloud-shadow, especially in middle distance, he shows himself a master.

That the Shavian wit of expression is often in full play has, I take it, been sufficiently demonstrated. One prefers not to contemplate the feelings of Mr. Leopold Rivers on reading that his

> "On the Lydd: Lydd" is certainly the very paintiest painting ever painted, and the title will but incite punsters to crime.

Still, Shaw himself cannot resist such incitements, and will go quite out of his way for a pun or a wisecrack. So he concludes a paragraph about the collected works of John Gould, the ornithologist, by saying:

> A bird coloured by hand is worth any two of the same species I have ever seen in the bush.

It was in April 1886 that the members of the New English Art Club held their first exhibition. One might suppose that Shaw, with his usual willingness to espouse revolutionary causes, would be found carrying the journalistic banner for the Impressionists. But though he addresses some words that were meant to be encouraging to the exhibitors, they must have shaken their heads as they read his comments:

> Mr. Maurice Geiffenhagen's "Ophelia" has her mouth full of snow, which might with advantage be replaced by a set of teeth . . . Impressionism, or the misfortune of having indefinite impressions, which can happily be cured by attentive observation and a suitable pair of spectacles, is responsible for Mr. Sydney Starr's "St. John's Wood."

A year later he is prepared to make some concessions to Whistler and Sargent, implying that for them the new movement is simply a lark. But for the movement itself he has nothing good to say:

> The value of impressionism depends on the accuracy of the impressions . . . These gentlemen are painting shortsightedly in more senses than one. The trick of drawing or colouring badly as if you did it on purpose is easily acquired; and the market will be swamped with "new English art," and the public tired of it, in a year or two.

Seven months later he has reversed his opinion — possibly because in the interim he visited art galleries on the Continent, though he does not indicate that as yet he knew any of the French Impressionists but Monet. His espousal of the movement is expressed in a curious paragraph, in which he says that

> just as, when a cherished acquaintance turns out to be a swindler, we cannot resist the illusion that somehow we saw through him all along, so, looking at the more elderly British wall-ornaments at the Institute, it is hard to admit that such airless, lightless, sunless crudities, coloured in the taste of a third-rate toy-maker, and full of shadows put in *a priori*, as a matter of applied physics, could ever have seemed satisfactory pictures . . . [The elderly school] is now getting a tremendous lesson from the men who are trying to paint no more and no less than they see . . .

Yet his apparent adoption of the Impressionist cause is deceptive. He followed it up with a series of sporadic attacks on the Academicians; but it was a year and a half before he so much as mentioned the Impressionists again. Then, after praising highly the work of Corot as well as Monet, he went on, apropos of the painter who is now regarded by many as the greatest of the English Impressionists, to give the New English Art Club some astonishing advice. Commenting on one of Sickert's music-hall pieces, he said:

> The chairman's face and cigar would be recognized by everyone as happy examples of impressionism, although there must be many people who can see a pin where Mr. Walter Sickert cannot see a tenpenny nail. It would save some misunderstanding if the members of the New English Art Club would visit Mr. Galton's anthropometric laboratory at South Kensington, and ascertain, for publication in the catalogue, the number of inches at which they can read diamond print. The critics could do the same, and allow for the difference in visual power in judging the impressions. Account should also be taken of how far off the artist saw his subject.

Even if — and in view of his lifelong respect for "anthropometry" the *if* is a large one — even if this is a Shavian joke, there is nothing in it, and little in anything that he wrote, to suggest that Shaw had any real sympathy for the Impressionists except in so far as he recognized that they were in revolt against academic convention.

Indeed, one is forced to the conclusion that — his youthful haunting of the National Gallery of Ireland notwithstanding — he had not much insight into visual art and in truth cared little about it. As we have seen, in his boyhood he had never really come to terms with the sensuous and passional world — he was alien to it, and withdrawn. Because this was so, it was impossible for him ever to understand the excited acceptance of the visual experience of *what is,* without which the artist is academic indeed. Rembrandt could find that excitement by observing the light playing about the headless carcass of an ox in a butcher's cellar; El Greco saw it in the curiously angular grace of drapery about a human figure too unselfconscious to pose; Canaletto, in the sunlit colours of a Venetian vegetable market. The experience did not make voluptuaries of them, as Shaw was apt to imply; they would not have been artists without it.

In music, Shaw was acutely responsive to the expression of excitement about experience and ideas. In painting, however, the one artist to whom he responded richly seems to have been Michelangelo, whose more-than-human figures chimed with Shaw's intuitions of the superman. Indeed, the clue to Shaw's ideas about art is in his religion, and the best things that he said about it were said in relation to religion and morality rather than to painting and sculpture. In the essay on "Parents and Children" which he wrote in 1910 as a preface to *Misalliance*, he had some wise comments to make on the importance of good art in the education of the young. Yet on the strength of his comments on individual works of art, especially in the period I have been discussing, it seems clear that his remarks about Oscar Wilde might well have been made about himself:

> Now it was quite evident to me . . . that Oscar knew no more about pictures than anyone of his general culture and with his opportunities can pick up as he goes along. He could be witty about Art, as I could be witty about engineering; but that is no use when you have to seize and hold the attention and interest of people who really love music and painting.[4]

One suspects that he was more genuinely at ease among cameras than among easels, just as in his reviewing days he was

[4] "My Memories of Oscar Wilde": Appendix A of Frank Harris's *Oscar Wilde* (Michigan State University Press, 1959), p. 336.

more at ease at an exhibition of handicrafts than in a gallery of impressionist paintings:

> It has been for a long time past evident that the first step towards making our picture-galleries endurable is to get rid of the pictures — the detestable pictures — the silly British pictures, the vicious foreign pictures, and venal popular pictures, the pigheaded academic pictures, signboards all of them of the wasted talent and perverted ambition of men who might have been passably useful as architects, engineers, potters, and cabinet-makers, smiths, or bookbinders. But there comes an end to all things; and perhaps the beginning of the end of the easel-picture despotism is the appearance in the New Gallery of the handicrafts-man with his pots and pans, textiles and fictiles, and things in general that have some other use than to hang on a nail and collect bacteria . . .

So he wrote in the *World* in October 1888. Some of the handicraftsmen were of course pleased. But it is notable that the greatest of them, William Morris, who worked at socialism with Shaw for many years, would not discuss art with him before 1895 — as Shaw himself testifies.[5] For the rest, we may let Sir Jacob Epstein, who had Shaw as a subject long after his journalistic days, speak:

> Shaw sat with exemplary patience, and even eagerness . . . He wise-cracked, of course. In matters of Art he aired definite opinions, mostly wrong, and I often had to believe that he wished to say smart, clever things to amuse me . . .
>
> Throughout my life in England, Shaw has been an outspoken champion for my work . . . I will not say that he understands what I have made. He seems deficient in all

[5] "Morris as I Knew Him," in Preface to May Morris: *William Morris* (Oxford: Basil Blackwell, 1936), p. xxii.

sense of the plastic, but has a lively notion of how stupid the newspapers can be over new works of sculpture and painting. He is generous to young talent, but seems likely to be taken in by cleverness or pretence. I would say that Shaw is not really interested in the plastic Arts, although he can be got to take a passing or journalistic interest in controversial work.[6]

Shaw's own estimate of his performance was — as we should expect — different from Epstein's. He ended his art criticisms for the *World* in 1889, and except for some incidental comment, wrote nothing more about painting until 1895. In that year he was invited by an American editor to write a reply to an essay in which Max Nordau had maintained that modern art is the work of degenerates and is itself immoral. Shaw responded with his famous essay *The Sanity of Art*, in which — as he later recalled with gratification — he "wiped the floor with Nordau." What is interesting for our purposes, however, is not his conversion of Nordau into a mop, but his surprising account of himself:

> When I was engaged chiefly in the criticism of pictures, the Impressionist movement was struggling for life in London; and I supported it vigorously because, being the outcome of heightened attention and quickened consciousness on the part of its disciples, it was evidently destined to improve pictures greatly by substituting a natural, observant, real style for a conventional, taken-for-granted, ideal one. The result has entirely justified my choice of sides.[7]

Even allowing for Shavian exaggeration on the point of his

[6] Jacob Epstein: *Let There Be Sculpture* (London: Michael Joseph, 1940), pp. 99–101. Epstein's head of Shaw, in the National Gallery of Canada, makes a devastating comment on the later Shaw's arrogance.

[7] *Major Critical Essays*, p. 291.

being "chiefly" engaged in art criticism, it is impossible to translate what he wrote into vigorous support for the Impressionists, or evidence that he understood what they were about. It is hardly conceivable that he had forgotten the nature of the reviews that he wrote, much as he may have wished to do so. Why then did he present himself as a sort of *ex post facto* champion of Whistler and the English Impressionists?

We may contrast with this vain — not to say self-deceptive — estimate of his art criticism the very modest comment which Shaw had made in the previous year about his early work as a critic of music. I have told how his first success in journalism came a few months after he arrived in London, when under the aegis of G. J. Lee he wrote musical criticism for *The Hornet.* This he did for almost a year, until September 1877. In 1894, he looked back on this criticism with embarrassment at its demerits, which he said he could not describe

> without overstepping the bounds of decorum. They made me miserable at the time; but I did not know even enough to understand that what was torturing me was the guilt and shame which attend ignorance and incompetence.[8]

Still, the plain fact is that this earliest of his criticism, though it is apt to be self-consciously pontifical, and though its style is sometimes heavy-handed or awkward, is far from incompetent. The writer knows what he is talking about and comments without fear or favour. What he has to say is infinitely sounder than the art criticism that he referred to with such complacency.

Nevertheless, when his work for the *Hornet* ended, he did

[8] *Ibid.*, Introduction, p. xviii.

no more regular musical criticism for many years. Meanwhile he vastly increased both his technical knowledge of music and his skill in prose; so that when in the summer of 1888 he began work as assistant critic to Belfort Bax of the *Star* he won the admiration of the editor, T. P. O'Connor. His delightful account of his being hired by O'Connor, which has been accepted by all his biographers, has recently been shown by Dan H. Laurence to be altogether a fabrication. Still, it is enough that when the opportunity came in February 1889, he replaced Bax and began his column of "Musical Mems" over the signature "Corno di Bassetto" — the title being perhaps in part a playful allusion to an attack that he had made on the adoption of foreign names by British artists. A little more than a year later he went to the *World*, which was still under the editorship of Edmund Yates, and for more than four years did a weekly column over the initials G.B.S.

In the fifth edition of *Grove's Dictionary of Music and Musicians* (1954) Eric Blom, the editor, gave almost a page to an article on Bernard Shaw, beginning with this comment:

> His literary career is not properly the subject of a musical dictionary, but he must be mentioned as one of the most brilliant critics, not only of the drama but also of music, who have ever worked in London, or indeed anywhere.

Few compliments would have pleased Shaw more. The admirable Sir George Grove himself had not included him in his great dictionary; but he once — when Shaw's concert-reviewing days were over — wrote him a letter in the crabbed hand of an old and arthritic man, commenting on his review of Grove's *Beethoven and His Nine Symphonies* — one of the most graceful pieces Shaw ever penned: [9]

[9] *Pen Portraits and Reviews*, pp. 104–110.

You are the only person who has exactly seized the point of view and the kind of feeling which have been mine during my long education in Beethoven; and I am sure that I could not have described it all in so happy and pleasant a way as you have done. Again let me thank (in my language bless) you for it, and don't think me impertinent if I say that by this article, and by such real appreciation, you have added one more pang to those which almost every Saturday assail me when I look to my left and see that again you are not there . . .

Good-bye, my friend. Let us some day sit together during a Beethoven Symphony or Concerto and meanwhile allow me to think myself yours gratefully and affectionately.[10]

The excellence of Shaw's musical criticism is recognized universally — not by Shavians only, but by many who seem in most respects quite out of sympathy with him. B. H. Haggin, for example, hardly conceals his distress over the fact that Shaw's criticism was written by Shaw:

For music criticism comparable with Berlioz's — for the finest written in English, and some of the finest in any language — read the concert reviews and articles of Bernard Shaw. You may be surprised to hear that he did such writing; but the fact is you will do better to read what he said about a performance at Covent Garden in 1890 than what you will find in a newspaper about a performance at the Metropolitan today . . . He was not a great spirit; but the music criticism he wrote in his early thirties reveals a genial and attractive human being astonishingly different from the perversely unpleasant and silly world-figure of later years. And it reveals him, at that early period, using vast resources of literary brilliance, fun, and wit in the service of a distinguished critical

[10] British Museum, Shaw Papers for 1896.

perception and taste in music that is an agreeable surprise to someone familiar only with the later Shaw.[11]

I do not propose to attempt a general discussion of the criticism here.[12] To the writing of it Shaw brought resources of the kind that he simply could not bring to the discussion of painting because he did not have them. He had an acute natural sensitivity to sound and rhythm, and he had been surrounded by good music throughout his childhood. In the course of the lessons he had given himself and those his mother had given him, and his varied experiences as arranger, conductor and critic under the aegis of Vandaleur Lee, he had wrestled with the problems of composition, orchestration, vocalization, and various instrumental techniques until he had reached a very clear understanding of many of them (which is not of course to say that he had solved them). He had a great and astonishingly detailed knowledge of European music from J. S. Bach onward, especially of operatic music.

One consequence of all this was that he knew what demands to make of a performance, and he was extremely sensitive to any failure to meet them. Even his earliest *Hornet* pieces make it clear that for him nothing less than mastery would do — mastery which was revealed not only in precision and polish, but still more in the ease and grace which are the evidence of the strength that is beyond violence. Another consequence was that, because he had so fully mastered his subject, Shaw could frequently display those same qualities in his criticism. It was in his writing about music, earlier than anywhere else, that the possibilities of his prose — in deftness,

[11] B. H. Haggin: "A Music Critic Looks at Music Criticism," *Yale Review*, Vol. XLV, No. 3 (March 1959), p. 338.

[12] The best short account of the music criticism is Carlyle King's essay "GBS and Music" (*Queen's Quarterly*, Vol. LXIII, No. 2).

precision, and athletic control as to both form and meaning — first became clear. The *Hornet* reviews of 1876-1877, though their tone is, not surprisingly, somewhat self-conscious, have both energy and grace such as Shaw's prose seldom achieved in the next five years. Here, for example, is the single paragraph that constituted his fourth *Hornet* piece, written just at the end of 1876:

> The past fortnight has been, musically speaking, nearly a blank. At Christmas the divine art is wont to retreat into private life! There are plenty of carols, but no concerts; and even the bells, in hopelessly false intervals, ring out a special appeal to the public to be taken down from their cold eminence and consigned to the crucible. And as, in spite of our protests, they daily assert beyond dispute our national insensibility to music, it would be as well to comply with their demand and allow the hours to pass away undisturbed.

The later work, for the *Star* and the *World*, was done almost always with dash and vigour and an enormous sense of fun, Corno di Bassetto being the first full journalistic version of the persona whom Shaw placed between himself and the London public.

Yet it would be a gross mistake not to recognize what accompanied the sense of fun. Shaw's family had given little scope for the development and expression of feeling through human relationships. It did, however, provide in very rich measure the outlets of music. I have said that art and life are not the same thing and that a whole range of experience was forever closed to Shaw. Still, that fact does not mean that he was without feelings or that they were not real or intense; it means only that they did not find expression through human contacts, which Shaw knew little and trusted less. They did find it in music, which he both knew and trusted. So that whatever the other effects of his unusual family background may have been, it is clear that in music his feelings — his passions — were continually and profoundly involved. In his criticism of painting, his gaiety and wit are only a disguise for his lack of feeling; in his musical criticism they are the evidence of his control of it. It was precisely because his passions were so involved in a subject in which his knowledge was so great that Shaw's judgments of music and musicians were what they were. Nothing else could account for the passage — for example — which Sir George Grove was to praise:

> Beethoven was the first man who used music with absolute integrity as the expression of his own emotional life. Others had shewn how it could be done — had done it themselves as a curiosity of their art in rare, self-indulgent, *unprofessional* moments — but Beethoven made this, and nothing else, his business. Stupendous as the resultant difference was between his music and any other ever heard in the world before his time, the distinction is not clearly apprehended to this day, because there was nothing new in the musical expression of emotion: every progression in Bach is sanctified by emotion; and Mozart's subtlety, delicacy, and exquisite tender touch and noble feeling were the despair of all the musical world. But Bach's theme was not himself, but his religion; and Mozart was always the dramatist and story-teller, making the men and women of his imagination speak, and dramatizing even the instruments in his orchestra, so that you know their very sex the moment their voices reach you. Haydn really came nearer to Beethoven, for he is neither the praiser of God nor the dramatist, but, always within the limits of good manners and of his primary function as a purveyor of formal decorative music, a man of moods. This is how he created the symphony and put it ready-made into Beethoven's hand.

> The revolutionary giant at once seized it, and throwing supernatural religion, conventional good manners, dramatic fiction, and all external standards and objects into the lumber room, took his own humanity as the material of his music, and expressed it all without compromise, from its roughest jocularity to its holiest aspiration after that purely human reign of intense life — of Freude — when
>
> Alle Menschen werden Brüder
> Wo dein sanfter Flügel weilt.
>
> In thus fearlessly expressing himself, he has, by his common humanity, expressed us as well, and shewn us how beautifully, how strongly, how trustworthily we can build with our own real selves.[13]

> I was still a child [Wanda Landowska tells us] when my master said to me, "No sentiment, Mademoiselle, more style!" I listened to him attentively, and had afterwards all the trouble in the world to unlearn what he taught me.[14]

The effects of the strange emotional milieu of Shaw's boyhood were not all admirable ones; but in turning the currents of his feelings into the channels of music, it at least saved him forever from the critical blunder of valuing style above sentiment.

Richness and integrity of feeling and thought — these were what Shaw looked for in both composition and performance. It follows that so far as the latter was concerned he was both traditionalist and anti-traditionalist. The composer's original experience and intention must be understood and observed as

[13] *Pen Portraits and Reviews*, p. 107. Shaw's review of Sir George Grove's book, *Beethoven and His Nine Symphonies*.

[14] Wanda Landowska: *Music of the Past*, trans. W. A. Bradley (London: Geoffrey Bles, 1926), p. 77.

far as is humanly possible if his music is to have its rightful effect. Shaw could never condone the incessant tampering with scores that conductors of a certain type indulge in: the alteration of tempi in the interest of showmanship; the excision of passages as a concession to the laziness of an audience; the conversion of a Hallelujah Chorus intended for forty clear voices into the oceanic roar of four thousand in order that the listeners may be stunned into submission rather than awakened to aspiration. On the other hand, no two individual performers, or groups of performers, or conductors can possibly be identical either in physical endowments, emotional experience, or intellectual insights. Their job then is simply to seek out as fully as they can what in themselves responds to the composer's revelation of himself and to mediate that to the audience with all possible honesty. Shaw expressed his thoughts on the matter in 1889, when a visit to Bayreuth had convinced him that the Wagner Festival was destroying Wagner's music by its determined effort to establish a rigid pattern of performance:

> The London branch of the Wagner Society . . . seems to have come to the conclusion that the best thing it can do for its cause is to support Bayreuth. It has not yet dawned on it that the traditional way of playing Tristan and Isolde will, in the common course of mortality, inevitably come to what the traditional way of playing Mozart's G minor symphony had come to when Wagner heard Lachner conduct it . . . The law of traditional performances is, "Do what was done last time": the law of all living and fruitful performance is, "Obey the innermost impulse which the music gives, and obey it to the most exhaustive satisfaction." And as that impulse is never, in a fertile artistic nature, the impulse to do what was done last time, the two laws are incompatible, being

> virtually laws respectively of death and life in art. Bayreuth has chosen the law of death.[15]

Wagner is the composer whom many readers are most likely to think of in connection with Shaw, forgetting that it was Bach, Handel, Mozart and Beethoven who provided his musical abiding-place. They do so partly because of the famous essay of 1898 — "The Perfect Wagnerite" — in which Shaw discussed, with brilliance and energy, the Ring Cycle, giving it a philosophical interpretation in the light of the social and religious beliefs that he himself then held, and taking rather heavily into consideration Wagner's own record as a revolutionary. In addition, it is easy to be deceived by some of Shaw's assertions about himself which have been too readily accepted by his biographers and critics. In 1935, writing the preface to the collection of pieces written by "Corno di Bassetto" in 1888–89, he referred to Wagner as the composer

> who was then the furiously abused coming man in London. Only his early works were known or tolerated. Half a dozen bars of Tristan or The Mastersingers made professional musicians put their fingers in their ears . . . The wars of religion were not more bloodthirsty than the discussions of the Wagnerites and the Anti-Wagnerites. I was, of course, a violent Wagnerite . . .[16]

> Few were so quick as Shaw in recognizing the genius of Wagner —

says Dan H. Laurence.[17]

15 "Wagner in Bayreuth," *The English Illustrated Magazine,* October 1889 (included in *How to Become a Musical Critic,* ed. Laurence, pp. 158–172).
16 *London Music in 1888–89 as Heard by Corno di Bassetto,* p. 29.
17 Introduction to *How to Become a Musical Critic,* p. xix.

There is of course no question as to Shaw's having been a Wagnerite, or as to the value of his essay on Wagner, which Eric Blom, while disagreeing with its interpretation of the Ring Cycle, nevertheless balances against Nietzsche's attack on the composer. All the same, the notion that Shaw was one of the early champions of Wagner is almost as inaccurate as the notion that he championed Impressionism. The great battle over Wagner, like that over Impressionism, was fought before Shaw arrived on the scene. One of his earliest reviews (June 6, 1877) marked the eighth and last concert of the Wagner Festival that had been celebrated at the Albert Hall, with the composer himself as the chief guest and — nominally at least — conductor. Shaw remarked (what was certainly true) that

> Herr Wagner, as a conductor, must be very unsatisfactory to an orchestra unused to his peculiarities.[18]

His further comments are concerned only with the quality of the performances, however, though he notes that

> At each concert Herr Wagner was received with tempestuous applause.

Elsewhere in his *Hornet* reviews, references to Wagner are respectful but certainly not "violent." Shaw regrets (somewhat inaccurately for once) the retrospective nature of London's Wagnerian education, which began with *Lohengrin* and proceeded to *Tannhäuser* and *The Flying Dutchman.* (Actually it began with the *Dutchman* in an Italian translation, and then *Rienzi.*) Wagner is "the greatest of modern composers," though Tannhäuser presents an "incongruous

[18] *How to Become a Musical Critic*, p. 24.

mixture of old forms and new effects," and the operas — except *The Flying Dutchman* — "grievously lack human interest."

The Festival of 1877 had actually marked the defeat of anti-Wagnerism in Britain.

> From this year [writes Percy A. Scholes] we may say that in the view of the British musical public, Wagner had at last "arrived." [19]

It is quite true that the controversy did not end — has not ended yet, for that matter: arguments about taste have a way of going on interminably, in spite of Latin proverbs. Some of the critics intensified their abuse in the face of Wagner's success. Dan H. Laurence has quoted John Ruskin's vertiginously abusive comments on *Die Meistersinger*, made in June 1882 in a letter to Fuller Maitland, after Ruskin had been dragged by some misguidedly enthusiastic friends to a performance at Drury Lane.[20] Ruskin, however, is a dubious witness, whose ideas about music are found wanting when weighed in the Shavian scales, at least. In the year before his Wagnerian venture he had written in wonderment to Dr. John Brown:

> What you say of Turner is such a joy to me, but how did you get to understand Beethoven? He always sounds to me like the upsetting of bags of nails, with here and there an also dropped hammer.[21]

[19] Percy A. Scholes: *The Mirror of Music 1844–1944* (London: Novello, 1947), vol. 1, p. 254. The point is also made by William Blissett in "Bernard Shaw: Imperfect Wagnerite," *University of Toronto Quarterly*, Vol. xxvii, No. 2 (Jan. 1958).

[20] Introduction to *How to Become a Musical Critic*, p. xix.

[21] John Ruskin: *Works* (London: George Allen, 1909), Vol. XXVII, p. 340. Shaw made his assessment of Ruskin as music critic in an article in the *World* (2 May 1894).

One of Corno di Bassetto's earliest notes (23 January 1889) refers to the fact that the critics who opposed Dr. Francis Hueffer's efforts on behalf of Wagner (in the 1870's) have recognized their folly. Fifteen months later he describes the anti-Wagner party:

> It consists of six old gentlemen, more or less like the Duke of Cambridge in personal appearance, who make faces and stop their ears whenever an unprepared major ninth occurs in the harmony. As the audience was some thousands strong, and enthusiastically opposed to the veterans, they did not make much headway.[22]

The evidence, indeed, all suggests that Shaw was a good deal more worried over the threat of idolatry of Wagner than of neglect:

> Here, under our very noses, is Wagner held up on all hands as the founder of a school and the arch-musical innovator of our age. He himself knew better; but since his death I appear to be the only person who shares his view of the matter,[23]

he wrote in December 1891.

The real clue to Shaw's Wagnerism lies in his acceptance of socialism and the growth of his religious belief. His rich background in music, coupled with his early interest in theatre and his natural bent, led him to respond to Wagner in his *Hornet* days; but it was as he developed his own social and religious beliefs and recognized Wagner, with his political and musical revolutionism, as the artistic spokesman and protagonist of both, that his particular brand of Wagnerism emerged. *The Perfect Wagnerite* was the climactic result.

[22] *London Music in 1889*, p. 349.
[23] *Music in London 1890–94*, Vol. 1, p. 294.

That essay constitutes, so far as music is concerned, Shaw's fullest statement of the relationship between art and belief. The passage which I have already quoted[24] from his article on Sir George Grove shows how much emphasis he placed on that relationship. Depth and integrity of musical expression must rest on depth and integrity of belief; greatness in art is the product, then, of greatness in belief. The critic — though his concern is with the art rather than the belief — must nevertheless recognize the relationship and take full account of it. It was Shaw's profound sense of this principle that, added to his wide knowledge and his highly cultivated sensitivity, gave his musical criticism its great strength. Nor did he ever renounce it. In 1942, when he was 85, he was invited by Anthony Weymouth of the B.B.C. to participate in its celebration of the 200th anniversary of the first performance of Handel's *Messiah* by giving a talk on the subject. He declined, by postcard, as follows:

1. No: it wouldn't do. Messiah cannot be performed with its original instrumentation. For this you need to have at least half a dozen oboes specially made with special reeds to double the violins — Henry Wood has one that Mahillon made for him.
2. Handel is dead and cannot put in the original harmonies he supplied on the organ.
3. Without these the original score is dull and inferior to Mozart's version of it.
4. The subject of the work is the Atonement; yet it can still make people cry who, like myself, abhor the Scapegoat doctrine as perniciously demoralizing and ungentlemanly.
5. I should say all this; and A. W. would get the sack.

— G.B.S.[25]

[24] *Supra*, p. 67.
[25] Anthony Weymouth: *Journal of the War Years and One Year Later* (Worcester: Littleburg & Co. Limited, 1948).

# 5
# *Evolution of a Socialist*

IF SUCCESS in journalism was slow in coming to Shaw, in at least one other activity it came more promptly. In *Sixteen Self-Sketches*, he gives an account of his training as a public speaker, relating how James Lecky "dragged" him to a meeting of a debating society called The Zetetical, in the winter of 1879.[1]

> . . . I had never spoken in public. I knew nothing about public meetings or their order. I had an air of impudence, but was really an arrant coward, nervous and self-conscious to a heartbreaking degree. Yet I could not hold my tongue. I started up and said something in the debate, and then feeling that I had made a fool of myself, as in fact I had, I was so ashamed that I vowed I would join the Society; go every week; speak in every debate; and become a speaker or perish in the attempt.

He goes on to tell that he was too nervous to use notes or remember his main points:

> The Society must have hated me; for I seemed so uppish and self-possessed that at my third meeting I was asked to take the chair. I consented as offhandedly as if I were the Speaker of the House of Commons; and the secretary probably got his first inkling of my hidden terror by seeing that my hand

[1] *Sixteen Self-Sketches*, pp. 56–64.

shook so that I could hardly sign the minutes of the previous meeting.

The subjects that the society debated were those which were fashionable among the intellectual avant-garde of the day. The tone, Shaw tells us, was "strongly individualistic, atheistic, Malthusian, Ingersollian, Darwinian, and Herbert Spencerian." [2] What his own part may have been, and how long he remained a member, it is difficult to say. In December 1881 he had some correspondence about a paper that he was to deliver in which, apparently, he proposed the killing off of unsound and deformed children, and advocated "applying the principles of artificial selection to human beings." Whether the paper was in fact read is uncertain; a full year later Lecky was writing to urge him not to withdraw from a commitment he had made to read his essay on "The Sacredness of Human Life." Whether this was the same piece, still looking for a reader and an audience, is not clear.[3]

If Shaw attempted to withdraw at that time, it was probably not through nervousness, since he had now had almost three years of the Zetetical, had also joined its senior partner, the Dialectical, and had adopted the practice of going to meetings of all sorts. It is much more likely that what prompted him was an experience that he had had three months earlier (September 1882) when he attended a meeting that touched on a subject which both the Zetetical and the Dialectical regarded as passé: Socialism. At that meeting he had heard the American Henry George, who had just returned to London after a British tour in the course of which he had, among other experiences, been arrested in Ireland as a "suspi-

[2] *Ibid.*, p. 56.
[3] British Museum, Shaw Papers for 1881, 1882.

cious stranger." George's subject was, of course, economics — and specifically, his theory of the Single Tax. His effect on Shaw was crucial.

The reader of the novels — four of which had been written by this time, each of them expressing some socialist sympathies — may wonder that Shaw had not yet made contact with any of the socialist groups which were active in London: the International Working Men's Association; the Radical groups within the Liberal party; the various Land Reform societies. The novels, however, though they express socialistic ideas about the class structure of society, some of the effects of industrialism, and a variety of other matters, do not indicate that their author had any recognition of the fact — becoming yearly more pressing in an increasingly industrialized society — that economics is a branch of politics, and that socialism goes nowhere until that relationship is understood.

It was this recognition that George brought to Shaw. Its effect on him, if less dramatic than his own account suggests, was nevertheless profound and permanent. He studied George's *Progress and Poverty*, engaged in a debate-by-letter with an opponent of George's ideas, and in July 1883 joined the Land Reform Union, a society dedicated to the practical application of the Single Tax theory. At about this time also he came into contact with an organization that had been founded two years earlier for the furtherance of Marxian Socialism, under the leadership of the colourful and erratic H. M. Hyndman: The Democratic Federation. The effect of his contact with Hyndman and his followers was to set Shaw reading the first volume of *Das Kapital*, in a French translation — no English one having as yet been made. The range and power of Marx's mind made George seem narrow and innocuous; and Shaw, unable to convert the Land Reform

Union to an interest in full-scale socialism, withdrew from it before his first year of membership expired. He was on the point of joining the Democratic Federation, when in May 1884 he was told of the recently founded Fabian Society, and began attending its meetings; on September 5 he was elected a member.

Socialism had now provided him with a gospel, and Shaw was rapidly being prepared for preaching it; for he was becoming a practised speaker and debater — lively, resourceful, and confident. During the next fifteen years he delivered literally hundreds of speeches under the most diverse circumstances, and learned every conceivable platform trick. W. B. Yeats describes him as he first knew him, in 1888:

> . . . an obscure man, known only for a witty speaker at street corners and in Park demonstrations. He had, with an assumed truculence and fury, cold logic, an invariable gentleness, an unruffled courtesy . . .

A glimpse of a different sort is provided by the bookseller Dan Rider, who was a member of a small, obscure branch of Hyndman's organization (now called the Social Democratic Federation), which Shaw was invited to address on a winter evening, probably in the same year.[4]

> Punctually to the minute, Bernard Shaw arrived. The audience, including myself, numbered four. Shaw was not at all perturbed. He walked up to the raised platform and took a seat at the speaker's table and quietly went through his notes. It was perishingly cold, so we gathered round the stove in the middle of the room and smoked our pipes to the accom-

[4] Dan Rider: *Adventures with Bernard Shaw* (London: Morley and Mitchell Kennerley, Jr.).

paniment of the smoke that puffed out of the stove in gusts and gradually filled the room . . .

Shaw . . . spoke with great ease and fluency . . . and I was surprised and (to tell the truth) rather disappointed to find he did not play the buffoon. He applied himself seriously and logically to destroying the theory of Karl Marx. We all sat deep in thought, cuddling up to the stove and puffing away at our pipes. As the ventilation of the room was as defective as the stovepipe, the air became misty and we all of us got more or less drowsy . . . The chairman kept on nodding and nodding until at last his head came to rest in his hands upon the table, and he fell into a sweet sleep . . .

When Shaw ended, the chairman awoke with a start, thanked Shaw for the intellectual evening, and invited questions. No one had any, and the meeting was dismissed. Subsequently, in the course of a debate with Hyndman, Shaw again attacked Marx. Then, when Hyndman had spoken, Shaw proceeded to assure the audience that in fact Hyndman's own followers in the Social Democratic Federation had long since accepted Shaw's criticism of Marx as sound, and indeed obvious. He reported how

. . . at one meeting, actually at the most important of their branches, the chairman was so bored at the commonplace nature of [Shaw's] arguments that, failing to find anything to disagree with, he went to sleep; and the audience passed him [Shaw] a unanimous vote of thanks for having given them an intellectual treat, and an intellectual treat was the clear expression of a man's own belief.

This [Rider goes on] was more than Hyndman could endure. Jumping to his feet, and stroking his flowing beard, and shooting out his cuffs . . . he shouted out, "That's a lie, and you know it. We are debating a serious matter and you refuse to debate it seriously. I appeal to the meeting against such tomfoolery."

"But it is the truth," said Shaw with suppressed laughter —

and threw the meeting into turmoil.

Yeats had noted Shaw's "assumed truculence." Rider's account turns the light on his irrepressible, gay audacity — a quality that endeared Shaw to audiences even though it sometimes alienated not only his opponents but those who might have been his allies. It points up as well another Shavian characteristic — the theatricality of Shaw's performances as a speaker. He had come to see very clearly the importance of the irrelevant in intellectual discussion — of temperament, of timing, of style; and his mastery of these led him more than once to a platform victory which in retrospect must have looked perilously like defeat. The most famous of such occasions, perhaps, came in 1906, in the course of the events that resulted in the departure of H. G. Wells from the Fabian Society. Wells, an ardent and ambitious socialist who was not yet convinced of the inevitability of gradualness, had criticized the Society for its lack of imagination and the Executive for lack of vigor — and of high seriousness. After a debate that had in fact lasted for months, Wells — an ineffectual speaker with a miserably squeaky voice — presented what was on paper a very able speech, in support of an amendment that would have swept the Executive from office. At the next meeting Shaw replied for the Executive in a speech:

> probably the most impressive he has ever made in the Society . . . to a large and keenly appreciative audience, in a state of extreme excitement.[5]

[5] E. R. Pease: *The History of the Fabian Society* (London: The Fabian Society, 1925), p. 174.

S. G. Hobson described how, toward the end of the reply, Shaw said:

> Mr. Wells in his speech complained of the long delay by the "Old Gang" in replying to his report. But they took no longer than he. During his Committee's deliberations he produced a book on America. And a very good book too. But whilst I was drafting our reply I produced a play. (Here he paused, his eyes vacantly glancing round the ceiling. It really seemed that he had lost his train of thought. When we were all thoroughly uncomfortable he resumed.) Ladies and gentlemen, I paused there to enable Mr. Wells to say: "And a very good play too!"
>
> We laughed [says the narrator], and went on laughing. Shaw has always been an adept at the unexpected: never did he put his gift to such purpose. He stood on the platform waiting. Wells, also on the platform, smiled self-consciously; but the audience went on laughing. Finally, when we were too exhausted to laugh longer, Wells withdrew his amendment and we all went trooping out in search of refreshment. Keats was snuffed out by an article; Wells was squelched by a joke.

Shaw — and the Executive — won the victory, both at the meeting and subsequently in the Society elections; but Wells was lost to them.[6]

[6] See S. G. Hobson: *Pilgrim to the Left* (London, 1938), pp. 106–107. While Hobson's account serves to illustrate the point I am making, it should not be taken with complete literalness, for it greatly oversimplifies the termination of a complex chapter in Fabian history, a chapter which Shaw thought of complacently in later years as "a glorious episode." See F. E. Loewenstein's article, "The Shaw — Wells Controversy of 1904–1908," in the *Fabian Quarterly*, No. 41 (April 1944), pp. 15–20. A precis of Shaw's speech was contained in *Fabian News* for January 1907, with no mention of the incident reported by Hobson; see C. E. M. Joad, ed.: *Shaw and Society* (London: Odhams Press Ltd., 1953), pp. 158–165.

It was not only his fellow intellectuals who sometimes found Shaw's jesting inept: not all the people who suffered from the poverty and inequity that he was attacking could join in his laughter. H. M. Hyndman's recollections are not always reliable, any more than Shaw's; yet there must surely have been occasions such as one that Hyndman describes when Shaw, having delivered to a working-class audience in Holborn a "clever, satirical speech," found himself greeted not with laughter and applause, but with the wrath of a Trade Unionist to whom unemployment was no subject for joking.

> Then Shaw for once in his life had the opportunity of listening to such a rush of conclusive argument, thorough exposure, and bitter ridicule turned upon himself, as he has only experienced in speech or writing a few times in his life.[7]

The heightened tone of Hyndman's description undoubtedly reflects a degree of wishful thinking as well as his long irritation at Shaw; but the central facts in his account need not be doubted.

Still, Shaw's stage sense won for him uncounted platform triumphs. His irrepressible humour may — as is sometimes said — have softened many a blow; but sometimes also it was the weapon with which the blow was struck. Nor need we imagine that he showed any great compunction about utilizing his superior techniques. He was scrupulously fair over the external conditions of debate, but, once satisfied about them, he fought to win and enjoyed the fruits. At eighty-five he could still recall with gratification his first success at the Zetetical

> when the Society paid to Art, of which it was utterly ignorant, the tribute of setting aside an evening for a paper on it

[7] H. M. Hyndman: *Further Reminiscences* (London: Macmillan & Co. Ltd., 1912), p. 264.

> by a lady in the esthetic dress momentarily fashionable in Morrisan cliques just then. I wiped the floor with that meeting . . .[8]

At all events, the Zetetical, the Dialectical, the Fabian and the Democratic Federation could not among them provide enough platforms for Shaw, once he had been launched as a speaker, nor did economics entirely engross him. In 1884, for example, he belonged also to the Browning Society and the Bedford Debating Society, and went to the meetings of the New Shakspeare Society; and when, two years later, the Shelley Society was formed, he attended the first meeting and became a member. It would be impossible even to guess at the number of meetings of other groups he attended from time to time. Almost always he spoke; and laughter was his ensign.

> It is by jingling the bell of a jester's cap that I, like Heine, have made people listen to me. All genuinely intellectual work is humorous.

So he wrote to Florence Farr Emery in 1892.[9]

It must not be imagined for a moment that the man wearing the cap was not serious. Shaw's conversion to socialism was complete; and it is doubtful that any person anywhere devoted more time and energy to its propagation — as lecturer, debater, committee man, essayist, editor, letter-writer, theorist, and adviser — than Shaw did, without the slightest expectation of remuneration, in the two decades after 1885. Nor was the jester's cap continually being shaken, even in the presence of an audience. His sister Lucy's friend Georgina

[8] *Sixteen Self-Sketches*, p. 57.
[9] Clifford Bax, ed.: *Florence Farr, Bernard Shaw, W. B. Yeats, Letters* (New York: Dodd, Mead & Co., 1942), p. 10.

Sime watched him one evening at a meeting of socialists in Morris's converted coach house at Hammersmith:

> . . . I caught sight of Bernard Shaw not seated but leaning against the wall, close to the door. His face came out very distinctly in the unshaded light of the stable-room, and as he listened it seemed to me to be lit up not only by that outside light but also, and in a particular way, by some inner lamp, as if Morris's words had lighted a candle of great and incandescent power within him. Shaw's face that night burned itself in on me; I have never seen any face like it since. Its expression was as clear and incisive as one of his own prefaces; his eyes were fixed on the lecturer. . . . His pale skin, his hair that the light above it turned to gold, and his strong, gleaming teeth, made a picture that no one, I think, could ever forget . . .
>
> . . . Shaw, standing there in the crowd and making one of them, yet looked as if he were alone, surrounded by nothing but space. He seemed a bit of pure Calvinism, a chapter of the 'Institutes' come to life . . .[10]

It is quite true also that for some of his hearers, the bells on the jester's cap may have seemed rather to jangle than to jingle:

> George Mercutio Bernard Shaw may, perhaps, be able to jest with a sword in his vitals. *Perhaps*—for the laughter is never quite healthy, is a little phosphorescent, has somewhat the appearance of bravado.

Such was the comment of his Fabian friends, the actress Janet

[10] Georgina Sime and Frank Nicholson: *Brave Spirits* (Simpkin, Marshall & Co. Privately printed, 1952), pp. 13–14.

Achurch and her husband Charles Charrington, in 1894.[11] The seeming levity of the Fabian Executive was one of the causes of Wells's dissatisfaction with the Society:

> I can assure you that constant flow of rather foolish laughter, or rather forced jesting, is no small defect in our work. It flows over and obscures all sorts of grave issues, and chills and kills enthusiasm. Its particular victim in this society is Mr. Bernard Shaw.[12]

Wells did not make the mistake of assuming that Shaw was not serious; but he did feel that the Fabians' devotion to laughter was damaging. Shaw, on the contrary, prized it. For him it was

> the invaluable habit of freely laughing at ourselves which has always distinguished us, and which has saved us from becoming hampered by the gushing enthusiasts who mistake their own emotions for public movements. From the first, such people fled after one glance at us, declaring that we were not serious.[13]

Recently J. B. Priestley has suggested that Shaw's astonishing equanimity resulted from the fact that

> being a *persona*-figure or a permanent character part, he was not emotionally committed to his ideas.[14]

[11] Janet Achurch and Charles Charrington: "A Confession of Their Crimes," in *The New Review*, Vol. X (1894), p. 492.

[12] Quoted in Henderson: *George Bernard Shaw: Man of the Century* (New York: Appleton-Century-Crofts, 1956), p. 252.

[13] *The Fabian Society: Its Early History* (Fabian Tract No. 41), p. 4.

[14] J. B. Priestley: *Literature and Western Man* (London: Heinemann, 1960), pp. 347-351.

The equanimity, however, was an aspect of the *persona;* so, often, was the laughter.

At all events, the story of Shaw's career as a Fabian is nothing so simple as the story of a successful platform orator and wit; it is much more that of an eager and perceptive student of the two complementary aspects of socialism — economics and politics — throwing himself with energy into its cause, and learning as he goes.

Henry George led him to economics and gave him the notion of the possibility — the necessity — of securing economic change by political action; Karl Marx provided him simultaneously with a vast historic perspective from which to view such action and a passionate motive for engaging in it. In the winter of 1883–84, Shaw became a member of a circle which met fortnightly at a private house in Hampstead to study and discuss Marx and, later, Proudhon. Though he recognized Marx's intellectual heroism, his conversion was not complete — partly because of an innate rebellious mistrust of saviours, but also because of some other doubts. As Graham Wallas — who along with Sidney Webb and Sidney Olivier was also a member of the group — recorded:

> We expected to agree with Marx, but found ourselves from the beginning criticizing him.[15]

In Hyndman's magazine *Justice*, in March 1884, there appeared a letter signed "G. B. S. Larking" — under the heading "Who is the Thief?" — in which the writer put his finger on the flaw in the Marxian theory of value and jocularly invited an explanation. Shaw later confessed that he raised the question in the form of a joke because, knowing himself a

[15] Graham Wallas: *Men and Ideas*, p. 103.

mere novice in economics, he assumed that it would readily be answered. In fact it was not, and Shaw was honestly confused. On April 15 he wrote a long letter to his friend McNulty, which he asked him to return, and which he later noted

> marks the beginning of my lecturing & shews the economic muddle I was in then.[16]

The "beginning" lecture in question was at the Invicta Club in Woolwich, the letter states. In the main, however, the document is a long, rambling discussion of economic problems, including a passage of dialogue between "Chum," a worker, and "Cap," a capitalist. Shaw is in admitted confusion about the value theory, the problem of monopolies, and other questions; but on one matter he is perfectly clear:

> The essential point is that a state of things exists in which a man can produce more than he consumes. In such a state of things a man can live idle if he can force another to work for him.

The comment is worth noting because of its suggestion that from the first Shaw's motives in socialism were moral and intellectual rather than humanitarian and compassionate: he scorned idleness, and he hated slavery.

Six months later there appeared in *To-Day* an article by the Jevonian economist Wicksteed, in which Marx's value theory was exploded; and Shaw, with more loyalty to his new hero than good judgment — especially in view of the *Justice* letter — set out to reply. What he produced, however, was not much more than an admission that Wicksteed had thoroughly shaken him, and that indeed the effect might have

[16] British Museum, Shaw Papers for 1884.

been worse had Shaw understood mathematics better. There followed a rejoinder by Wicksteed, containing one comment in particular that Shaw must have greeted with a shout of laughter:

> Mr. Shaw . . . renounced mathematical reasoning in favour of the literary method which enables a clever man to follow equally fallacious arguments to equally absurd conclusions *without seeing that they are absurd.* This is the exact difference between the mathematical and the literary treatment of the pure theory of political economy.[17]

In the following winter, in addition to attending the meetings of the Hampstead group (now the "Hampstead Historical Society"), Shaw joined the "Economic Circle," meeting at the home of a wealthy stockbroker named Beeton, in Belsize Square. Its director was Wicksteed.

Not that Shaw's approach was for a moment that of the humble scholar. E. I. Fripp, a member of the circle, recalled the newcomer's first appearance there:

> He stood up with red hair and beard, in a grey suit (most of the company being in evening dress), and chaffed both Wicksteed and the rest of us with an audacious wit, sometimes too pointed to be entirely relished . . . [He] drew pictures of his own and Beeton's profiles, to illustrate his argument that the curves of a man's profile had more to do with his control of the market than the curves of supply and demand.[18]

[17] *To-day,* April 1885. Shaw's exchange with Wicksteed and his subsequent review of *Das Kapital* in the *National Reformer* were published as *Bernard Shaw and Karl Marx. A Symposium 1884–1889* by Random House, New York, in 1930.

[18] C. H. Herford: *Philip Henry Wicksteed* (London: Dent, 1931).

In the next two or three years Shaw read and reread, discussed and rediscussed, lectured on and debated Marx and Jevons, until he had mastered them both — and a great deal besides. One result of his study was a series of three articles for the *National Reformer* in the summer of 1887, under the general title, "Karl Marx and 'Das Kapital.' " The articles are not calculated to give comfort either to those who like to denigrate Shaw by calling him Marxist because he disturbs their consciences, or to the Marxists themselves. For the first of them contains, along with an admission of Marx's greatness, a forthright attack on "Marxolaters" who were making *Das Kapital* their Bible when only part of it had been published, and when moreover that part itself contained a fatal flaw.

> Whatever may be the ultimate verdict as to Marx, it must be borne in mind that the extraordinary impression he makes does not depend on the soundness of his views, but on their magnificent scope and on his own imperturbable conviction of their validity.
>
> . . . But it is one thing to give an extraordinary man his due, and quite another to encourage or acquiesce in the setting up of his book as a Holy Scripture.[19]

The second and third articles comprise a careful examination and, at least from a Jevonian point of view, refutation of Marx's theories of value, surplus value, monopoly. Finally, Shaw states again his conviction of Marx's greatness and explains what he took to be his chief limitation:

> To me it seems that his errors arose from several causes. He was a born materialist; and when he attempted to carve a

[19] *National Reformer* (Aug. 7, 1887).

theory with the tools of the born metaphysician, he cut his fingers . . .

My last word for the present is — read Jevons and the rest for your economics; and read Marx for the history of their working in the past, and the conditions of their application in the present. And never mind the metaphysics.[20]

Shaw repeatedly — both before and after writing these articles — challenged the English Marxists, especially H. M. Hyndman and Edward Aveling, to refute his arguments; but the challenge went unheeded. It is only fair to add that Hyndman, in his autobiography, claims that he once challenged the entire Jevonian brotherhood — "professors and Fabians, students and sciolists, lecturers, authors, and pamphleteers" — to debate economic theory with him at the National Liberal Club. "Not one of them turned up to effect my immolation."[21]

"Shaw . . . is not of real importance as a Socialist thinker," writes G. D. H. Cole, in an interesting passage of polite depreciation;[22] and he goes on to deny that there was any real originality in Shaw's ideas. It may be so; yet Shaw's attack on Marx was "original" at least in the sense that it was not

[20] *The National Reformer* (Aug. 21, 1887).

[21] H. M. Hyndman, *Further Reminiscences* (London: Macmillan, 1912), pp. 217–218.

[22] G. D. H. Cole: *A History of Socialist Thought,* Vol. III, Part I, "The Second International 1889–1914" (London: Macmillan, 1956), p. 220. The paragraph in question concludes an account of Shaw that is factually accurate but antagonistic in tone. One wonders when — if ever — his successors among the theorists will face up to the discomfort that Shaw causes them. It is strange to find a university professor writing a book on *Philosophical Foundations of English Socialism* in which he devotes an entire chapter to *Fabian Essays,* praises them as still alive, relevant, and interesting, yet contrives never to mention the man who wrote two of the eight essays and edited the volume with scrupulous care. (A. B. Ulam: *Philosophical Foundations of English Socialism.* Harvard University Press, 1951.)

secondhand, and he was among the first to recognize that there is no essential difference between the economic rent on land and that on other kinds of capital. What was certainly original in his contribution to economics was the lucidity of his prose. To turn from the writings of contemporary academics and theorists to Shaw's essay "The Economic Basis of Socialism" is to step from the darkness of some of the gloomier groves of academe into daylight and champian. In fact Shaw's lucidity and style were what made his contribution to Socialism unique: for he was above all — in lectures and letters, essays and debates — an incomparable teacher. Again and again his task was the elucidation of materials gathered by the Webbs and other Fabians, and the presentation of socialist economics to audiences as diverse as the Economic Section of the British Association (which he addressed in September 1888), the Sunday crowds in Hyde Park, the Clapham Labour League, and the Rectory Road Literary Society.

Certainly in the main Shaw's socialist theory was simply Fabian socialist theory. He drew his economics from Jevons, modifying it somewhat in the light of some of Sidney Webb's findings and his own thought. He accepted the notion that the state must be the principal instrument of bringing about socialism, though he was never a "state-worshipper," as Hesketh Pearson claimed.[23] He believed — with the other Fabians — that there must be a very large degree of control through local governmental institutions, if socialism were to be effective; he agreed that change must come by legislation rather than by violence, and that it would therefore be gradual. He did pursue one idea a good deal further than his fellows — for him, the objective of socialism must be complete

[23] Hesketh Pearson: *The Life of Oscar Wilde* (London: Methuen & Co. Ltd., 1954), p. 158.

equality of income for all, including women. As A. M. McBriar has pointed out,[24] the official Fabian view as stated in 1896 was that the Society

> opposes all pretensions to hamper the socialization of industry with equal wages, equal hours of labor, equal official status, or equal authority for everyone.[25]

Presumably Shaw concurred in this view, at first. Subsequently, however, he altered his opinion. In 1913, before the Political and Economic Circle of the National Liberal Club, he spoke brilliantly on what he called "The Case for Equality." Like Rousseau a century and a half before him, Shaw accepted fully the fact — and the value — of the "natural" inequalities that distinguish individuals from one another. Rousseau, however, was content merely to try to trace the sources of social and economic inequality — the effects of which he recognized as vicious — and to answer his question "What, then, is to be done?" by a fervent appeal to a nobility of character which he has just been announcing that mankind no longer has. Shaw took up Rousseau's question and had the courage to provide the blunt and simple answer which neither the economists nor anyone else really cares to contemplate: "Equalize incomes!"

Except on this point — which is after all not so much a question of economic theory as of moral attitude — his economics were not startingly unconventional. As I have said, however, he recognized from the time of his acceptance of it that socialism had a dual nature — that it was necessarily con-

[24] A. M. McBriar: *Fabian Socialism and English Politics 1884–1918* (Cambridge University Press, 1962), p. 57.

[25] *Report on Fabian Policy* (Fabian Tract No. 70), p. 7.

cerned with politics as well as economics. He therefore worked at both simultaneously.

The Fabian Society itself had no political affiliation or ambition; indeed, at its inception it was not even socialist. It began as an offshoot from a society that had been established in 1883 and had modestly taken as its declared object

> The cultivation of a perfect character in each and all.[26]

After a few months a number of the members — perhaps wanting something more easily defined than perfection, to cultivate — organized a separate body which was to devote itself to reconstituting society "in such manner as to secure the general welfare and happiness." [27]

By the time Shaw joined it — four months later — it had become avowedly socialistic. Yet it did not at first ally itself with any particular political group. There were a number of socialist organizations in London with political (though not necessarily Parliamentary) ambitions of various kinds, which vied with each other for a following. They included the Radical wing of the Liberal Party, which hoped to push Mr. Gladstone a good deal further in the direction of social reform than he was disposed to go; the Democratic (later Social Democratic) Federation, led by the dogmatic Marxist Hyndman; several anarchist societies; and other groups. The position of the Fabians with respect to these has been described in this way:

> The object of the Fabian Society was to persuade the nation to make their political constitution thoroughly democratic,

[26] E. R. Pease: *op cit.*, p. 32.
[27] *Ibid.*, p. 32.

> and so to socialize their industries as to make the livelihood of the people entirely independent of capitalism. The Fabian Society, far from holding aloof from other bodies, was urging its members to join them and was permeating them with Fabian ideas.[28]

A. M. McBriar has traced the connections of the Fabians with the establishment of distinctive Labour organizations in politics. The position of the Society was reasoned out in its Election Manifesto of 1892:

> . . . the Fabian Society, though convinced of the need of a new political party devoted solely to the interests of the Working Class, would be trifling with the public if it pretended that there was any such thing yet in existence as a Labor Party, or that the present movement of popular feeling in that direction is worth sufficient pounds, shillings, pence and votes, to run twenty genuine Labor candidates . . .[29]

It is true that in the course of time the Fabians became strong supporters of the idea of such an organization. But at the conference held at Bradford in 1893, at which the first Independent Labour Party was brought into being, the London Fabian Delegation, led by Shaw, was almost denied participation because of its active connections with the Liberal Party. Shaw avowed subsequently that the Fabians in effect dominated the conference; but the truth is that they had a very uncomfortable time, for they clearly had no intention of merging with any political party that might be formed. Instead, "permeation" remained the Society's policy (though a much-disputed one) for many years.

[28] M. Beer: *A History of British Socialism* (London: George Allen & Unwin Ltd., 1919), p. 284.
[29] *Fabian Election Manifesto 1892* (Fabian Tract No. 40), p. 10.

It was natural, then, that Shaw should regard it as his duty to speak to meetings of socialists of every stripe, and to contribute articles and letters to their journals; indeed, a considerable amount of mutual aid (as well as mutual denigration) was practised by the various socialist groups.

It is difficult to say with assurance what Shaw's political views were in his first years as a Fabian. Presumably, since he joined the Society in preference to the Democratic Federation, he was not prepared to accept either the program of Hyndman (who presented the curious spectacle of a doctrinaire Marxist flirting with the Conservatives) or that of William Morris, who in this period was an outright revolutionary. There is an interesting possibility that Shaw's early sympathies were for a time with the Anarchists. The group that he joined in 1884 to study Marx met fortnightly at the home of Mrs. Charlotte Wilson, in Hampstead. Mrs. Wilson, a supporter of Kropotkin, was elected to the executive of the Fabian Society at the same time as Shaw (December 1884), and remained in the Society for some years as its only avowedly Anarchist member. It was at about the end of 1884 that Shaw wrote an article for the first issue of a new journal. The journal was called *The Anarchist*, and the article was "What's in a Name?" In it Shaw speaks, as *Fabian Tract No. 4* was to do two years later, of the two distinct kinds of socialism, the Collectivist and the Anarchist; and he goes on to argue that

> the sole valid protest against Tzardom, individual or collective, is that of the Anarchist who would call no man Master. Slavery is the complement of authority, and must disappear with it. If the slave indeed make the master, then the workers are slaves by choice, and to emancipate them is tyr-

> anny. But if, as we believe, it is the master that makes the slave, we shall never get rid of slavery until we have got rid of authority. In favour of authority . . . there is much to be said on every ground except that of experience. Were there twice as much, it is the mission of the Anarchist to obstruct its coming and to hasten its banishment; to mistrust its expediency, however specious the instance; and to maintain incessant protest against all its forms throughout the world.

Having written the article, Shaw sent it to the editor of the *Anarchist,* Henry Seymour, unsigned; and received, in consequence, a letter enquiring whether he wished his name to appear. With un-Shavian caution, he then wrote to Seymour to ask what company he would be keeping in the columns of the journal. The reply must have been partly reassuring, for in fact the article did bear Shaw's full name: but it also carried, beneath the title, the curiously protective parenthesis, "How an Anarchist might put it." Was Shaw, then, actually on the point of accepting the anarchist position? Or was he simply, perhaps as a favour to Mrs. Wilson, stating the case of the Anarchists with a good deal more of journalistic *savoir-faire* than they themselves could have mustered? Perhaps there was a certain amount of personal retrospection in some of the comments that he wrote, in 1906, in the preface to *Major Barbara:*

> When some huge change in social conditions, such as the industrial revolution of the eighteenth and nineteenth centuries, throws our legal and industrial institutions out of date, Anarchism becomes almost a religion. The whole force of the most energetic geniuses of the time in philosophy, economics, and art, concentrates itself on demonstrations and re-

minders that morality and law are only conventions, fallible and continually obsolescing.

If Shaw did entertain the idea of joining the Anarchists, it cannot have been for long; when in 1886 the Fabians, at a meeting which was so rowdy that they were not allowed to use the meeting place again, debated a resolution intended to "smoke out" the Anarchists in the Society, he was firmly on the side of law and order — in opposition to Mrs. Wilson, William Morris, and a handful of others. Yet he retained a good deal of sympathy for the Anarchists and greatly admired Kropotkin. On the occasion of the latter's seventieth birthday, in 1912, he was one of the speakers at the public celebration, and

> went so far in his praise as to say that he was beginning at last to wonder whether Kropotkin had not been all these years in the right and he and his friends in the wrong.[30]

In his early Fabian days, or perhaps before them, Shaw had undoubtedly read Bakunin also; there are numerous parallels in the thought of the two men. Still, it is probable that in the main, having accepted the Fabian idea of promoting socialism through permeation of existing parties, he at first took the view that socialists must work with the existing institutions of government. In an article on "Socialism and Property," apparently written in the autumn of 1887, he argued the collectivist position in this way:

> There is no human action of which it can now be confidently affirmed that it will affect no one except the agent, or that the

[30] Woodcock and Avakumonis: *The Anarchist Prince* (London: T. V. Boardman and Co., Ltd., 1950), p. 265.

> agent's freedom to do it will "infringe not the equal freedom of any other men." Consequently "freedom" in this sense may be dismissed as a mere dialectical figment, of which the very expositions — Stuart Mill's "Essay on Liberty" and Mr. Spencer's "Social Statics," for example — are now patent reductions to absurdity. Theoretically, since there are no indifferent actions, there is for every man a rigid line of conduct from which he cannot swerve one hair's breadth in the minutest detail without injury to the community; and if the community could ascertain that line it would be justified in compelling him to keep to that line, to the entire abolition of his "freedom." Conscientious educated men seek the guidance of that line throughout their lives, and never for a moment think of themselves as free agents.[31]

He went on to say that

> the acceptance of the state as supreme and the individual as merely its tenant and delegate is quite as consistent with freedom of action and possession as the individualist doctrine that the liberty and property of the individual are paramount, and that the activity of the state must be jealously restricted to the protection of these.

But the only state that can be entrusted with such supremacy, he maintained, is a democratic one; for only a democratic state will be concerned equally with the welfare of every member.

Along with this expression of socialistic Calvinism, it is well to consider what Shaw's reaction had been to a practical situation that had scandalized many socialists not long before. Early in 1885 there had been a general election, in which Hyndman's Social Democratic Federation had entered candidates for two London seats. Both had been badly defeated,

[31] British Museum, Shaw Mss. No. 50690 (8).

and very soon it became public knowledge that their election expenses had been paid by the Tories in an effort to split the Liberal votes. The resulting scandal shocked the nation and caused other groups of socialists — notably Morris's Socialist League and the Fabians — to pass motions of censorship against the S.D.F. for behavior "calculated to disgrace the Socialist movement in England." Shaw shared in the sense of outrage, and wrote to Andreas Scheu:

> The Federation are convicted of offering to sell their fictitious numbers to the highest bidder (in money, not reforms) . . . All England is satisfied that we are a paltry handful of blackguards.[32]

Interestingly, however, when he wrote an account of the affair seven years later (February 1892) he was prepared to maintain that Hyndman's only error in connection with the "Tory gold" was a tactical one:

> From the point of view of the abstract moralist there was nothing to be said against the transaction . . . and Mr. Hyndman's classical quotation, "Non olet" — "It does not smell," meaning that there is no difference in the flavour of Tory and Whig gold once it comes into the Socialist treasury — was a sufficient retort to the accusations of moral corruption that were levelled at him,[33]

he commented, reminding one of the argument that he was to advance in *Major Barbara*, in respect of Undershaft's money and the Salvation Army. Still, in his *Plan of Campaign for*

[32] Quoted in C. Tsuzuki: *H. M. Hyndman and British Socialism* (Oxford University Press, 1961), p. 71.
[33] *Fabian Tract No. 41.*

*Labour*, published as *Fabian Tract No. 49* in January 1894, Shaw made a further reference to "Tory gold," and cautioned Labour candidates against accepting money from the Conservatives:

> The temptation to spoil the Egyptians will be great; but it must be resisted on the ground of expediency even by those who cannot see any principle at stake in the matter, because the experience of 1885 . . . proves conclusively that Conservative money utterly destroys a candidate's chances instead of helping him . . .

The critical word is "expediency." In the interval since 1885 Shaw had been coming to terms with the exigencies of "practical" politics, and recognizing that though with their watchwords "Educate, Agitate, Organize," the Fabians might be looking towards the establishment of a Utopia, yet in the meanwhile compromise was the law of political life.

We need not be surprised, therefore, to find him attending Liberal caucuses as well as the meetings of avowedly socialist groups. He became well known in Liberal circles; so that in the spring of 1889 he received two invitations to become a candidate in the coming election. The first of these — from the Battersea Liberal and Radical Association — he rejected at once because he "could not afford it." The second — from the Chelsea Liberal Association — he found more tempting, and — since his financial position had not perceptibly improved — one is bound to wonder why: did Chelsea perhaps appeal to his ingrained class consciousness, as Battersea could not? At all events, he agreed to seek the nomination as "a Liberal candidate prepared to support Mr. Gladstone." On the back of the letter of invitation, he scribbled some notes which suggest the lines of his political thought at the time:

10/4/89
consented.
My own pol[itics] the S[ocial]. D[emocratic]. pol[itics]
Thorough democratization of rep[resentative] bodies — Co. Councils above all.
Municipalization of land and industry.
Taxation of unearned incomes to the point of entirely recovering them for the use of the com[muni]ty.
Payment of election expenses & members.
Shorter parliament.
Suffrage for women on exactly the same terms as for men.
Rad. reform of our penal system.
Abolition of Protection for private as against public enterprise.
Establishment of Church on dem[ocratic] basis so as to devote the parish church to the use of parish[io]ners for address by Mr. Bradlaugh or General Booth if they wished.
Support Gladstone on
Home Rule
Disestablishment of Ho. of Lords
Call myself a Social Democrat.
Without hearty support of E——[34] & rad[ical] working-class voters should not have the ghost of a chance.[35]

We do not know whether or not these notes indicate the line that Shaw took in his speech to the nominating body; they suggest clearly that, whatever he had learned about compromise and the policy of permeation, he had no intention of deceiving his would-be supporters — and one suspects that Gladstone would not have found him a very comfortable

[34] Word illegible.
[35] British Museum, Shaw Papers for 1889.

ally. Nevertheless, he seems to have impressed the caucus very favorably; on the day on which the secretary informed him that another candidate had been chosen, he received also a letter from his friend and fellow Fabian Graham Wallas, explaining the decision:

> They were without exception marvellously sweet on you, but funked the money business . . . Finally we adopted a report to the Club that we infinitely preferred you to any other candidate but that in the present state of the law as to election expenses we decided to go for Costelloe . . .

Shaw's socialism of course shines through the proposals contained in the notes; so also does his faith in democratic methods. This faith he had stated many times, in tracts and speeches. Here he indicates the ways in which he believes that democracy must be extended — in the County Councils and other bodies already in part representative; in the church, which he thought of as a public institution; in the electoral system, which continued to treat women as second-class citizens. Disestablishment of the House of Lords — that playhouse for would-be's and rest home for has-beens in British politics — was accepted by the Fabians from the start as a necessary reform. Whether Shaw would in fact have been in favour of going the rest of the way to republicanism is less clear. The *Fabian Election Manifesto 1892* refers to the "detested hereditary privileges of the House of Lords and the Crown," but in fact references to the monarchy are comparatively rare in the Society's literature. In 1900, Shaw engaged in a wordy debate with Belfort Bax, in the *Saturday Review*, on the question whether socialism implied republicanism. Bax maintained that "socialism of necessity presupposes republicanism"; Shaw, that on the contrary socialism "has always struggled to dissociate itself from the Republican tradition, which was inveterately individualistic," and that the public will always have to worship an image of some kind, and the Queen makes a better idol than the army of "some British Boulanger." Shaw's fellow Fabian Hubert Bland joined him in the debate at one point; but they did not by any means have the best of it.

The questionable judgment of the Chelsea Liberals in selecting another candidate seems not to have disturbed Shaw unduly, and certainly did nothing to lessen his socialist activity. As the election of July 1892 approached, he worked harder than ever, speech-making and permeating to the top of his bent. In the twelve months up to and including March of that year he gave eighty-two lectures and addresses. He prepared, for circulation by the Fabian Society, the Manifesto already referred to, in which the importance of the election was stressed and the issues, as they concerned the working classes, were analysed. Then, on the eve of the election itself, he prepared for distribution a leaflet which must have been the great-grandparent of those millions of posters now piously displayed by Chambers of Commerce all over North America, reading "Vote as you please — but vote!" Shaw's leaflet was more argumentative and more urgent. It began with the caption "VOTE! VOTE!! VOTE!!!" referred to the long struggles that had preceded the extension of the franchise, and went on to say:

> A political battle is about to begin. Choose your side according to your conscience; and strike the one blow that the law allows you. There is no excuse for not voting. Even when there is no candidate worth voting for, there is always some

> candidate worth voting against. It is impossible that the candidates should be so exactly alike that one does not represent your opinions better than the other. If you do not vote for that one, you will help his opponent to get in. Even if you think that both candidates are fools, make the best of it by voting for the opponent of the bigger fool of the two . . .

Although the work of getting out such a leaflet may suggest faith in the importance of the franchise, the language is scarcely that of a sanguine believer in the virtues of democracy. Indeed, to read carefully Shaw's writings of this period is to recognize that a new, discordant note of impatience — the beginning of disillusionment — has slowly crept in. It may have been detected by some of his correspondents as early as the summer of 1889; one of them, who had written Shaw in praise of his novel *Cashel Byron's Profession*, had received a disquieting reply. Clearly under the impression that the young novelist needed a blunt talking-to, he proceeded to administer it:

> Your notes and style make me unhappy; you have the *tone* of a disappointed man, and you will end by snarling as my dear friend Mr. Ruskin now does. What in hell's name does a man like you want to be messing around with clever, overlearned crackpots for? I know all the Russian leaders — assassins and others — but then they dare something: they hit hard iron with the bare fist while you go on punching a bolster. Heaven forbid that I should libel anyone; but I always feel when I meet your fellows that there is an element of mean envy in them. You might go on writing blessed books, and living a rich, full life: it makes me sick when I think how your temper will be ruined; how one scurvy knave after another will use you, and how all your wealth of wit and genuine manhood will at last be exhaled in a screech . . .

. . . Do you *smoke?* If you don't then I shall turn my face to the wall and be content to die. With sincere admiration, I am,

Yours,
J. Runciman

That Shaw should ever vaporize — in either a screech or a smoke ring — was as unthinkable to him as to us. But that he was beginning to feel that in his efforts to prod the British workingman into political action he was punching a bolster, we may well believe. In the essay "The Economic Basis of Socialism," which he contributed to *Fabian Essays*, in 1889, he could still profess confident optimism as to the future of socialism; in its companion piece, "The Transition to Social Democracy," there is implied a similar faith in democratic processes. But in the essay called *The Impossibilities of Anarchism*, which he wrote two years after the publication of *Fabian Essays*, there is a curious implied paradox that seems to have been unnoticed by him or anyone else. The essay is a refutation of the notion that anarchism is the way to social reform, and a statement of the claim of democracy to provide the way. Yet of what material is the democratic unit — the common voter, who holds the key to progress — made?

Could the institution of property as we know it [Shaw demanded] ever have come into existence unless nearly every man had been, not merely willing, but openly and shamelessly eager to quarter himself idly on the labor of his fellows, and to domineer over them whenever the mysterious workings of economic law enabled him to do so? It is useless to think of man as a fallen angel. If the fallacies of absolute morality are to be admitted in the discussion at all, he must be considered rather as an obstinate and selfish devil . . .

—not a very hopeful component of self-government! The paradox is not made sharp in the essay in question. It indicates, however, the beginning of a mistrust of the capacity of the common voter to make or act on a political judgment, and so of the democratic process itself. The *Election Manifesto* of 1892 carefully analysed the political situation, pointed out to the working classes what they ought in their own interests to do, and urged them to do it. Yet it also contained some candid and unhopeful comment. In the midst of a section in which he argued the ultimate need for an Independent Labour Party, he said—after examining the financial problem involved—

> The poverty of the workers is therefore no excuse for their slavish political apathy. They make greater sacrifices to support legions of publicans and sporting bookmakers than free political institutions would cost them; and there is no escaping the inference that they care more for drinking and gambling than for freedom. The same workman who pleads want of education and opportunity as an excuse for not understanding party politics is at no loss when the subject is football, or racing, or pigeon-flying, or any subject, however complicated, that he really wants to understand . . . The test of the political capacity of a class is shewn by its power to make the most of ordinary circumstances; and under ordinary circumstances the Working Class does nothing at all . . .
>
> Slavery [he comments tartly, a little further on] is popular in England provided the wages are regular.

It is beyond the scope of this book to trace the growth of his mistrust, which sometimes expressed itself in attacks on the Parliamentary system, sometimes on the electoral system, sometimes on the general principle of democracy, which merely — he remarked in 1903 —

> substitutes election by the incompetent many for appointment by the corrupt few.

Just occasionally one feels that he was on the verge of the kind of despair that his correspondent Runciman had predicted for him. In a letter to the *Saturday Review*, in 1899, he wrote:

> There is a moment in the oft-repeated history of civilization when mankind, carried by the pursuit of individual interests, pecuniary and salvational, to a point signalised by the culmination of Liberalism in Democracy, quite suddenly misses its way, and after struggling for a period in a morass of blackguardism, tumbles back to its starting-point in a disastrous degringolade. The point is always the same: it occurs when Liberalism has won political liberty, not for a people capable of freedom, but for a huge proletariat which has become convinced that its interest lies in having plenty of rich men to attach itself to like leeches.
>
> . . . It is the old story: commercial civilization has grown until it has raised problems which the men it has produced have neither the courage nor the knowledge to solve . . . Hence we get the iniquitous bastard Socialism which grabs at the social benefit proposed by the Socialists, but calmly passes a law to force some section of the community to pay the bill . . . When the next step in advance is Socialism, man proves too mean for it; and the policy of plundering a minority of voters to propitiate a majority is preferred, with finally ruinous results.

There is no difficulty in seeing the reasons for Shaw's misgivings. For years he and his fellow Fabians had, with the most astonishing and unselfish energy, studied and taught, lectured and debated and written for the cause of socialism, and with what results? Here and there the election of a progressive candidate for public office, now and then the enactment of some piece of enlightened legislation. Even these achievements had often been the products not of education, mainly, but of endless compromise and bargaining and even trickery — such as troubled the conscience of Beatrice Webb to the end of her days.

Shaw's candid account of one of the successes is worth considering. It has to do with the adoption by the Liberal Party, for its election program in 1892, of a series of proposed reforms drawn up by the Fabians. These came to be known collectively as the Newcastle Program, and they included (for example) Home Rule for Ireland, the Disestablishment of the Church in Scotland and Wales, a series of parliamentary, electoral and budgetary reforms, and extension of the Factory Acts.

> The exact facts of the launching of the Newcastle Program are these [Shaw wrote long afterward to E. R. Pease]. Webb gave me the Program in his own handwriting as a string of resolutions. I being then a permeative Fabian on the executive of the South St. Pancras Liberal and Radical Association . . . took them down to a meeting in Percy Hall, Percy Street, Tottenham Court Road, where the late Mr. Beale, then Liberal candidate and subscription milch cow of the constituency (without the ghost of a chance), was to address as many of the (Association) as might turn up under the impression that he was addressing a public meeting. There were certainly not 20 present, perhaps not 10. I asked him to move the resolutions. He said they looked complicated, and that if I would move them he would second them. I moved them, turning over Webb's pages by batches and not reading

most of them. Mr. Beale seconded. Passed unanimously. That night they went down to The Star with a report of an admirable speech that Mr. Beale was supposed to have delivered. Next day he found the National Liberal Club in an uproar at his revolutionary breakaway. But he played up; buttoned his coat determinedly; said we lived in progressive times and must move with them; and carried it off.[36]

A little more than a year after the election in which the Newcastle Program figured, Shaw was publicly castigating the Liberals for their trickery in dealing with the proposals that he had thus tricked them into adopting. That he was conscious that these tactics involved some sacrifice of his own integrity is certain; and yet — in spite of such sacrifices, of his years of unflagging effort, and of his misgivings about democratic processes — he kept his faith in the necessity of freedom and in socialism as the way to it.

That he did so is partly attributable to his courageous — not to say irrepressible — high spirits, his love of fun. Even in the period when his correspondent Runciman thought he detected the beginnings of bitterness in him, Shaw could write an ebullient account of what the House of Lords would be like after the Revolution, when Morris, Hyndman, Headlam, Belfort Bax, and the rest had all become peers. The account, entitled "A Curious Extract from the 'Times' of the 1st April, 1900," was published in the April 1888 issue of *To-Day* (No. 53, Vol. 9). If the article has a point, it is simply that the House of Lords is incapable of change, no matter who may sit in it; though it may receive and discuss reports from the Commons, such as one made by "Viscount Champion" (i.e., H. H. Champion, one of the most outspoken Socialists), who

36 Pease: *op. cit.*, p. 112.

> admitted that the Government had been unable to carry out the capital sentences passed by the Committee on Public Safety. But the Government could do no more than it had done. It had appointed the most eminent surgeon in England, Sir James Joynes, to the vacant post of public executioner. Sir James had travelled for three years at the public expense in order to study the methods of foreign executioners, and had come to the conclusion that the most humane system was that of allowing the criminal to die of old age. All summary methods, he reported, were attended with danger to the health of the convict. The Government could not, of course, disregard such an opinion; and the condemned men, of whom he might mention that he himself was one, were slowly dying in the manner recommended. The operation was being watched by Sir James, of whose advice the convicts freely availed themselves when they were ill. One of them had already paid the penalty of his crime at the ripe age of 106.

In spite of such high jinks, there is no mistaking the fact that a profound change had been taking place in Shaw's thought about politics. McBriar says that the years 1894–1896 were "years of crisis," and perhaps they were so. I suggest, however, that the seeds of disillusionment had begun to sprout at least as early as 1892, and that their growth was very largely due to Shaw's experience in practical politics. As he toiled away at Fabian speech-making, manifesto-writing, and permeating, it was gradually driven in on him that the mere changing of the machinery of government was a relatively unimportant matter. As his *Saturday Review* letter of 1899 makes clear, he came to see that the real roadblock in the way of socialism was not Parliament or Capitalism, but human nature. The effect of this recognition is a quandary indeed: the way to improve mankind is socialism, but in order to have socialism we must first improve mankind.

Had Shaw's thought been grounded only in economics and politics, we may well believe that the forecast made about him by Runciman, in the letter that I have quoted, might have come true: he would have ended by snarling like Ruskin, and expired in a screech. Setting aside Shaw's high spirits, there were two ways of meeting the quandary that I have described.

In the first place, mankind is not uniformly unimproved: some men stand high above the rest in intelligence, virtue, responsibility. Clearly, they are the ones fit to rule, and it is they who must be allowed to do so. Every political theorist from Plato to John Stuart Mill must have considered this question and speculated as to ways of discovering the best leaders for society. Rousseau argued that the law made judgments, but that it judged only actions, not people; that the only way to judge people themselves is through public esteem. Mill contemplated the possibility of weighting ballots so as to give a greater voice to the more intelligent voters. Shaw — with his logic if not his judgment firmly in hand — goes back to the notion that he had touched on in his art criticism, that the various capacities of men, including the political one, can and should be measured; the devising and acceptance of an appropriate "anthropometry" is the necessary step to full political health.

The most important force in sustaining Shaw in his quandary, however, was not his belief in the practicability of anthropometry; it was the religious faith that he had slowly developed and adopted. The development had taken place in the same period as his adoption of socialism, and when his doubts about the eventual feasibility and effect of that movement began to arise, he was able to place it against a background that was millennial, and so to see it in a perspective that made individual feelings — whether of optimism or despair — laughably irrelevant.

# 6

# *Evolution of a Believer*

If Shaw's thoughts about religion were very often misunderstood and sometimes led to his being grossly abused, he himself was at least partly to blame. As a journalist, he more than once commented sagely on the proverb about giving a dog a bad name. Yet he had already given himself a bad name, by publicly and repeatedly declaring himself an atheist. The reaction of the Anglo-Saxon world — especially of the Victorian world — was as certain as the reaction of water to flame, and almost as sibilant, especially as Shaw compounded the crime by his socialism and his other unconventionalities. The story is well known of his first attendance at a public meeting of Furnivall's Shelley Society, in which he arose and announced that he was, like Shelley, a Socialist, Atheist, and Vegetarian. The result, as he himself told it in a letter to G. K. Chesterton, was that

> two ladies, who had been palpitating with enthusiasm for Shelley under the impression that he was a devout Anglican, resigned on the spot.[1]

He does not add that Henry Arthur Jones, who was also present, turned to Furnivall and muttered, "Three good reasons for kicking the b—— out!" Shelley might be forgiven,

[1] Maisie Ward: *Gilbert Keith Chesterton* (London: Sheed and Ward, 1944), p. 197.

since he was a poet and died young; Shaw did not qualify on either of these grounds. Still, the reference to the poet is not inappropriate. A good deal of Shaw's early writing recalls, in both substance and manner, the author of the notes on *Queen Mab* — a fact which those who think of Shaw as preeminently an enemy of romance would do well to keep in mind.

Shaw's atheism was an expression of his rebellion against the conditions of his childhood. Given the bigotry of class-conscious Dublin Protestantism, a parental policy of noninterference, and the shrewd and passionate mind of the youthful Shaw, the rebellion was inevitable. The first of his many hundreds of letters-to-the-editor was addressed to the journal *Public Opinion;* in it he attacked full tilt the revivalists Moody and Sankey, claiming that in fact they were not dealing with religion at all, but only with unreflective, purposeless and objectionable emotional excitement. Shaw was then eighteen, and it was already some years since he had decided that Christianity as he saw it in operation about him was largely a blend of hypocrisy, bigotry, and superstition, and that in all intellectual honesty he could not continue going to church, or even saying his prayers. This did not mean, of course, that he at once became an atheist. Though he might rebel against conventional creeds and practices, he could not escape from concern with belief. It was not possible for him to abide in a state of "contented negation," like his countryman Yeats in his early years. Some idea of the ultimate nature of the cosmos and man's relation to it was essential to him; and his first decision was not to adopt atheism, but to found a new religion. When he conveyed this determination to his friend McNulty, however, the latter dissuaded him and made him promise to seek literary fame instead.

Nevertheless, atheism was a dimension of freedom, as Thomas Jefferson had argued in America, and it was inevitable that Shaw should sooner or later adopt it. You cannot freely believe in a god unless you are also free to deny him; and how can you know this freedom fully unless you commit yourself to denial and face the consequences? Looked at in this way, atheism is not only a dimension of freedom, but a dimension of faith, since it presumably takes no less an act of the individual imagination and will to believe in no-god than to believe in a god or some gods.

If it began as rebellion, his atheism must soon have become an affirmation of rationalism, which, interestingly enough, inspired him to attempt poetic drama: early in 1878 he attempted to express his religious (or irreligious) views in a Passion Play. Hesketh Pearson tells us that he "got no further than a character sketch of Our Lady as a shrew." But he did a good deal more — wrote, in fact, forty-nine pages of blank verse dialogue.[2] We need not regret his failure to complete the play; as he himself apparently recognized, much of it is, to say the least, tasteless: across one passage that he abandoned he wrote, "Vile Stuff"; and certainly it could never have found a producer. Yet it is valuable as a demonstration of Shaw's fresh sense of character and situation, as well as his outrageously heterodox views.

The play begins with a scene in the carpenter's shop at Nazareth, where Mary and Joseph — respectively a shrew and a shiftless bully — are arguing bitterly. The entry of their sons Jesus and John does not help matters, but presently a customer comes in — a wealthy traveller named Judas Iscariot. He is looking for a first-rate craftsman to do some work for him, and Joseph recommends his elder son. Jesus

[2] British Museum, Shaw Mss. for 1878.

agrees to go, Judas having given him directions in an exchange which the young playwright makes heavily ironic:

JUDAS Young man, thou knowest
The Way of Darkness, near the synagogue.
JESUS It is a broad and pleasant path, wherein
Many do enter. I'll attend you, sir.

When the two meet again, they have a long talk about a variety of subjects, culminating in a passage in which Jesus reveals his doubts as to the accepted notions of the God of Scripture — a "gloomy tyrant" — and his belief in

A grand, ineffable, benevolent Power
Throned in the clouds, and all composed of Love
Whose influence, though obscured by death and sin
(The origin of these inexplicable)
Yet gives us all that's noble in our nature
And draws our souls, aspiring, to its majesty.
Death is to me the portal to this presence
And sure I am, though worms destroy this body,
God shall not suffer me to see corruption.

Judas replies that Jesus is a poet who has been seduced by his imagination. Judas himself is content to live only for the truth. For him

The fittest study for a feeling man
Is ceaseless observation of his fellows
Whereby he comes to know himself by them
Having first learnt their nature from his own.
This knowledge reached, the student straight becomes
A solitary watcher of the world
A man whose sympathies are so enlarged

That he is lost above the vulgar crowd
Who straight cry "Joyless cynic," "Atheist!"
In parrot fashion. But the man, unmoved,
Feeling the stream of happiness steadily rising
Though but an inch gained midst a hundred ebbs
Exultingly foresees the distant age
When man shall conquer pain, and on the brow
Of Death place an imperishable wreath.

He goes on to sketch his vision of a far-distant future in which Man will live loftily, "impenetrable, calm, and knowing," in a time when such terms as Pain and Pleasure will have lost their meaning. To achieve this, no poetic myth of a God is needed — only a sufficient number of men like himself, who

a man unblinded
And trained to shun the snare of self-delusion
Know that my very dust will scarce exist
When man shall have no reason to despise himself.
I live, almost content, and set my hand
To pick a pebble from the mighty mountain
Whose giant shadow keeps the world in darkness,
Heaped, like the Pyramid, by throngs of slaves
Whose hands, to glorify their master, Ignorance,
Piled this dull mound of superstition up.
Thus I to reason trust, and thou to dreams
But, save that I ask no part for myself
Except the foretaste which my mind supplies
We look to the same end. Then let's take hands —

And he and his companion ride off together in the direction of Jerusalem.

It is easy to see in this Judas the young Shaw, pleased with and supremely confident in his capacity for objective reasoning and purposeful action, contemptuous of whatever looks like superstition, and treating Jesus not as an impostor, indeed, but as a poet whose imagination has overset his judgment. Clearly, too, the Man-of-the-future whom Judas describes foreshadows those unsatisfactory end-products of evolution whom Shaw was to introduce forty years later in the last section of *Back to Methuselah.* In the next incident of the play Shaw makes another point that he was to return to in later years — the harm done by well-intentioned persons when they let poetic imagination guide their actions instead of rational analysis. Jesus, having begun to teach in Jerusalem and won some followers, comes into the temple and angrily overturns the money-tables — thereby encouraging a group of ruffians led by Barabbas to engage in pillaging so excitedly that when a Roman soldier tries to interfere, Barabbas kills him. Jesus is horrified — the more so because he recognizes his own responsibility in the affair:

> O miserable vanity!
> Oh wretched worm, that came to mend the world
> Having served apprenticeship to mending sticks;
> That came to drive corruption from the temple
> And in its sacred hall let loose foul murder,

he exclaims, bitterly upbraiding himself.

After this incident, which is vividly conceived, the would-be playwright clearly does not know what to do with his characters, and having set them on their way to visit Bethany, where Mary Magdalene (Pilate's mistress of the moment) is living, he gives up.

It is obvious that the play was intended as an expression not only of Shaw's denial of conventional creeds but also of his affirmation of belief in the sufficiency of human reason and the capacity of man both to conceive of and to progress towards an ideal state. As always with him, the affirmation is more important than the denial. Yet for some years — possibly as much as a decade — he found atheism a necessary condition, offensive though it might be to many around him. A true rationalist, he was quite prepared to apply the experimental test. Among the Shaw papers for 1878 in the British Museum is an envelope containing a tiny, tarnished silver medal on a piece of blackened cord. With it is a pencilled note:

> Dear George,
>
> I enclose a little medal which I beg you to wear. And believe that I wish to be your sincere friend,
>
> E. A. Collier
>
> Unless you wear the medal send it back to me.

Across the top of the letter are two notes in Shaw's handwriting, one in ink:

> Received on the 21st March 1878, with a medal of the Virgin Mary enclosed;

and one in pencil:

> Agreed to wear same for 6 mos. & discarded it accordingly 21/9/78.

The incident is significant, for it makes it clear that there was — if one may use the term — nothing doctrinaire about his atheism, as there was about that of some of his friends. In adopting it he was simply following the promptings of his own mind and heart with as much honesty as he could. Yet his concern was with belief — not unbelief; and there is in his early notebooks a surprising number of jottings of Biblical verses and comments on them. There is also noted a fragment[3] of a conversation that he had with "Mr. C." — whom we may suppose to have been the sender of the medal. They were discussing conversion:

S. Remarkable that an infidel when converted invariably becomes an R. C. — never a Protestant.

Mr. C. (an R. C.) indignantly — It's not likely that God, if he took the trouble to save a soul, would only half do it!

After Shaw had recovered from this, Mr. C. observed:

A priest has a special gift of grace whereby he converts you.

S. (referring to a recent interview) But he didn't convert me.

Mr. C. That was your hardness & perversity, and not his lack of grace. (S. floored)

For Shaw there must be no priestcraft — only the operation of his own mind on his own experience and observation. Indeed, it is open to question whether his avowed atheism ever got much beyond being an exhilarating mode of rejecting authoritarianism in religion and declaring his individual freedom of thought. Atheism was a means to freedom, but freedom did not necessarily lead to atheism: it might lead to Protestantism. It would be pleasant to suppose (though there is no direct evidence for it) that Shaw was the man who rose up in what was obviously Irish wrath, at one of the Reverend Stewart Headlam's public discussions, and shouted:

[3] British Museum, Shaw Papers for 1878.

Atheist as I am, sir, atheist as I am, no man shall stand between my soul and my God! [4]

It goes deep, my lord [says the Earl of Warwick about Joan's heresy]. It is the protest of the individual soul against the interference of priest or peer between the private man and his God. I should call it Protestantism if I had to find a name for it.

Precisely when Shaw abandoned his atheism and replaced it with the Shavian religion it is difficult to say. The mysticism which he was to claim for himself was not of the sort that involved road-to-Damascus conversions. Like his atheism, it was the product of profound reflection on his own experience of men and books and art. It came slowly, therefore, and like a thief in the night; and all the available evidence suggests, significantly, that it began at the same time as his conversion to socialism, and that its development and his deepening concern with socialism went hand in hand. It is interesting to observe, for example, that on May 3, 1884, his militantly atheistic friend Belfort Bax wrote to Shaw an outraged note in response to a comment which the latter had made on Bax's secularist materialism:

Shaw! I always did believe you honest, but now, alas! what do I find to be the result of two months hobnobbing with "baptized Christians"? [5]

Bax demanded. It was just two days later that a letter came from a new acquaintance, Hubert Bland, who wrote to tell Shaw more about "the Fabian about which I spoke to you last night," to invite him to the next Fabian meeting, and to

[4] F. G. Bettany: *Stewart Headlam* (London: John Murray, 1926).
[5] British Museum, Shaw Papers for 1884.

enclose "the only tract we have yet issued." That summer Bax continued to harangue Shaw about religion, but finally gave him up for lost. "No, Shaw," he wrote on August 21:

> I regret to see you have still the *bourgeois* in your blood. Wishing you a successful purification of your intellectual system . . .

If Shaw's hobnobbing with Christians distressed Bax, it must equally have distressed the Christians; for it did not connote anything remotely resembling a return to his childhood fold. There must have been countless occasions more or less like the meeting of the Browning Society in May 1888 at which Anna M. Stoddard read a paper on Browning's "Saul," concerning which Shaw had something to say, as the secretary noted:

> Mr. Shaw thought the poem a very beautiful one. Apart from his admiration and enjoyment of the poem as a poem, he did not see how anyone in this century could accept the cardinal statement in it, where David informs Saul that "all is love and all is law." Miss Stoddard did, on the ground that that optimism was just as valid in the present day in an address from her to them, as it was from David to Saul. Looking round at what took place today, how could anyone accept David's statement, that these were the works of God? He had some experience as to how Christianity enabled people to endure sorrow. He must say that they bore the misfortunes of others with the most extraordinary magnanimity. Although not a Christian, he would like to say a word or two on Christ from a purely secular point of view. In regard to the statement that Christ is always with us, he thought if Christ were to come on the earth and see what was taking place, he would be very greatly hurt to be told that it was the

> influence of his spirit, for he thought this the most desperately mean, sordid, selfish, rascally, dastardly century that anyone could wish to live in. They found wretched men, women, and children working and sweating from twelve to eighteen hours a day for a bare subsistence, in order to produce the dividends on which these very Christian people lived pleasantly, and went to church on Sunday to thank God that they were not as other men.[6]

All the same, a profound change had been taking place in Shaw, and Bax had been right in discerning it, if wrong in his diagnosis.

It may come about some day that Shaw's socialist activities will be seen as simply an episode — though a major one — in his religious development. Even if the major plays are all that survive, this may still be true; for they comprise, as he himself maintained, much more a statement of religious faith than a political manifesto; and he was to comment that even socialism was never more for him than a program of specific reforms that he thought desirable. Nevertheless the introduction to socialism preceded the beginning of his new religious faith, and it was not the philosophers or the mystics who "rent the veil," but Karl Marx. He did so, Shaw told Pearson,[7] by opening his eyes to the facts of history and civilization, giving him a fresh conception of the universe, and providing him with a mission and purpose in life. For the connection between ideas and experience has to be made by each individual in a way suitable to him. Until he read Marx, Shaw's thought had been to a large extent divorced from life; the

[6] The Browning Society's Papers 1888–89, Part X (London: N. Trubner & Co., 1888), p. 266.

[7] Hesketh Pearson: *Bernard Shaw, His Life and Personality* (London: Collins, 1942), p. 68.

ideas he discussed were not grounded in experience. They were therefore in the true sense academic, as a debate about the Trinity might be to a Buddhist. They were not felt. Marx served as the fire that fused ideas and life, thought and passion. Shaw's account and Pearson's suggest an abrupt and dramatic change; in fact what occurred took place gradually — as became a Fabian — with much analysis and discussion and many interruptions.

We have already seen that Shaw made his first close study of socialist economics as a member of a group organized about the beginning of 1884. That group was concerned primarily with Marx. Yet, in view of the fact that its founder and hostess was the anarchist Charlotte Wilson, it is reasonable to suppose that it gave some attention also to the teachings of Marx's principal rival in revolution, Michael Bakunin. It is true that Marx's economic and social theory fascinated Shaw more than anything else; but it is hard to resist the impression that the anarchism of Bakunin, with its emphasis on individual liberty, on puritanical morality, and on destruction as an aspect of creation, was in the long run hardly less significant.

Perhaps, however, the remarkable P. H. Wicksteed, who was the leader of the group, had more to do with the renewal of Shaw's specific interest in religion. Wicksteed, as well as being an economist, was a Dante scholar and a clergyman — one of several who influenced Shaw in this period. They were cultivated and liberal-minded men, and with them he went over the ground of his disbelief, and found them not aghast, but prepared for informed and good-natured debate. Whatever their influence may have been, it is certain that in the mid-1880's he was becoming increasingly dissatisfied with the ultimate aridity to which atheism, despite the noble and disinterested social purposes that many of its followers pursued, inevitably led. Those followers had adopted Darwinism, and Shaw's acquaintance Edward Aveling — then living with Karl Marx's daughter Eleanor, who was presently to commit suicide on his account — had written an essay called "The Gospel of Evolution" for *The Atheist Platform* of 1884. Unquestionably Shaw accepted the idea of evolution. Early in 1887, however, he read, reread, and reviewed Samuel Butler's *Luck, or Cunning?* — and his eyes began to be opened to the full horror of the idea of a universe that was not only materialistic, but mindless. In the next year or two he read or reread, among other writers, Blake, Bunyan, and Schopenhauer, and his rejection of materialist atheism as a valid and practicable creed was completed. Late in 1884, in the course of a letter to Hubert Bland, he had written:

> The ordinary man, leading the ordinary life, never becomes conscious of the will or impulse in him that sets his brain at work devising ways and reasons. He supposes his life to be a mere matter of logical consequences from a few bodily appetites and externally appointed "duties" with their attendant pains and penalties . . . If such a man is to attain consciousness of himself as a vessel of the Zeitgeist or will or whatever it may be, he must pay the price of turning his back on the loaves and fishes, the duties, the ready-made logic, the systems and the creeds. He must do what he likes instead of doing what, on second-hand principles, he ought — You and I have followed our original impulse, and our reward is that we have been conscious of its existence and can rejoice therein. The coming into clearer light of this consciousness has not occurred to me as a crisis. It has been gradual . . .[8]

Obviously Shaw saw himself even then as moving to a new, mystical relationship with the cosmos. In fact he had begun to

[8] Doris Langley Moore: *E. Nesbit, A Biography* (London: Ernest Benn Ltd., 1933), p. 100.

set in place of his atheism a hypothesis of the universe and man's place in it that gave him simultaneously a fresh sense of individual significance and a cosmic sanction for his socialism. Twelve years later, in a remarkable essay that he wrote for the opening number of the *Savoy*, he announced the final futility not only of atheism but of rationalism and proclaimed himself a churchgoer. We need not take the phrase with too much literal seriousness, though his declaration is not merely a piece of Shavian blarney. For him "churchgoing" has a broad and unorthodox meaning. Nevertheless the essay shows how completely his view of the nature of man and his destiny had changed. The consequence was that he became a man of faith — not in the Pauline sense that makes faith the substance of things hoped for, but in that older definition which calls it the resolution to stand or fall by the noblest hypothesis.

What he had needed was a hypothesis that would in the first place be credible. Since boyhood he had been revolted by "the mass of mean superstition and misunderstood prophecies which is still rammed down the throats of children in this country."[9] A Bible that was filled not only with self-contradictions but with much that was patently contrary to what modern man has learned about the world could never content him: he must have a hypothesis that would allow for the free advance of knowledge without the periodic turmoil into which the church was thrown by Galileos and Darwins. Moreover, it must be one that avoided the inherent contradictions that troubled the minds of Victorians from Mill to Hardy, and had been threshed over endlessly in the various debating and literary societies that Shaw belonged to: the incompatibility of divine omnipotence with divine benevolence;

[9] "Mr. Bernard Shaw Explains His Religion," *The Freethinker* (Nov. 1, 1908).

of divine omniscience with freedom of choice; of teleology with natural law.

> The Author of the Sermon on the Mount [Mill had written] is assuredly a far more benignant Being than the author of Nature. But unfortunately, the believer in the Christian revelation is obliged to believe that the same being is the author of both.[10]

In 1888 Shaw, turning for the moment from arguing for the economic basis of socialism to considering some of its philosophical bases, observed that

> if the guiding hand were indeed benevolent, then it could not be omnipotent; so that our trust in it was broken: if it were omnipotent, it could not be benevolent; so that our love of it turned to fear and hatred . . .[11]

He must, then, have a hypothesis that the reason could accept; but that did not mean, though he passed through a phase of rationalism, that he remained a rationalist. In 1908 he wrote bluntly:

> I am contemptuously and implacably anti-rationalist and anti-materialist.[12]

The point was that while he must be able to accept his hypothesis in all intellectual honesty, he also recognized (as twentieth-century physicists are beginning to do) that human reason is severely limited, and that there are whole ranges of

[10] John Stuart Mill: *Three Essays on Religion* (New York: Henry Holt & Co., 1874), p. 112.
[11] "The Economic Basis of Socialism," in *Fabian Essays in Socialism,* p. 43.
[12] "Mr. Bernard Shaw Explains His Religion."

experience that it is incompetent to deal with. It is an instrument of analysis and reflection, by which we may see what is possible and by what means the possible may be achieved; but it is powerless to make us move towards — or even wish for — that possibility.

"Reason is never a root, neither of act nor desire," says Robinson Jeffers, summing up a truth that Hamlet also had discovered.

Yet all the ranges of experience have meaning, even though it may not be statable in the terms of the reason; indeed, it is precisely the attempt to rationalize certain of them which leads to the unintelligible contradictions and impossible rigidities of creed and dogma. Near the end of the essay "On Going to Church" Shaw reaffirms his claim that the church is essential to man's deepest need; but he adds that that need cannot be met even in the church

> save when we leave outside the door the materialisations that help us to believe the incredible, and the intellectualisations that help us to think the unthinkable, completing the refuse-heap of "isms" and creeds with our vain lust for truth and happiness, and going in without thought or belief or prayer or any other vanity, so that the soul, freed from all that crushing lumber, may open all its avenues of life to the holy air of the true Catholic church.

Shaw's hypothesis must be rational, but not rationalistic. Also, it must take honest account of the insufficiencies of man and nature, and provide for the possibility of improvement. He was repelled by the doctrine of Original Sin, with its unremitting perpetuation of inherent evil in the heart of man; he was completely outraged by the doctrine of the Atonement, whereby sinners were cleared of their responsibility through the gratuitous murder of an innocent Jew two thousand years ago. He was prepared to stand or fall by the noblest hypothesis — but not by this ignoble evasion.

The theory of Creative Evolution at which he arrived underlay everything he wrote after the mid-1890's. He stated it and explored its implications over and over again, in plays and essays and speeches, often without his audience's recognizing that he was doing so. Yet he never forgot that it was only a theory — a piece of cosmic guesswork, "basically as hypothetical and provisional as any of the creeds." This being so, and because of his impatience of rationalism, he made no attempt to turn it into a philosophical "system" — much less a theological one. He was not interested in the refinements of epistemology, eschatology, or the like abstractions, and would probably have agreed with Thomas Mann that the satisfaction to be derived from the contemplation of "systems" is a private and aesthetic one only. What he wanted — without in the least disvaluing purposive contemplation — was a credible cosmic perspective and a frame of reference for the discussion of moral and social questions.

He found it in the concept — which may be stated briefly here — of a force which, though in itself without vision or intelligence, nevertheless works endlessly, in and through matter, towards an ever fuller and higher realization of itself. Its ultimate goal is a state of pure intelligence, in which matter will be dispensed with. Because it is imperfect and fumbling, it makes mistakes — sometimes hideous ones — in its millennially slow advance towards that goal; it has to discard them and begin again; and the works of geologists and palaeontologists are full of the evidence of its having done so. Nevertheless it fills the universe, not with chaos and accident, but with purpose and design. It is not intelligence, though mind is as yet its highest instrument and achievement. It is not love, though love is sometimes its best device. Miraculous and mysterious and ineffable, this force is Life itself.

There is no need to attempt here to trace the sources of the concept; it is clear enough that many strands of nineteenth-century thought are caught up in it. In so far as Shaw is concerned, the last stage of its development seems to have begun with his reading of *Luck, or Cunning?* in 1887. Yet the review of Butler's book that he wrote for the *Pall Mall Gazette* in May of that year is not at all conclusive. It sketches wittily the nature of the Darwin-Butler controversy and praises Butler's quality as a writer, but sidesteps the issue itself:

> It is not expedient to discuss here the main point raised by Mr. Butler, particularly as he is evidently quite capable of writing another book on the scientific attainments of the Pall Mall Gazette, if provoked by contradiction.

In the course of time he came to take Butler's view of evolution, it is true, and he fully acknowledged that author's primacy in the fight to present the theory with something better than the arid mechanism of Darwin. All the same, Shaw was not one to let other people do his thinking for him and he differs from Butler in several respects. The most important of these is the one noticed by C. E. M. Joad, who pointed out how divergent the views of the two writers are on the role of intellect:

> Butler regards the operations of the speculative intellect as a pedantic futility, and appears to look forward with equanimity to the merging of the practical intellect in unconscious instinct. There is nothing in his writing to show that he does not think man would be better off without intellect alto-

gether, and that its gradual supersession may be expected as the next stage in human progress towards the goal of evolution. For Shaw, on the other hand, the unfettered operations of intellect are the goal of evolution.[13]

In comparing Shaw's discussions of Creative Evolution with Butler's, too — the Preface to *Man and Superman*, say, with *God the Known and God the Unknown* — one cannot fail to see how much freer Shaw is than Butler of the lesions of a bigoted upbringing and education. Butler could no more clear himself of the effects of "country parsonage unsociability and evangelical bigotry" — to use Shaw's phrase — than Shaw could overcome those of upper-middle-class snobbishness.

At all events, Shaw had little interest in efforts to trace the sources of his ideas about Creative Evolution. Certainly he did not claim originality for the theory, and was quite content, when Bergson's work appeared, to acknowledge him as its philosopher.[14] For the technical criticisms of scholars he cared little — they were only rationalizing, after all. He may perhaps have noted with approval Bertrand Russell's comment, even though it occurred in a sweeping attack which the latter made on Bergson, that

[13] C. E. M. Joad: *Samuel Butler* (London: Leonard Parsons Ltd., 1924), p. 165.

[14] Not with the humility of discipleship, of course. Bertrand Russell tells of a luncheon in London in honour of Bergson, "to which Shaw had been invited as an admirer, along with a number of professional philosophers whose attitude to Bergson was more critical. Shaw set to work to expound Bergson's philosophy in the style of the preface to *Methusaleh*. In this version, the philosophy was hardly one to recommend itself to professionals, and Bergson mildly interjected, 'Ah, no-o! It is not qvite zat!' But Shaw was quite unabashed, and replied, 'Oh, my dear fellow, I understand your philosophy much better than you do.' Bergson clenched his fists and nearly exploded with rage; but, with a great effort, he controlled himself, and Shaw's expository monologue continued." (Russell: *Portraits from Memory and Other Essays*. London: George Allen and Unwin, 1956, p. 73.)

> when we have shown that this or that doctrine is self-contradictory, we have only shown that it does not appeal to the intellect; if the intellect is in fact misleading, as Bergson contends, it is useless to employ it against him.[15]

At the elegantly disdainful question of Santayana he would have laughed — and perhaps introduced it into a play:

> What is this *élan vital,* that a little fall in temperature would banish altogether from the universe? [16]

It must be noted that although the full nature and operation of the Life Force are beyond the scope of reason, it is nevertheless working in the direction of mind; and while man must recognize that reason is yet a very primitive instrument, it is the best one available, and must be cultivated in every possible way. If, considered as impulse, the Life Force is comparable to the Schopenhauerian Will, Shaw sees no opposition between it and Intellect, as Schopenhauer had done.

> Ability to reason accurately is as desirable as ever; for by accurate reason only can we calculate our actions so as to do what we intend to do: that is, fulfil our will —

Shaw wrote in 1890 — an idea that must already have been forming in his mind when he introduced the temple scene into his Passion Play.

Certain of the broad implications of the hypothesis of Creative Evolution were of special value to Shaw. In the first place, it provided a philosophical justification for his attitude

[15] Bertrand Russell: *The Philosophy of Bergson* (Cambridge: Bowes and Bowes, 1914), p. 36.

[16] George Santayana: *Winds of Doctrine* (London: J. M. Dent & Sons Ltd., 1913), p. 107.

to authority, by doing away with absolutes of any sort whatever. If there is not and never has been a being that was perfect, and perfection is only a goal that is millions of years in the future, then no individual or institution can properly lay claim to power or authority other than that which may have arisen within itself. There are no divine beings and there are no divine laws; and Good and Evil are relative terms only. Not even life itself is sacred, since its various forms continually and inevitably destroy one another. The mysterious Life Force that surges through all living forms on its tortuous evolutionary path is eternal, its purposes are holy. Shaw nevertheless — for all his hatred of cruelty, his humanitarianism, vegetarianism, anti-vivisectionism, and so on — held no sentimental regard for the individual forms themselves. He was to write in 1915:

> I see no logical nor spiritual escape from the theory that evolution involves a deliberate intentional destruction by the higher forms of life of the lower.[17]

It follows that no reasoning individual can properly expect some other individual or an institution to determine for him what is the ultimate nature of his relationship with the cosmos and what his behavior ought to be: these are things that he must discover by his own honest reflection on his own experience; and having discovered them, he is under the highest obligation to deal with them in such a way as to help the Life Force in its evolving purpose. The Kingdom of Heaven is within you indeed; it exists nowhere else; and you will find it only by strenuously seeking to serve the purposes of the Life

[17] *Killing for Sport,* ed. Henry S. Salt (London: G. Bell & Sons Ltd., 1915), Preface, p. xvii.

Force in every thought and action. In short, the individual is freed from the need of deferring to external authority.

But he is also deprived of its support. He can no longer ask others, "What must I do?" He must ask himself. And truth to oneself becomes the highest canon.

The will to be true to oneself, which has inspired the noblest achievements of men throughout history, Shaw conceived as a passion, and called it "the moral passion." Truth to oneself, however, postulates a will to find the truth as well as a will to act it. Therefore alongside the moral passion he places a second one: intellect.

> I should say [he remarked as he began his brilliant Foundation Oration at the University of London in 1920] that one of the first things that a student at a university has got to feel, if he has any business at the university at all, is that intellect is a passion, that intellect is really the noblest of the passions, and that it is the most enjoyable of the passions, and the most lasting of them.

Beside these two, the other passions are of secondary importance, and indeed some of them are downright nuisances. Even the sexual passion is one of these. True, it is still biologically necessary to evolving life; in this sense certainly it is crucial, and the study of its proper role and of the social framework in which it may function best is of the greatest importance. Still, aside from this utilitarian aspect the sexual passion is a mischievous hindrance. As man evolves further in the direction of mind he will gradually leave it and the other vestigial physical passions behind. Yet it does not follow that intellect and morality, the newest passions, are the strongest. On the contrary, at the present stage of evolution they are weak — often mere toys of the others.

If the individual's highest responsibility is to realize as fully as possible the purposes of the Life Force within himself, then obviously he must be left free to do so. And in this conception lay the philosophical justification for Shaw's socialism. Only in a democratic and socialist society, where the state is responsible to the citizen as well as the citizen to the state, can the individual be free to think, to act, and — most especially, since the Life Force still depends on biological devices — to mate.

Free — not equal. The relativism implicit in the theory of Creative Evolution necessitates a fresh examination of the concept of equality in human affairs. What use in talking of men's equality in the sight of the Absolute if there is no Absolute? How can there be equality of opportunity when opportunity is visibly the product of inevitably unequal environments and inherently unequal endowments? Phrases such as "equality before the law" may describe objectives well worth striving for, even though we can never be quite sure whether we have attained them; and many artificially induced inequalities can indeed — and must — be swept away as obstructions in the way of the Life Force: those of rank and class, for example, which so seriously limit the freedom of individuals to marry. Still, equality is after all a mathematical conception, and (setting anthropometry aside) only one aspect of human behavior is susceptible to the measurement it implies: the economic. Let us bring about equality of income, then, for we shall find that by doing so we abolish other artificial inequalities and go a long way towards making men free.

It is easy to see, then, how Shaw's socialism is in effect an aspect of his religion. For him socialism is the Church Militant — the embodiment and forefront of the upward struggle of the Life Force; and his religion inspires and supports it at every point. He is at almost the opposite pole from Yeats, whom William Morris had brought into the Hammersmith circle of socialists. For a while Yeats was an enthusiastic supporter of the movement; but he broke from it after a discussion of religion in which, as he tells in *Autobiographies*, he spoke "with all the arrogance of raging youth," saying that "there must be a change of heart and only religion could make it," and questioning the common sense of "talking about some new revolution putting all things right, when the change must come . . . with astronomical slowness." Shaw must have agreed about the change of heart, and even about its slowness; but in his view, it and the revolution they were talking about were inextricably bound together. To do as Yeats was implying — keep the religion and not worry about the socialism, and so make the slowness only more astronomical — was the height of irresponsibility.

That men cannot be their best selves if they are not free to be them is clear enough; but it is also clear that by disposing of absolutes and making truth to oneself the basis of conduct, Shaw envelops the word "best" in a deep fog. If each person is to follow the good as he sees it in the light of his own experience and reason, then conduct becomes an entirely relative affair; and the individual can only proceed pragmatically, by trial and error. Shaw here presented himself with a problem that Mark Twain, his fellow rebel, had been confronted with only a few years earlier. Huckleberry Finn, however, when he had explored the society of the Mississippi Valley and found its institutions to be cruel shams and its religion hypocrisy (found, in short, that its sole effect on him was to prevent him from being true to himself), resolved to abandon it — "light out for the Territory" — and have done with civilization. But Shaw believed that there must be *more* civilization, not *less.* To reject utterly institutions and conventions and laws was to create moral anarchy. And as he was to write many years later:

> the only definition of scoundrelism known to me is anarchism in morals.[18]

He perforce came to a very different conclusion from Mark Twain's. It was one that involved an important modification of the view that I have described of the nature of the individual's role in evolution and in society. For the continued development of the Life Force through evolution, it may be necessary for the individual to be free from the twin authorities of law and convention, free to be true to himself; but — the recognition was forced on Shaw by his political experience — the plain fact is that most men at the present stage of evolution cannot be trusted with such freedom and indeed do not want it. Neither the intellectual nor the moral passion has sufficiently developed in them. It follows that laws and conventions to codify standards of behavior, and institutions to enforce them, are social necessities; in making them effectual, even myth and dogma may have their place.

The civilization that Shaw wanted to see extended and enlarged was — curiously enough, in view of his numberless assaults on its institutions — British civilization. When the Boer war broke out, he was firmly on the side of the Empire; and in the tract that he wrote stating the position of the Fabian Society in regard to the war, he argued for economic imperialism on the basis of international socialism:

> The notion that a nation has a right to do what it pleases with its own territory, without reference to the interests of the

[18] Preface to *London Music in 1888–89.*

rest of the world is no more tenable from the International Socialist point of view — that is, from the point of view of the twentieth century — than the notion that a landlord has a right to do what he likes with his estate without reference to the interests of his neighbors . . . [In China] we are asserting and enforcing international rights of travel and trade. But the right to trade is a very comprehensive one: it involves a right to insist on a settled government which can keep the peace and enforce agreements. When a native government of this order is impossible, the foreign trading power must set one up.[19]

For such purposes war might, apparently, be an instrument of the Life Force. At about the same time as he wrote *Fabianism and the Empire*, Shaw sent a letter to the *Saturday Review* discussing the British actions in China following the outbreak of the Boxer uprising:

> The war in China is part of a series of inevitable wars for the establishment of an international level of civilization. If the Western level of civilization gets reduced by the passions which war excites to the level of the refractory civilizations which it attacks, the world-force which is flinging the West on the East will vanish; and the victory will be to the hardiest and skillfullest slayer . . . We are belying the ground on which all our wars must now be fought: to wit, the superiority of British civilization to the civilizations that come in conflict with it.[20]

The quotations are doubly interesting, for they expose two serious flaws in Shaw's thinking. The implied notion that British civilization, being a superior one, should *ipso facto* be able

[19] *Fabianism and the Empire* (London: The Fabian Society, 1900).
[20] *Saturday Review* (July 28, 1900).

to wage war in some high-minded fashion and not be "reduced by the passions that war excites" is the measure of his insight into the nature of passion. It was to betray him into what was by far the most confused writing he ever did: his comments on World War I, collected in the volume called *What I Really Wrote About the War.* Allied to confusion about the problem of war is his confusion about the problem of means and ends. He could argue with the greatest eloquence that man has no right to pursue knowledge (much less, as so often happens, compound his ignorance) by torturing animals. If the end cannot be achieved by some better means than vivisection and the cruelty it involves, the end will have to wait, and indeed we may have to forego it. On the other hand, he was equally prepared to argue in effect that mass vivisection of human beings — war — for the purposes of international trade and civilization is justified by the end in view.

He does, it is true, suggest two important considerations. In the first place, the conventions and the codes of civilization must be seen and stated honestly, not made billboard advertisements for morality behind which iniquity may flourish. It may — to adopt a common Shavian example — be necessary on occasion for society to take the life of an individual. Let the necessity then be stated clearly and objectively, not in terms of such impossible abstractions as justice, loyalty, and the like — which so easily become mere euphemisms for revenge, envy, or the lust for blood. In this respect Shaw is directly in the line of all great satirists, from Aristophanes to Swift; he differs only in the specific religious sanction of his attacks. In the second place, the law and the convention, the myth and the dogma must not be made absolute. Since the Life Force is evolving towards some unimaginable perfection from visible imperfection, the imperfection must not be permitted to impede the process by becoming crystallized and static. Change is indeed the law of life, as much for those recent evolutionary arrivals, the moral and intellectual passions, as for the primitive protoplasm.

Yet no specific change establishes itself throughout an entire species simultaneously; to stay with the two passions referred to, no new intellectual or moral attitude or concept becomes established throughout an entire society simultaneously. Rather, it begins with particular individuals who are strong enough in intellect to see more clearly than their fellows, and endowed with sufficient moral passion to act according to what they see, at all costs — even of life itself. These are the individuals who find impossible the conventions that the masses of their fellows submit to, because those conventions prevent them from being true to the new vision of life that they have seen. They therefore rebel against the conventions — and for doing so are sometimes persecuted by their fellows even to martyrdom. Nevertheless, by their vision they show the way to the rest, and their persecutors become their followers, and the Life Force reaches forward a little further. These are the individuals who change the world — they are the heretics, the rebels, the geniuses of history.

It is clear that Shaw had seen all this by the early 1890's; for in a letter to Florence Farr, in January 1892, he wrote:

> There are two sorts of genius in this world. One is produced by the breed throwing forward to the godlike man, exactly as it sometimes throws backward to the apelike. The other is the mere monster produced by an accidental excess of some faculty — musical, muscular, sexual even. A giant belongs properly to this category; he has a genius for altitude. Now the second order of genius requires no education: he (or she) does at once and without effort his feat, whatever it may be,

> and scoffs at laborious practice. The first order finds it far otherwise. It is immature at thirty, and though desperately in need of education (being less a child of Nature by so much more as it is advanced in evolution) can find nothing but misleading until it laboriously teaches itself. I am a genius of the first order . . . but I know my order and the price I must pay for excellence . . .[21]

It follows that Shaw saw the necessity, for the masses of ordinary people, of conventional morality and law as guides to conduct. Individuals who wrote him — as many did — about their problems were often surprised, and sometimes offended, by the conventionality of his advice, as, for example, when he consistently advised young women to adhere to the accepted pattern in respect to marriage. He argued that the day will come when we shall have a society in which some system of "Free Love" will displace the present institution of marriage and that it will be a vast improvement when this happens; all the same, in the present state of the law regarding property and women's rights, a woman is foolish to run the risks involved in defying convention. The essential point, of course, is that people who are not by nature unconventional — for whom in fact being true to themselves really means being conventional — only invite disaster if they force themselves to rebel. And the naturally unconventional person does not ask for advice about his behavior. The most that can be hoped is that the conventional majority will not persecute the unconventional few among whom is the spearhead of the Life Force's advance. Especially they must not persecute new and unaccustomed ideas. Shaw's lifelong war against literary and dramatic censorship was an expression of this view; but it too

[21] *Florence Farr, Bernard Shaw, W. B. Yeats, Letters,* ed. Clifford Bax (New York: Dodd, Mead, 1942), p. 9.

must not be misunderstood. Society, he believed, has a perfect right to examine and try in its courts or other institutions ideas that are offensive to its ordinary standards, and persons who propagate those ideas: there must always be Inquisitions. What is wrong is not the existence of them, but the placing of their functions in the hands of officials who are not held publicly accountable for their decisions, and the introduction of dogmatic absolutes into their judgments and cruelty into their sentences. Spectators of *Saint Joan* — especially Protestant spectators — are too apt to see it as an attack on the Inquisition. Yet Shaw could hardly have explained more carefully that it is not: he devotes a large part of the Preface to making the point that the church had a perfect right — even duty — to try Joan in the courts, examine her heresy and its effects, and excommunicate her forthwith; and indeed that her trial was a model of fairness. What neither the church nor the state nor any other institution had the right to do was to persecute and destroy her for her ideas, especially with such cruelty. Nevertheless, that was the only point at which her judges went wrong: "the final and dreadful wrong of the lying sentence and the pitiless fire," as Ladvenu describes it in the Epilogue.

The impact on Shaw's life of his conversion — if we may use that term — to Creative Evolution can hardly be overestimated. The eccentric socialist now had a religious basis for both eccentricity and socialism; the man who had struggled to find an aim and had battled long against his own indolence found his being flooded with the purpose and energy of fully awakened genius. And at least some of the gates of Hell were not to prevail against him. He was saved forever from the gloom that so often darkens the work of his great contemporaries in letters: Hardy, Conrad, Galsworthy. It was not another chronicler of Crass Casualty who took the Stage in the 1890's; instead it was G.B.S., with his vast and dauntless egotism, supported not merely by his class-consciousness, his sense of intellectual power, and his passion for freedom and truth, but also by a cosmic philosophy which he was prepared to proclaim to the world with ringing conviction.

> My passion [he wrote to a fellow playwright in 1894], like that of all artists, is for efficiency, which means intensity of life and breadth and variety of experience; and already I find, as a dramatist, that I can go at one stroke to the centre of matters that reduce the purely literary man to colourless platitudes.
>
> Do you now begin to understand, O Henry Arthur Jones, that you have to deal with a man who habitually thinks of himself as one of the great geniuses of all time? — just as you necessarily do yourself. We may be deceiving ourselves; but why add to the heavy chances of that, the absolute certainty of such a deception as would be involved in the notion that we thought ourselves common fellows with a bit of talent.][22]

It could not be expected that the attitude of mind implied in this passage should not harden through the years into a vanity that at times seemed monumental. Nor can one fail to see how closely Shaw's religion suited his own individuality — what a made-to-measure creed it was. The man who concluded that intellect and morality (which he at least took to be his own passions) were the highest of the passions, and that the commoner human feelings — love, anger, grief, and so on — were of a lower order, confessed by that very fact that the range of his sympathy with the mass of humanity was a se-

[22] *Life and Letters of Henry Arthur Jones* (London: Victor Gollancz Ltd., 1930), p. 141.

verely limited one, and that to a large extent he set himself apart from it. The effects were sometimes bizarre. Shaw once described his Shelley Society friend, Furnivall, as a Muscular Christian who "could not forgive Jesus for not putting up a fight in Gethsemane." But in a similar way Shaw, as a genius of Creative Evolution and believing Jesus also to be a man of genius, could not forgive him for failing to put up an argument before Pilate, and indeed went so far as to provide a belated script for him.

One of the forms that his vanity took was a species of hindsight that led him to falsify — perhaps quite unconsciously — his own past. As a genius of the intellectual and moral passions, it was to be expected not that he would be infallible but that he would always have shown a degree of insight and responsibility beyond the ordinary. Accordingly, when in 1895 he looked back at the art criticism which he had written only a few years before, he came, as we have seen, to the surprising conclusion that he had always been on the side of the Impressionists. Similarly, he liked to affirm that he never sacrificed political duty to private pleasure — especially sexual pleasure — and "never refused or broke an engagement to speak on Socialism, to pass a gallant evening." The diaries make clear that this statement is a good deal short of the truth; and surely no candid reader of them can accept for a moment his statement that "I did not pursue women: I was pursued by them." In the same way the notion that he was always essentially in control, and that "like Goethe, I knew all along," was necessary to the G.B.S. myth; but that is all.

Yet all this is nothing beside the positive effects of Shaw's adoption of his new faith. The fact that his creed has had few if any followers, and that it raises at least as many questions as it answers, is beside the point. It is true that it is a religion in which, though much is holy, nothing is sacred; in which God is not the beginning but the end — not the Creator but the created; and man's chief function is not to glorify and enjoy Him forever, but only to help, in the brief moment allowed, to bring Him into existence. Yet Shaw found in it a credible framework in which to view man and the cosmos; and he found much more — a pattern of ideas that simultaneously excited, organized, and released his phenomenal energy. He became a man with not only one cause, but a dozen — all of them expressions of his resolution to stand or fall by what was for him the noblest hypothesis. Without it his socialism would have lost half its fire — and his plays would never have existed at all:

> . . . the best established truth in the world [he wrote to Henry Arthur Jones in 1899] is that no man produces a work of art of the very first order except under the pressure of a strong conviction and definite meaning as to the constitution of the world. Dante, Goethe, and Bunyan could not possibly have produced their masterpieces if they had been mere art-voluptuaries. It may be that the artistic by-product is more valuable than the doctrine; but there is no other way of getting the by-product than by the effort and penetrating force that doctrine braces a man to. Go straight to the by-product and you get Gounod instead of Wagner.[23]

For the Creative Evolutionist, art could never be a compromise — not even a "joyous compromise," as Lawrence Durrell has called it; it must be nothing less than a ringing statement of faith.

Having experienced the transformation that his religion

[23] *Life and Letters of Henry Arthur Jones* (London: Gollancz, 1930), p. 143.

effected in himself, Shaw could not fail to conclude that it ought similarly to transform others; and indeed came eventually to believe that only the religious impulse could bring about the social changes that he wanted to see. In 1908, in an address at the City Temple, he looked back over his activities as social and intellectual rebel, and drew some conclusions:

> After the experience that I have had of various forward movements, I have discovered that the only people who are dangerous are the religious people. I have been in movements which, as you know, in some ways have been very highly intellectualized. They have been able to give very convincing demonstrations, for instance, to the working men of this country that whenever they produce a pound somebody robs them of ten shillings. There was a time about the middle of the last century when many able men — Karl Marx was one — really did believe that if you could only bring that intellectual demonstration and the fact of that robbery home to the working men of Europe they would combine together and rise up against that robbery and put an end to it. I don't know that I hadn't some hopes in that direction myself . . . but I discovered by experience that no man has the slightest objection to being robbed of ten shillings out of a pound if the remaining ten shillings will make him reasonably comfortable.

He went on to appeal to his hearers to go out and place before men an ideal of citizenship that will involve the highest sense of social responsibility:

> Take poverty and illness in extremely bad part; and when you meet a man whose wife is ill or who is poor . . . don't say to him that it is the will of God, which is a horrible blasphemy. Tell him in solemn Scriptural language that it is a

> damnable thing, and that you have come to try and put a stop to it because *you* are the will of God. And then you will have put the man you are talking to on the high road to understand that his will is the will of God too.[24]

For the reordering of society is only a means to the regeneration of man, so that the Life Force may, through him, reach further towards its goal.

> Communism [Shaw wrote in 1935 at the age of 79], is the fairy godmother who can transform Bosses into "servants of the rest"; but only a creed of Creative Evolution can set the souls of the people free.[25]

[24] R. J. Campbell: *The New Theology* (London: Mills & Boon Ltd., 1909), pp. 258ff.

[25] Preface to *The Millionairess.*

# 7
# *Philandering and "The Philanderer"*

I HAVE BEEN trying to show that the emergence of the mature Shaw — especially of Shaw the playwright — followed and was largely the result of a complex of experiences that he underwent in the years 1885–1892; and that these experiences included his acceptance of socialism as a practical mission of his life, the shaping through journalism and debating of his thought about the arts — especially music and the theatre — as well as his prose style, and his gradual adoption of a belief about the cosmos and man's place in it sufficiently comprehensive and profound to support both socialism and art and to be felt by him as essentially religious.

There is another aspect of his life in this period that strikes the reader of his letters and diaries as having taken up almost as much time and energy as both art and socialism. For that reason, and because of the light that it throws on his character and the effect it had on his plays, it has to be taken into account. It was the subject of an oddly defensive note that Shaw addressed to Frank Harris in 1930, beginning in this way:

> First, O sex-obsessed Biographer, get it into your mind that you can learn nothing about your biographees from their sex histories. The sex relation is not a personal relation.[1]

[1] *Sixteen Self-Sketches*, p. 113.

A biographee who says that the sex relation is not a personal relation is telling a good deal about himself, and certainly justifying the biographer in looking more closely at the "relation" as it concerns his subject. The biographer is entitled to ask, for example, whether those who shared in the relation also had the impression that it was impersonal.

Archibald Henderson described Shaw as "ruthlessly antiromantic" from the age of fifteen; the evidence suggests, on the contrary, an unusually susceptible and romantic youth, finding in daydreams what he was too mistrustful and self-conscious (and poor) to pursue in reality. Shaw himself said in later years that, although sexual experience was delayed for him to a much later age than for most men, he was like Rousseau, whose blood boiled with sexual longings from childhood on. In one of his letters to Mrs. Patrick Campbell he told her of how

> Once, in my calfish teens, I fell wildly in love with a lady of your complexion; and she, good woman, having a sister to provide for, set to work to marry me to the sister. Whereupon I shot back into the skies from which I had descended, and never saw her again.[2]

This however was not by any means his only early and earthly romance. The letters that he kept — one wonders what prompted him to do so — make it clear that he carried on flirtations on all sides, turning from one to another with great dexterity, and laying a firm basis for the skill in philandering that he subsequently displayed. A number of cryptic notes among the diaries obviously refer to youthful attachments, the details of which are concealed behind asterisks and

[2] *Bernard Shaw and Mrs. Patrick Campbell: Their Correspondence*, ed. Alan Dent (London: Victor Gollancz Ltd., 1952), p. 41.

exotic pseudonyms. There are the "L*** Episode," the "Calypso infatuation," the "Catastrophe, or the indiscretion of No. 2," the "Terpsichorean episode," "La Carbonaja," and Leonora — and a good many others. Leonora, who "gains the ascendant" suddenly on January 11, 1879 — by which time Shaw had been in London for almost three years — may have been the daughter of the Lawson family, whom he had recently met. There is nothing to be gained by tracing the record in detail. It makes clear that the young Shaw was highly susceptible to female charms, and that he did not altogether confine his romancing to the dream world that was so accessible to him. Nor did he always take it seriously. On April 11, 1882, he found the seat next to his in the British Museum Reading Room — not the likeliest place for roses and raptures — occupied by a young lady who disturbed his judgment. He recorded the effect:

> Violet Beverley
> No matter how cleverly
> I try to work when you sit beside me
> At set of sun
> There is nothing done
> Only the unwritten page to chide me
> Only your empty chair to deride me.
>
> It is something to have learned your name
> And something more to have heard your voice
> Though I came not hither with any such aim,
> Though you sat beside me by chance, not choice.
> Oh Violet, Violet, why do you come
> To read about your primeval kind
> To a place where men must be deaf and dumb
> But where, alas! they must not be blind?

I came to write, and I stayed to look.
I dared not offend, yet could not refrain,
And so, whilst you sat there deep in your book
I studied your face again and again.

And thus, Miss Beverley,
No matter how cleverly
I strive to work as you sit beside me,
At set of sun
I have nothing done
There is only my unwritten page to chide me
Only your empty chair to deride me.[3]

There is nothing to show whether Shaw presented this cri du coeur to the studious young lady. At all events, he later added a note which showed that his lyric resources had not been exhausted:

Subsequently there is reason to believe that her name, after all, is not Violet Beverley, but Mabel Crofton. Consequently —

Mabel Crofton,
No matter how often
I turn to my work when you sit, etc. etc.

and — Oh Mabel Crofton, why do you come
or — Oh moidering Mabel, why —

On the other hand, he was sometimes genuinely moved — or thought he was. Apparently it was the treachery of Calypso in marrying and going off to "an exquisite gaol by the sea," as he tells with heavy irony, that produced an outburst of self-conscious misery. Besides Calypso, that outburst introduces two other charmers whose attractions Shaw has felt:

[3] British Museum, Shaw Ms. 50721B.

Hail, Folly! and flourish Delusion,
Continue, whilst man remains brute
Of Passions and Dreams and Confusion
To bring forth your fruit.

All the fiends take each black-eyed enslaver,
Calypso, Queen Mab & Yolande.
Love philtres were tempting of savour
In the mouth turn to sand.

Queen Mab has her home in the city
Yolande has her foot on the stage
But Calypso, though tender her pity
And furious her rage,
Though so prone to each impulse of passion
That she gasps for a breath of romance,
Has succumbed to the cruel old fashion,
The bitter old chance.[4]

In short, she has married; and the poet, after raging at some length, bids her farewell in a stanza which suggests that he is already recovering:

Then farewell, oh bewitching Calypso,
Thou didst shake my philosophy well.
But believe me, the next time I trip so
No poem shall tell.

It was not until 1885 that Shaw had a full sexual experience. In the seven years which followed it he arrived at the ideas about women and the sex relation which were so profoundly to affect his plays. It was among his mother's music pupils that he found a woman as ready to round out his education as

[4] British Museum, Shaw Ms. 50720.

Madame de Warens was with the young Rousseau. Jenny Patterson of Brompton Square was, by a combination of luck and cunning, precisely qualified to overcome all the obstacles of which Shaw was conscious. She was wealthy — and his poverty mattered nothing to her; she was a widow — and his inexperience did not frighten her; she was unconventional — and his fear of imprisonment through marriage did not concern her; and she was physically attractive and so intransigently passionate that the one remaining barrier, his profound mistrust of the senses, was swept aside.

Not, it is true, without a struggle. The forces of physical desire and psychological revulsion must have made Shaw's mind a turmoil in the summer of 1885. Some extracts from the Diary sketch the story:

> (July 10) . . . Found Mrs. Patterson here when I came home. Walked to her house by way of the park. Supper, music & curious conversation, & a declaration of passion. Left at 3. Virgo intacta still.

> (July 13) . . . In the evening wrote to E. McN. an account of what had passed on Friday evening.

> (July 17) . . . Mrs. Patterson came. Saw her for a few moments. Blush etc. Spoke at Fabian in the evening & walked with Mrs. Besant to her gate. Sat up to write to Mrs. Patterson.

> (July 18) . . . Went to Inventions[5] & heard Dutch choir . . . May Morris also there. Went with her & thence to J. Patterson. Forced caresses. Thence to Lady Wilde's where I met Stuart Glennie, Mrs. Kingsford, & others. Thence to Barton's where I discussed socialism with Baker. Called at Brompton Sq. on my [way] back, but she had not yet come in, & I did not wait.

[5] An exhibition of musical instruments.

(July 19) . . . Went to Brompton Sq. but was too late to see J. P. who was going to bed, so walked home. Wrote to her.

(July 20) . . . Missed again as to J. P. Wrote her a good letter in reply to hers . . .

(July 21) . . . Satisfactory letter from J. P. . . .

(July 25) . . . to J. P. where I found M. [i.e., Shaw's mother] Had something to eat and saw them into Inventions . . . (At 11) . . . went back to Brompton Sq. where I met Mrs. P. & M. returning from Inventions. We walked along the Brompton Road looking for a bus, but they were all full. So on the corner of Montpelier St. M. went on by herself, & I returned to the Square with J. P. & stayed there until 3 o'clock on my 29th birthday which I celebrated by a new experience. Was watched by an old woman next door, whose evil interpretation of the lateness of my departure greatly alarmed us.

(July 27) No work done. Went to museum & wrote a letter to J. P.

(July 29) . . . Walked from Farringdon St. along the Embankment to Westminster with May Morris. Thence home.

(July 31) . . . Went with M. Morris to Hammersmith & had to walk back by Fulham . . . Wrote to J. P. & to May Morris before going to bed.

(Aug. 2) . . . Did nothing but write a few letters. Went in the evening to J. P.

(Aug. 3) Wrote full circumstantial account of affair with J. P. to E. McN. . . . Spent evening with Sidney Webb at Colonial Office. He told me about his love affair and disappointment. Wrote a rather fierce letter to J. P. on my return.

(Aug. 4) Did nothing practically. Called on Eleanor Aveling in the afternoon. Resolved to begin a new Pilgrim's Progress at once . . . Wrote to J. P. in reply to her answer to yesterday's explosion.

(Aug. 5) Alice Lockett & Mrs. Shenstone here in the morning. Wrote the beginning of Pilgrim's Progress. To Inventions from 5 to 7:45. Thence to J. P. to eat and make love until 1:20.

The record suggests the deep ambivalence in Shaw's mind about sex. On the one hand, we may be quite certain — regardless of his later spider-and-fly theories about women's attraction of men — that he was not just passively or unwillingly consumed by the amorous fires of Mrs. Patterson. He had at least the normal amount of sexual drive, including sexual curiosity. It is probable that this was seconded by something of which he was less conscious: a deep longing for human affection of the sort that his childhood had never provided. It does not take a Freudian to notice that the affair with Mrs. Patterson was only the first and longest of many that Shaw had with women who were or had been married: Mrs. Edith Bland, Mrs. Annie Besant, Mrs. Florence Farr Emery, Mrs. May Morris Sparling, Mrs. Janet Achurch Charrington, Mrs. Patrick Campbell. How many of them reached or came near to sexual consummation we shall never know, but certainly some of them did. Shaw of course disliked Freud, as a scientist "utterly void of delicacy." His own utilitarian explanation of his tastes was that he "preferred fully matured women who knew what they were doing."[6] He might have added, in the same vein, that with them he was a good deal safer.

Opposing these feelings was that strong grain of fastidious-

[6] *Sixteen Self-Sketches*, p. 113.

ness and hypersensitivity to direct human contacts that was also a product of his childhood environment. His other passions, too — for the higher life of the mind, for freedom of the spirit — were not to be denied. His initiation outraged something deep in his nature; it was followed at once by a sense of revulsion that led him to write a letter of confession — a "full circumstantial account" — to Edward McNulty; then to turn wrathfully on his companion in sin; and finally to commence an act of penance: bringing Bunyan up to date. The latter project did not advance far: perhaps Mrs. Patterson was more persuasive than Messrs. Obstinate and Pliable. Shaw soon returned to her and they began a long, if sometimes tempestuous, liaison. He kept for many months in his diary a sort of statistical record of its course which ought to settle decisively the doubts that are sometimes expressed about his virility. From time to time he resolved to put an end to the affair. His reasons doubtless varied; but the diaries make it clear that his comment to Frank Harris that he never "had any scruples or remorses or misgivings of conscience about [sexual intercourse]," [7] though it may sound supermanly, is unreliable.

The diaries reveal other things besides his curious ambivalence towards sex. They make nonsense of the claim which he was so often to assert — and out of which he was to make such comedy — that in his experience woman was the pursuer, man the victim. It was sometimes so: the wife of his friend Hubert Bland, overcome by Shaw's sexual attractiveness, pursued him with unquestionably amorous intentions, and he had finally to send her away from his house

> after an unpleasant scene caused by my telling her I wished her to go, as I was afraid that a visit to me alone would compromise her.

[7] *Loc. cit.*

Moreover, just as he sometimes felt attracted to women who were quite unconscious of him, so he sometimes unwittingly attracted them. In May 1887 a sensitive young socialist named Grace Black appealed to him in a letter to bring more humanity to his socialism.

> What I fear is that you do not care for nor believe in people sufficiently, and you won't be able to understand them unless you do; and your socialism must be warped, if you don't understand human nature.[8]

In reply Shaw used a gambit which it had pleased his vanity to use before: he accused Miss Black of being in love with him. She answered thoughtfully:

> I guessed you would think I was in love with you. So I am, but that has nothing to do with my letter and it is a pity if that thought has clouded my meaning. My personal happiness is certainly connected with your success as a teacher of socialism . . . But apart from that I do love you, & why do you wish to dissuade me from that and from believing in you?

And in a postscript she added:

> Why do you accuse me of being in love with you, if you do not want the truth? But the triumph is stale: you knew it before.

Nevertheless, though he may sometimes have been cast in the role of Lancelot to some luckless Elaine, the Mozartian hero Don Giovanni was a good deal more congenial than the Tennysonian knight; and Shaw was much more often the pursuer

[8] British Museum, Shaw Papers for 1887.

than the pursued. His affair with Mrs. Patterson lasted for seven and a half years, and he had many an opportunity to break it off, had he genuinely wanted to do so.

It is clear, too, that even from the beginning she could not absorb all his interest. An astonishing number of women shared it in varying degrees — not only those already mentioned, but also Alice Lockett, Geraldine Spooner, Eleanor Aveling, Grace Gilchrist, Bertha Newcombe; the list seems endless. Certainly both the degree and the direction of the interest varied — sometimes it was more on Shaw's side, sometimes less; and it may be that — at least until the Florence Farr episode began in October 1890 — he was sexually faithful to Mrs. Patterson. But that his conversation with these women was kept to the level of discourses on economics, and their shared activities to playing piano duets and drinking tea at the Wheatsheaf vegetarian restaurant, is not to be supposed for a moment. Leonard Charteris — that unmistakable self-portrait by Shaw, in *The Philanderer* — protests his innocence, and is even supported by Sylvia Craven as he does so:

CHARTERIS: Then you know that I never pay any special attention to a woman.

SYLVIA (*thoughtfully*) Do you know, Leonard, I really believe you. I don't think you care a bit more about one woman than another.

CHARTERIS: You mean I don't care a bit less for one woman than another.

SYLVIA: That makes it worse. But what I mean is that you never bother about their being only women: you talk to them just as you do to me or any other fellow. That's the secret of your success. You can't think how sick they get of being treated with the respect due to their sex.

CHARTERIS: Ah, if only Julia had your wisdom, Craven!

Yet the behavior of Charteris towards Grace Tranfield and Julia Craven makes it clear enough that while he may be paying them the unexpected compliment of talking to them intelligently and ignoring the respect due to their sex, it does not follow that he is ignoring their sex itself. If Mrs. Patterson recognized herself in Julia Craven, and Florence Farr knew she was Grace Tranfield, it is doubtful that any of Shaw's acquaintances would have cast herself in the role of Sylvia.

Long after he had abandoned his new Pilgrim's Progress, Shaw was sometimes embarrassed and remorseful over his philanderings, however much he may later have denied that he had any cause for such feelings. He told Hesketh Pearson a story of how his friendship with Annie Besant culminated in her drawing up a contract (her husband being alive and she unable to remarry)

> setting forth the terms on which [Shaw and she] were to live together as man and wife, and presented it to [Shaw] for signature. He read it. "Good God!" he exclaimed, "this is worse than all the vows of all the churches on earth. I had rather be legally married to you ten times over."
>
> She would have nothing less than her contract, which she had expected him to sign with his heart's blood; and when he not only laughed at it, but was evidently quite serious in refusing to be bound by it, she demanded her letters back. He collected what he could of them, and at a further and final interview gave them to her. She produced a casket in which she had kept all his letters, and, convulsed with suppressed tears, handed them to him. "What! You won't even keep my letters!" he said. "I don't want them." The correspondence went into the fire. And that was the end of their private relations.[9]

[9] Hesketh Pearson: *Bernard Shaw* (London: Methuen, 1961), p. 112.

Whether or not that account is largely a piece of Shavian fiction, the Diary describes a different course of events. On December 23, 1887, by which time he and Mrs. Besant had been on terms of close friendship for more than a year, he noted that

> Mrs. B. gave me back my letters —

and on the following day:

> Brought Mrs. Besant's letters down to Fleet Street [i.e., to her office] but she had gone . . . I left the letters at Avenue Road . . . On my return I found that J[enny] P[atterson] had been here and had read my letters to Mrs. B., which I had incautiously left on my table.

A week or so later, when he came to write his annual commentary on the events of the preceding year, he remarked:

> The intimacy with Mrs. Besant . . . reached in January a point at which it threatened to become a vulgar intrigue, chiefly through my fault. But I roused myself in time and avoided this. I however frequently went to her house on Monday evenings and played pianoforte duets (mostly Haydn's symphonies) with her. At Xmas, I returned all her letters and she mine. Reading over my letters before destroying them rather disgusted me with the trifling of the last 2 years with women.

There is no mention of either the casket or the marriage contract; and the Diary's account of the end of the correspondence itself cannot be brought into line with that given to Pearson in later years.

In a similar way, we may contrast the story that Shaw

was to tell in 1936 of his relations with May Morris with the one revealed by the Diary and some other sources. When he wrote *William Morris as I Knew Him,* as an introduction to the second volume of May's study of her father, he provided an account of a "Mystic Betrothal" between himself and her:

> One Sunday evening after lecturing and supping, I was on the threshold of the Hammersmith house [i.e. Morris's house] when I turned to make my farewell, and at this moment she came from the diningroom into the hall. I looked at her, rejoicing in her lovely dress and lovely self; and she looked at me very carefully and quite deliberately made a gesture of assent with her eyes. I was immediately conscious that a Mystic Betrothal was registered in heaven, to be fulfilled when all the material obstacles should melt away, and my own position rescued from the squalors of my poverty and unsuccess; for subconsciously I had no doubt of my rank as a man of genius. Less reasonably I had no doubt that she, too, knew her own value, a knowledge that involved a knowledge of everyone else's. I did not think it necessary to say anything. To engage her in any way — to go to Morris and announce that I was taking advantage of the access granted to me as comrade-Communist to commit his beautiful daughter to desperately insolvent marriage, did not occur to me as a socially possible proceeding. It did not occur to me even that fidelity to the Mystic Betrothal need interfere with the ordinary course of my relations with other women. I made no sign at all: I had no doubt that the thing was written on the skies for both of us.
>
> Suddenly, to my utter stupefaction, and I suspect to that of Morris also, the beautiful daughter married one of the comrades.
>
> This was perfectly natural, and entirely my own fault for

taking the Mystic Betrothal for granted; but I regarded it, and still regard it in spite of all reason, as the most monstrous breach of faith in the history of romance . . . Apparently my limitless imagination had deceived me in the matter of the Mystical Betrothal.

But it had not deceived me in the least. For it presently happened that the overwork and irregular habits of the combination of continual propaganda with professional artistic activities, which killed Morris ten years before his time, reduced me to a condition in which I needed rest and change very pressingly; and holidays of the usual sort were beyond my means. The young couple thereupon invited me to stay with them for a while. I accepted, and so found myself most blessedly resting and content in their house, which had the Morris charm; for she had inherited her father's sense of beauty . . . Everything went well for a time in that *ménage à trois*. She was glad to have me in the house; and he was glad to have me because I kept her in good humor and produced a cuisine that no mere husband could elicit. It was probably the happiest passage in our three lives.

But the violated Betrothal was avenging itself. It made me from the first the centre of the household; and when I had quite recovered and there was no longer any excuse for staying unless I proposed to do so permanently and parasitically, her legal marriage had dissolved as all illusions do; and the mystic marriage asserted itself irresistibly. I had to consummate it or vanish.

. . . When it became evident that the Betrothal would not suffer this [*ménage à trois*] to be an innocent arrangement the case became complicated. To begin with, the legal husband was a friend whose conduct towards me had always been irreproachable. To be welcomed in his house and then steal his wife was revolting to my sense of honour and socially inexcusable; for though I was as extreme a free-thinker on sexual and religious questions as any sane human being could be, I was not the dupe of the Bohemian Anarchism that is very common in socialist and literary circles. I knew that a scandal would damage both of us and damage The Cause as well. It seems easy in view of my later position to have sat down together as three friends and arranged a divorce; but at that time I could not afford to marry, and I was by no means sure that he could afford to be divorced. Besides, I hated the idea of a prosaic and even mercenary marriage: that, somehow or other, was not in the plane of the Mystic Betrothal. The more I reasoned about the situation the worse it was doomed to appear. So I did not argue about it. I vanished.

Then the vengeance of the violated Betrothal consummated itself in a transport of tragedy and comedy. For the husband vanished too! . . . This marriage which all the mystic powers had forbidden from the first went to pieces when the unlucky parties no longer had me between them. Of the particulars of the rupture I know nothing; but in the upshot he fled to the Continent and eventually submitted chivalrously to being divorced as the guilty party, though the alternative was technically arranged for him . . .

The beautiful one abolished him root and branch, resuming her famous maiden name, and for all I could prove, abolished me too.[10]

It is a pleasant story, and Hesketh Pearson states that May's husband confirmed the account of the *ménage à trois*, but was convinced that Shaw had betrayed him.

He told Holbrook Jackson (from whom I had it) that after completely captivating his wife Shaw suddenly disappeared, leaving behind him a desolated female who might have been

[10] May Morris: *William Morris* (Oxford: Basil Blackwell, 1936), Vol. 2, pp. xxviiff.

an iceberg so far as her future relations with her husband went.[11]

Shaw's role in the entire affair may have been technically quite innocent, and in fact Pearson suggests that if he erred it was in being too loyal to H. H. Sparling, May's husband; but the plain truth is that for a man concerned about either scandal or friendship Shaw's behavior was far from circumspect. His close friendship with May lasted for almost ten years, beginning early in 1885. On April 4, 1886, Sparling told him about his love affair with May. In August 1888 the three of them spent a few days together at Kelmscott. In this period they were all very active in socialism, of course. May and Sparling were married on June 14, 1890, and late in 1892 or early in 1893 Shaw began a stay of some weeks with them at their home in Hammersmith Terrace — presumably the period of the *ménage à trois*. After mid-January he seems to have stayed mainly at Fitzroy Square, where he and his mother lived; though in the succeeding months, having by no means vanished, he went frequently to the Sparlings for meals, music, or talk, and sometimes spent the night there. He was much occupied with both Jenny Patterson and Florence Farr, but he found time to skate, walk, play duets, and at least once to have what he called "rather an emotional" conversation, with May. On May 21, Sparling being in Paris, Shaw "rushed off to Hammersmith" to have a long walk, tea, and an evening of music with May, and stay the night at the Terrace. On the next day the two had a long walk, a siesta in Richmond Park, and dinner, and then parted — Shaw to go off to see Florence Farr. On the 23rd he was again with May, and on the 24th with Florence. Kate (i.e., Mrs. H. S.) Salt, an intimate friend

[11] H. Pearson: *op. cit.*, p. 97.

of both May and Shaw (herself in love with him, according to Janet Dunbar), was scandalized and angry at their behaviour. Yet Shaw continued to visit the Sparlings and especially to see a good deal of May until the end of 1893, and perhaps until some time in 1894—the Diary becomes very sketchy at the beginning of that year. All things considered, it is hardly surprising that Sparling should have been doubtful of him—especially since, however innocent he may have been, there seems no question about May's feelings. In a letter written in July 1901, Shaw's sister Lucy says:

> I did not know William Morris, but my mother did, and he was a close friend of my brother's. I know May Sparling, now May Morris again, having sent Sparling to the "right about" through the divorce court. She was a beautiful damsel of the Rossetti and Burne-Jones type . . . May made a fool of herself over G.B.S. and there is no doubt ruined the whole of the romantic side of her life. I believe her only object in divorcing Sparling was to give G. the chance of marrying her. She obtained her decree absolute the very day he was married. The worst of it was, she always wore her heart on her sleeve, and everyone knew about her madness for G. . . .
>
> She used frequently to come to our house, but has never been since G. married.[12]

Lucy demonstrates incidentally that she had her own sense of drama. Actually, Shaw was married on June 1, 1898. May's initial decree was granted on July 18, and did not become absolute for another six months. Still, there was at least one meeting between them in the period when her divorce was

[12] H. G. Farmer: *Bernard Shaw's Sister and Her Friends* (Leiden: E. J. Brill, 1959), p. 140.

pending. On March 12, 1898 — two and a half months before her sudden marriage to Shaw — Charlotte Payne-Townshend left London on a trip to Rome; and Shaw, in a note apparently intended for her benefit, recorded that he "divided the rest of the day between tears and answering letters," and that his digestion wholly ceased. By the next day, however, he had recovered sufficiently to go out for lunch — to May's, where he joined Emery Walker and some others. But even Shaw could not turn this occasion into one of easy gaiety:

> Walker goes. May and I disconcert one another extremely, carefully avoiding the subject we are both thinking of. I mount my bike and fly.[13]

Shaw may sometimes have been touched with remorse about his behaviour with women, as in the Annie Besant affair, but Jenny Patterson was made frantic with jealous rage. Though there was evidently never any thought of marriage between her and Shaw, she was furiously possessive, and she had no compunctions even about going into his house and reading his mail — in which, to be sure, she sometimes found reason for her doubts. On one occasion, after coming out of a Fabian Society meeting with him and Annie Besant, she deliberately separated herself from them in order that she might follow them. Fortunately for Shaw on this occasion, he merely walked a short distance with Mrs. Besant, then saw her onto a bus — and turned to find Mrs. Patterson watching. He accompanied her to her door, then went home and wrote to Mrs. Besant. Many times, however — over one or other of Shaw's women friends, or some supposed slight to herself — Mrs. Patterson was thrown into ungovernable anger; and there were days like a Sunday in 1888 when

[13] British Museum, Add. Mss. 46505–6, No's. 93, 94.

> In the afternoon J.P. came, raged, wept, flung a book at my head, etc. At 6:30 I left her & went off to Archer for tea . . .

or a June evening in 1890 when Shaw

> went to J.P. . . . but found her so fractious that I presently shook the dust off my feet and came away.

Sometimes the relationship seemed about to end. But it was not until February 1893 that the finale came — in a scene that Shaw soon incorporated into a play.

In the autumn of 1890 he had met the actress Florence Farr (at that time Mrs. Florence Emery, by which name Shaw consistently refers to her. Her husband had left her, and she eventually divorced him). Mrs. Patterson went to the East in January, and returned in April to find that Shaw had been both overworking — for he had had a furious spate of lecturing and writing — and overplaying (in hot pursuit of Florence). There was a series of scenes that he later described alternately as "fearful" and "terrific." Nevertheless he somehow pacified Mrs. Patterson, and for almost two years — punctuated by periods of tempestuous jealousy on her part — the affair continued, Shaw switching his attention back and forth between the two women with the dexterity of a circus performer. At last Mrs. Patterson could stand no more. On the evening of February 4, 1893, Shaw went to see Florence Farr.

> J.P. burst in on us very late in the evening. There was a most shocking scene; J.P. violent and using atrocious language. At last I sent F.E. out of the room, having to restrain J.P. by force from attacking her. I was two hours getting her out of

> the house & did not get her home to Brompton Sq. until near 1, nor could I get away myself until 3. I was horribly tired & upset; but I kept patience & did not behave badly nor ungently. Did not go to bed until 4 & had a disturbed night. I made J.P. write a letter to me expressing her regret & promising not to annoy F.E. again. This was sent to F.E. to reassure her.

So the Patterson affair ended. Shaw's philandering, of course, did not. Within a few months he was angering Kate Salt by his conduct with May Morris Sparling; he continued to see much of Florence Farr until 1894, when W. B. Yeats took her attention; and there were various minor centres of interest. But he was now becoming deeply involved in the theatre, as critic and playwright, and as busy as he had ever been with socialist activities and miscellaneous journalism. In 1896, at the age of forty, he met the woman whom he was to marry.

What then — one is bound to ask — was the significance of his decade of philandering, and what effect did it have on his thought? At least twice he attempted to formulate his ideas dramatically, in plays that had their beginnings in his own experiences. In August 1889 he began work on a play that he proposed to call *The Cassone*, set it aside after a few days, took it up again more than a year later, and finally abandoned it. It was probably in November 1890 that he wrote the fragment of dialogue that follows:

> [Ashton — a Shavian figure — has tried to persuade Lady Eleanor to make Mr. Castlemaine fall in love with her.]
>
> C. I know . . . He's mad on the subject. He told me he was going to do it.
>
> E. (furious) He *told* you! Actually told you — to your face!!!

C. I'm really extremely sorry, Lady Eleanor: It's quite inexcusable in him; but he has some insane theory about it. He falls in love with every woman he sees, and says that it does him good — keeps him from becoming the slave of his ordinary intelligence, he says. You see his theory is like this. He declares that it is never prudent to take a step in advance, because you cannot be sure of what will happen to you where you have never been before.

E. That's true.

C. Exactly. Therefore every step in advance is an imprudence — a folly. That's clear, isn't it?

E. Yes.

C. Very well. Now, says Ashton,[14] no man will deliberately commit a folly except under the impulse of a feeling that is too strong for his common sense. Consequently he will never advance except under the influence of a series of impulses from feeling. But no feeling overpowers a man's common sense so effectually as love; none is so pleasant: none acts with such certainty on all sorts of people. Therefore if you want to keep going — advancing, you understand — you must keep constantly falling in love.

E. With a fresh person every time?

C. That's the point of my case according to Ashton. He declares that since I married, a sense of duty & a reluctance to hurt my wife's feelings have restrained me from allowing myself to form any fresh attachments; whilst my affection for Lily has become a matter of habit, and lost its stimulating power — otherwise its power of getting the better of my common sense. Necessarily, therefore, according to him, I have ceased to advance. All married men, he says, suffer in the same way, for the same reason . . .[15]

[14] Shaw wrote "Castlemaine," but "Ashton" is obviously intended.
[15] British Museum, Shaw Ms. 50690.

How seriously Shaw intended this pleasant piece of rationalizing may be questioned. Yet in the piece he addressed to Frank Harris he said:

> During the 14 years before my marriage at 43 there was always some lady in the case; and I tried all the experiments and learned what there was to be learnt from them . . .[16]

And the fact that he returned to the Cassone manuscript suggests that he was interested in Ashton and his argument, perplexed by the problem of the philanderer, and concerned to account for him in some reasonable — and not wholly discreditable — way. The thesis that the advanced person must be a philanderer, and that his continuing to advance depends on his continuing to philander, was soon discarded; the concept of the philanderer as a man of advanced ideas and the courage to live up to them was more persistent.

Accordingly, in March 1893, a few weeks after the episode that ended the Patterson affair, Shaw began to write *The Philanderer*. It is not one of his major plays, and did not receive even a copyright performance until 1898. But it is interesting for its self-portrait of the author in the role of the hero, Leonard Charteris. In the printed version of the play, Charteris's appearance is described in some detail. In the manuscript with which he began, Shaw is content to call him a

> Promising young writer on philosophic subjects. Age between 36 & 40. Bachelor. Pleasant appearance, smart but unconventional.[17]

As the play opens, Charteris, the philanderer, who entirely

[16] *Sixteen Self-Sketches*, p. 114.
[17] British Museum, Shaw Ms. 50690.

mistrusts marriage, is nevertheless proposing to his most recent "flame," Grace Tranfield, in order to escape from her immediate predecessor, Julia Craven. They are interrupted by the stormy arrival of Julia herself, and the Patterson-Shaw-Farr episode is re-enacted. As the play proceeds, against a background of supposedly Ibsenist fads, Charteris succeeds in ridding himself of both entanglements; and at the end he stands triumphant and gay, while Julia — now engaged to marry a man whom she does not love — is supported by Grace as she almost faints under the emotional strain of the moment.

> Charteris, amused and untouched, shakes his head laughingly. The rest look at Julia with concern, and even a little awe, feeling for the first time the presence of a keen sorrow.

As Charteris thus looks on amused, Grace Tranfield speaks the final line of the play:

> Never make a hero of a philanderer.

Charteris, however, unquestionably is the hero — the quick-witted, self-possessed Shavian. He has understood Ibsen in the Shavian way, and so come to regard ideals — and the conventions and institutions that supposedly embody them — as shams, traps that hamper the freedom and prevent the development of those who want to live their individual lives to the full. He recognizes, too, that many people who fancy themselves in this class are in fact constitutionally conformist, and have taken to the superficial unconventionalities of Ibsenism only as a fad. In a passage that Shaw excised from the play, he had Charteris say to Julia:

> . . . I have always told you that you are a thoroughly womanly woman, and that the conventional lines are the right lines for you. Believe me, the only people who can afford to be-

have exceptionally in this world are the genuinely exceptional people. Not the people who talk about it, but those who do it naturally without thinking about it.

But what are we to make of Charteris's triumphant gaiety as he watches the pain — however momentary — of the two women from whom he has most recently "escaped," and presumably relishes the feeling that he is now free to "escape" from others? Is the man who so behaves superior in the least to the doctor who is deliberately cruel for the sake — as he claims — of medical science? That Shaw was aware of the difficulty is clear; in the third act of *The Philanderer* as he first wrote it, there was a long and at times impassioned discussion of cruelty and the guilt of the vivisector, a subject on which he was fond of holding forth. In the final form of the play, there is left only this passage (Julia has just told Charteris of her engagement to the medical scientist, Dr. Paramore):

CHARTERIS. . . . Our vivisecting friend has made a successful experiment at last.

JULIA (earnestly). It is you who are the vivisector: a far crueller, more wanton vivisector than he.

CHARTERIS. Yes; but then I learn so much more from my experiments than he does! And the victims learn as much as I do. That's where my moral superiority comes in.

It is a harsh comment and a vain one — even though in the play Julia responds to it with "rueful humor"; and one is bound to wonder whether in fact Shaw did not derive some subtle, unacknowledged satisfaction from the pain — as well as the pleasure — that his philanderings gave: pain which was perhaps related to the emptiness and hurt of his own childhood. How much of self-revelation may be contained in the speech that he wrote for Charteris to speak to Julia, the second and third sentences of which he then crossed out?

> Never mind, dearest: you never did understand me and you never will. *It doesn't matter. I don't want you to: I only want you to like me . . .*

On the other hand, how much philosophical illumination had come to him through his sexual experiences? In *The Quintessence of Ibsenism*, two years before he wrote *The Philanderer*, he had argued the Platonist view:

> Tannhauser may die in the conviction that one moment of the emotion he felt with St. Elizabeth was fuller and happier than all the hours of passion he spent with Venus; but that does not alter the fact that love began for him with Venus, and that its earlier tentatives towards the final goal were attended with relapses. Now Tannhauser's passion for Venus is a development of the humdrum fondness of the bourgeois Jack for his Jill, a development at once higher and more dangerous, just as idealism is at once higher and more dangerous than Philistinism. The fondness is the germ of the passion: the passion is the germ of the more perfect love. When Blake told men that through excess they would learn moderation he knew that the way for the present lay through Venusberg, and that the race would assuredly not perish there as some individuals have, and as the Puritan fears we all shall unless we find a way round.[18]

Forty years later he wrote to Frank Harris:

> I was never duped by sex as a basis of permanent relations, nor dreamt of marriage in connection with it. . . . I valued sexual experience because of its power of producing a celestial flood of emotion and exaltation which, however momen-

[18] *Major Critical Essays*, p. 36.

tary, gave me a sample of the ecstasy that may one day be the normal condition of conscious intellectual activity.[19]

It is not difficult to perceive how Shaw tried to see his sexual activity in relation to the process of religious and philosophic development that occurred in the period with which I have been dealing. Perhaps Schopenhauer, whose *Metaphysics of the Love of the Sexes* he read in October 1888, helped him to see his sexual experiences as an aspect of his religion: they showed that the energy of the Life Force was throbbing in him, that he was in its grip as surely as Don Juan had been and John Tanner was to be. And his religion provided a rationale: his philandering was justified not only as manifestation of the Life Force, but also because it revealed to him the ineffable wonder of celestial intellectuality. We may be pardoned for asking whether this is "ruthless antiromanticism" or merely the replacement of the rose-tinted spectacles that Shaw disliked by a pair of some other colour — shamrock green, perhaps.

Whatever view we take of his philandering and the probably complex motives behind it, it is clear that he remained, as he had been from his boyhood, a divided self, that his early mistrust of the passions persisted. For the passions as he saw them — he is at precisely the opposite extreme to D. H. Lawrence — becloud the mind and lead us into false relations with one another; false relations have a way of becoming institutionalized; and institutions become oppressive and permanent: the passion of vengeance creates the institution of justice; greed creates property; sexual love creates marriage — false gods, all of them, protected by rituals of falsehood. Not that Shaw wanted to sweep them away forthwith — he had long ago perceived the dangers of too sudden revolution and ar-

[19] *Sixteen Self Sketches*, p. 115.

gued against it because of them. In a review that he wrote for *The Commonwealth* in 1885, which that magazine rejected, he had said:

> . . . Free Love would prove just such another delusion as Free Contract for the labourer . . . It may be hard on many a dutiful wife and mother at present to know that her husband keeps another woman for his pleasure in a suburban villa; but if marriage were abolished he would simply keep her at home in the drawingroom whilst his wife, when she grew old, would be sent to the kitchen or nursery . . . [or] into the streets . . . Wedlock is a heavy chain for a man to rivet upon himself; but the woman is born with the chain on: to her wedlock only means rivetting the other end of it to a man. Abolish wedlock, and the man is free; but the woman is left to bear the whole weight of her servitude alone.[20]

Still, a chain is a chain, and it is only natural that one should avoid rivetting it on if possible; and if other people choose bondage, that is not a reason for disturbing one's habits unduly. When his sister Lucy married, December 17, 1887, Shaw made the following note in his diary:

> Went to the stores to get some whiskey & cake for Lucy's wedding to Chas. Butterfield (St. John's Church, Charlotte St., 2:30). Went off to dine at Wheatsheaf as usual & did not get back to the church until the ceremony was over. Came back to tea after Image's lecture on Art at Willis's rooms . . .

Long before this time, in making jottings for an essay that he never wrote, he had commented that marriage for money is more likely to succeed than marriage for love, because in it the misleading and treacherous sexual passion is not a concern.

20 British Museum, Shaw Ms. 50690.

We need not conclude, however — despite the Fabian gossip of the time — that his marriage to the Irish heiress Charlotte was a mercenary one. When it took place, Shaw had passed the brink of financial success, and before long had an income greater than hers. Moreover, they had known each other intimately for many months — had worked together in the Fabian Society and holidayed together in company with the Webbs. The letters that he wrote her reveal the same divided purposes that his philandering indicates. He is concerned for her happiness — he wants her to be well and free; but he wants "to tell you lies face to face — close."[21] He has to be with her — he must see her —

> I *must;* and that "must," which "rather alarms" you, TERRIFIES me. If it were possible to run away — if it would do any good — I'd do it . . .[22]

He longs to be kept "deep in her heart." But he cannot endure her possessiveness:

> My nerves are shattered by the scenes of which I have been and am the innocent victim. I wonder are you at all ashamed of yourself. I have allied myself to a fountain of tears.[23]

At the end of March 1898, when Charlotte was in Rome, he wrote what is perhaps the most revealing letter of all:

> Somehow, I am beginning to feel like my old self again. After all, it is magnificent to be alone, with the ivy stripped off. As I walk round the park at night, looking at the other stars, I no longer feel 42. The hopples are off . . . I am nat-

[21] British Museum, Add. Mss. 46505–6.
[22] *Ibid.*
[23] *Ibid.*

> ural once more. You count that I have lost one Charlotte; but I have lost two; and one of the losses is a prodigious relief. I may miss die Schöne grünen Augen occasionally though the very privation throws me back, brutally great, to my natural dreamland; but then think of the other Charlotte, the terrible Charlotte, the lier-in-wait, the soul hypochondriac, always watching and dragging me into bondage, always planning nice sensible, comfortable, selfish destruction for me, wincing at every accent of freedom in my voice, so that at last I get the trick of hiding myself from her, hating me & longing for me with the absorbing passion of the spider for the fly. Now that she is gone, I realize for the first time the infernal tyranny of the past years which left me the leisure of the rebel, not the freedom of the man who stands alone. I will have no more of it: if you hate women who pull flowers, what do you think of women who cut down trees?[24]

Two months and two days later they were married — the marriage being precipitated by the fact that Shaw was suffering from a seriously injured foot, and Charlotte proceeded to carry him off and nurse him.

Was he, then, dragged into bondage? Did Charlotte become his jailer, his stage manager, or his second self? Or all three?

> "I should never have married at all," he said [to W. S. Blunt in 1906], "if I had not been dead at the time. I tumbled off my bicycle, and the surgeons made a hole in my foot which they kept open for a year, and me in bed. I thought I was dead, for it would not heal, and Charlotte had me at her mercy. I should never have married if I had thought I should get well . . ."[25]

[24] British Museum, Add. Mss. 46505–6 No. 90.

[25] W. S. Blunt: *My Diaries, Part Two* (London: Martin Secker, 1920), p. 136.

> I am in custody down here —[26]

he wrote Mrs. Campbell from Ayot St. Lawrence in 1913; in the context of a Shavian love letter the remark should not be given too much weight, yet there are many others in the same vein. Friends, acquaintances, and observers of the couple, from Beatrice Webb to Bertrand Russell to Professor Dover Wilson, commented on Charlotte's managing ways with her husband, though to what extent he welcomed her government or chafed under it is not clear. At all events their marriage lasted for forty-five years — until Charlotte's death in 1943: a childless, and indeed — so Ervine states — unconsummated marriage. Whether it was punctuated by other episodes of philandering than the notorious one with Mrs. Campbell — whether, for example, there is any truth at all in the colorful claims of Erica Cotterill[27] — we shall perhaps never know; nor can we guess what strains the husband and wife placed on each other — or what strength they found together. In the spring of 1944 Shaw told Hesketh Pearson:[28]

> If you had had forty odd years of love and devotion such as I have had, you would know what freedom meant, and I am enjoying this here for the first time.

And again:

[26] *Bernard Shaw and Mrs. Patrick Campbell: Their Correspondence*, p. 72.

[27] In 1916 Erica Cotterill published a book called *An Account*, an astonishing piece of erotica which purports to relate her experiences with the man to whom the book is dedicated: "Bernard Shaw, whom I love." Hesketh Pearson apparently regards the narrative as entirely the work of an inflamed imagination — which, whatever the other facts may be, the woman certainly had! (See Pearson, *Bernard Shaw*, pp. 123–124.)

[28] H. Pearson: *Bernard Shaw: His Life and Personality* (London: Methuen, 1961), p. 421.

> When one has been married for over forty years there is something quite indestructible that grows up between people which has nothing to do with emotions in any way.

"The sex relation is not a personal relation," he had written to Frank Harris. In a sense he was right — as prostitutes and their clients by the thousands could testify. But what is significant is his failure to acknowledge that the sex relation is capable of being a very important aspect of the personal relation — as even the jealous though virginal Charlotte clearly believed. Still, Shaw's reason for making the remark is not hard to understand. He had never been able to reconcile himself to the earthy facts of life, or to overcome that deep mistrust of the passions which had been bitterly born in him as a small child. When these forced themselves on him, he had to deny their validity — turning grief to laughter, for example, as when he amazed Granville-Barker by his merriment at his mother's cremation; or justifying his philandering as a process of scientific investigation. But for what was he looking? For freedom, certainly; but was it also for the secure affection that his mother had withheld from him? Perhaps it is not surprising after all that the great heroines of the plays — Candida, Lady Cicely, Ann Whitefield, Major Barbara — though they are by no means sexless, are less like sweethearts than mothers.

> I have written THE Mother Play — Candida —

he wrote to Ellen Terry; and again:

> Candida, between you and me, is the Virgin Mother and nobody else —

a comment that prompts one to speculate about the identities of Morell and Marchbanks, if not of Shaw himself. Lady

Cicely plays precisely the same role with respect to Brassbound as Candida does for Marchbanks. Ann Whitefield may look more like the girl in love — but her prototype, in the regions beyond, cries to the universe for — not a lover or husband for herself — but

> A father! A father for the Superman!

Barbara, accepting joyfully the facts of her father's armaments factory and his model town, sounds matronly and more than a bit snobbish as she considers the prospect of saving

> not weak souls in starved bodies, sobbing with gratitude for a scrap of bread and treacle, but fullfed, quarrelsome, snobbish, uppish creatures, all standing on their little rights and dignities . . . Let God's work be done for its own sake: the work he had to create us to do because it cannot be done except by living men and women. When I die, let him be in my debt, not I in his; and let me forgive him as becomes a woman of my rank.

For her it is true, of course, but incidental, that her marriage to Adolphus will go forward:

> I have my dear little Dolly boy still.

As for Joan, Shaw unsexes her — in the teeth of the historians — more completely than the spirits that tend on mortal thoughts succeeded in unsexing Lady Macbeth. The intellectual impact of the play is perhaps heightened as a result; if its humanity is correspondingly narrowed, that is a price Shaw was willing to pay — though he would not have admitted he was paying it.

# 8

# *Temple of Civilization: G.B.S. on the Theatre*

By the early 1890's Shaw's socialism was fully developed; his religious belief had taken shape, even if he did not yet call himself a "mystic"; and he was reaching conclusions about sex which, however limited and unsatisfactory they might seem to others, he himself thought not only to be consonant with that belief, but even to confirm it. With the adoption of a coherent hypothesis about life and conduct came the possibility of the organized release of his enormous energies through the theatre. To discuss fully the forms that the release found — the plays, from *Candida* onward — is beyond the scope of this book. But the way to the theatre lay through dramatic criticism as well as play writing, and it was with criticism that he began.

His thought about the theatre was doubtless influenced, if not actually shaped, by his long study of Wagner. Ernest Newman has commented that

> In his attitude towards the theatre . . . Wagner is the final term in the long, slow development of certain German culture-forces. We ask ourselves in amazement today how any artist could persuade himself that the theatre is at once the measure of a nation's civilisation and the most potent shaping factor of that civilisation, and how he could make his life one long agonized struggle to impose such a conception on the world.[1]

[1] Ernest Newman: *The Life of Richard Wagner* (New York: Alfred A. Knopf, 1946), Vol. 2, p. 130.

Shaw would have been less amazed. For him too the theatre was a temple of civilization, providing measurement, guidance, and impulsion. In his mature opinion, as in Wagner's, the quality of every work of art depended on two things, aside from technical excellence: an ordered, meaningful theory of the cosmos and man's place in it, and a conviction about that theory so strongly felt by the artist that its expression becomes a passionate necessity to him.

Precisely when these conditions were first fulfilled for Shaw as regards his own play-writing we can only guess: probably it was at the time when he came to write *Candida* (1894), since that is the first play that is clearly an expression of his philosophy. His acceptance of Creative Evolution as a faith was a gradual process, and inevitably — his mind being as complex as it was — he had to think through its implications in many fields before the whole was coherent.

It is certain that for many years he had been thinking profoundly about the theatre and its place in the scheme of things. As early as February 1889 he read a paper at a meeting of the Church and Stage Guild (a group formed under the influence of his friend the Reverend Stewart Headlam, in an attempt to bridge the dark Victorian gap between the church and the arts), his topic being "Acting, by one who does not believe in it; or, the place of the Stage in the Fool's Paradise of Art." In the course of it he remarked that

> Dramatic criticism is the quintessence of art criticism, which is itself the essence of human folly and ignorance.

Since he was himself just concluding his third year as an art critic, had written a number of theatre reviews for various journals, and was in due course to serve more than three years as a weekly drama critic, we may assume that he was mentally making at least one exception to his generalization; on the other hand, as would become a man in the process of religious conversion, there may have been some penitential self-flagellation involved — a hair shirt beneath the motley. At all events the paper, which greatly puzzled its hearers, was reported on at some length in the *Church Reformer*[2] for March, Shaw preparing the account. It is curious that it has been ignored by his biographers and critics alike — the more curious since it not only shows clearly the unorthodox direction that his thought was taking but proceeds with a zest and vigour that left the audience gasping. It has never been reprinted, though certainly it deserved a place in Professor West's valuable collection of Shaw's writings about theatre. As a point of departure for examining his dramatic criticism, it is unsurpassed.

It begins with an attack on the popular notion — accepted in those pre-Stanislavsky days even by actors and critics, as well as the general public — that acting is shamming: a notion which makes respect for the theatre impossible. It is true (said Shaw) that acting, like all other art, is play, and all play is make-believe; but it is at the opposite extreme from sham: acting is the art of "metaphysical self-realization" in the supreme degree.

> We go to see Coquelin because we know he will always be Coquelin, because every new part he plays will be some new side of Coquelin or some new light on a familiar side of him, because his best part will be that which shows all sides of him and realizes him wholly to us and to himself.

The actor's art, then, consists in his discovering more and more fully his own nature by entering and exploring sympa-

[2] *The Church Reformer*, London (March 1889), pp. 67-70.

thetically whatever character, situation, and experience the dramatist presents him with, and communicating to his audience the truth that he finds. Acting — and indeed the whole art of the theatre — is, properly understood, an instrument of truth, of life, of growth. In short — Shaw did not hesitate to say so — its function is didactic; and it follows that to make of it an instrument of mere self-display or empty "entertainment" is a prostitution and a betrayal, a means of continuing in a Fool's Paradise.

He proceeded to extend his observations to the rest of the arts, referring to his own earlier experiences of them, after his boyhood haunting of picture galleries, concert halls, and theatres:

> When at last I made a plunge into London, I soon found out that the artistic people were the shirkers of the community. They ran away from their political duties to portfolios of etchings; from their social duties to essays on the delicacies of their culture; and from their religious duties to the theatre. They were doing exactly what I had done myself, in short — keeping up a Fool's Paradise in order to save themselves the trouble of making the real world any better.

He had only saved himself, he confessed, by abandoning his own efforts at producing works of art (i.e., novels) and pursuing the Real by way of the incessant lecturing on Socialism which distinguished his present phase of self-realization.

This paper was by all odds the fullest and most candid statement that Shaw had made about the arts and his relation to them. The point of view that he expressed had been arrived at through reflection not only on his experiences as would-be artist and as critic, but also on his political and socialist activities of the preceding five years and the insights that he had had into the deepest meanings of life. In his call for moral earnestness and purpose, and for naturalism in treatment, he was echoing comments that he had made before — in his discussion of Holman Hunt, for example. But whereas in the art criticism he had been vacillating and even self-contradictory, he now was lucid and consistent; indeed the principles that he here enunciated were to remain valid for him through the rest of his life. All that he wrote in his three years as drama critic for the *Saturday Review* has them as its basis, though there they are of course extended, applied in many directions, and given a religious sanction in the light of Creative Evolution.

Even that is implicitly present, though not spelled out. If an actor at work is engaged in a process of "metaphysical self-realization" as he attempts to discover and fulfill the purposes of the dramatist, just so is every man engaged in such a process as he seeks to discover and fulfill the purposes of the Life Force. The play itself, if its author is a genuine artist, is an imaginative projection of his conception of the relation of man to the cosmos; and the performance in the theatre is the celebration in miniature of the mysterious workings of the Life Force, in which the spectators participate as surely as the actors. In a word, it is ritual. If for Shakespeare all the world was a stage, for Shaw the stage is all the cosmos. The point cannot be made too strongly; for critics who have attacked Shaw's plays, from Yeats to Francis Fergusson, have often failed to see that his purpose as artist is not a bit less profound than that of Shakespeare or Sophocles or Strindberg or Brecht. Fergusson[3] indeed denies that, except in *Heartbreak House*, Shaw's stage ever really signifies anything broader than the drawing room which it sometimes represents.

If the performance of a play is ritual, it follows that the theatre is a place of worship — a temple. Shaw does not hesitate to say that it is so — it is one of the two temples necessary

[3] In *The Idea of a Theatre* (Princeton University Press, 1949).

to man. In the essay that he wrote in 1896 on going to church, he claimed for the church its place as the centre of aspiration and holiness, where man may engage in an act of worship in which body, passions and mind merge — an act of mystical contemplation that is beyond the possibility of rationalizing, for the Life Force expresses itself in many other ways besides the conscious reason.

Yet Reason is an instrument of the Life Force, the highest that it has yet devised; and only through rationalizing can man convert the truths that he discovers in private, intuitive, supra-rational worship into conduct that he can consciously practise in the workaday world. Gilbert Murray wrote, in reviewing the 1913 edition of *The Quintessence of Ibsenism:*

> Mr. Shaw pours contempt on Reason as a blind guide, and what he means is right . . . The only hope is to think and think again; but you must think with your whole nature, with every sensitive feeler of your mind, and not merely with the fully conscious logical intellect.[4]

It is "thinking" in this sense, and — if one may use the term — "discussion" in this sense, in which individuals engage *as entire individuals*, that Shaw understands to be the prime function of the theatre; and because this is a holy function, he regards the theatre as a temple. It is a temple where the truths that the Life Force reaches to in acts of individual worship can be objectified and communicated and examined.

> The theatre is really the week-day church; and a good play is essentially identical with a church service as a combination of artistic ritual, profession of faith, and sermon.[5]

[4] *New Statesman* (1913), p. 665.
[5] *Our Theatres in the Nineties,* Vol. 1, p. 264.

Considered so, the theatre is indeed as sacred an institution as the church. It is older than the church; and it is also newer, for — perhaps because in order to exist it must in some sense represent the life about it — it resists the tendency of the church to pickle its message in dogmatic brine. When Shaw looked back from the vantage point of 1906 over the years during which he was writing drama criticism for the *Saturday Review*, he remarked of the theatre:

> In my time none of the critics would claim for it, as I claimed for it, that it is as important as the Church was in the Middle Ages and much more important than the Church was in London in the years under review. A theatre to me is a place "where two or three are gathered together." The apostolic succession from Eschylus to myself is as serious and as continuously inspired as that younger institution, the apostolic succession of the Christian Church . . . When I wrote, I was well aware of what an unofficial census of Sunday worshippers presently proved: that churchgoing in London has been largely replaced by playgoing. This would be a very good thing if the theatre took itself seriously as a factory of thought, a prompter of conscience, an elucidator of social conduct, an armory against despair and dullness, and a temple of the Ascent of Man.[6]

This theatre is not and must not be a place of mere entertainment, any more than a church is a place of mere entertainment. Throughout his life, Shaw despised playwrights and critics and producers who thought that

> intellectual seriousness is out of place on the stage; that the theatre is a place of shallow amusement; that people go there to be soothed after the enormous intellectual strain of a day

[6] *Ibid.*, "The Author's Apology," p. vi.

> in the city; in short, that a playwright is a person whose business it is to make unwholesome confectionery out of cheap emotions.[7]

The theatre has often fallen prey to persons with just such ideas; the ghost of Shaw himself must shriek with Irish rage at the spectacle of money-bent Americans blowing the brains out of one of his own plays, substituting catchy tunes for them, and completing the embalming process with a large injection of romance. Yet one of the sure signs of the theatre's enduring life (he called it "the eternal theatre") is that its best servants continually purge it of sensuousness and emotionalism, whereas the church relies increasingly on those very devices.

The idea that a theatre is essentially a place of worship has of course the sanction of history, as Shaw's friend Gilbert Murray helped to make clear in his studies of Greek drama, and as the body of medieval liturgical drama testifies. More recently some critics, such as Francis Fergusson, have attempted to justify it on the basis of the ritualistic argument also implied by Shaw.

> I suggest [writes Sir Tyrone Guthrie] that theatrical performance is a form of ritual, that the audience is not asked to subscribe to an illusion but to participate in the ritual.[8]

For Shaw, however, neither the historical nor the ritualistic argument was necessary; given the theatre's function as he conceived it, and the rest followed naturally.

Recognition of this idea and its implications for the relation-

[7] *Dramatic Opinions and Essays* (New York: Brentano's, 1906), Preface.
[8] Tyrone Guthrie: "Shakespeare at Stratford, Ontario," *Shakespeare Survey 8* (Cambridge University Press, 1955), p. 130.

ship between art and religion illuminates Shaw's criticism and his plays also. It does not of course follow that it is axiomatic, or even that it is generally accepted. Many an artist, in every field of art, would be on the side of Stravinsky discussing the Wagnerian Festival at Bayreuth:

> What I find revolting in the whole affair is the underlying conception which dictated it — the principle of putting a work of art on the same level as the sacred and symbolic ritual which constitutes a religious service . . . It is high time to put an end, once for all, to this unseemly and sacrilegious conception of art as religion and the theatre as a temple.[9]

But that the idea was vital to Shaw is certain.

It was in January 1895, by which time he was in fact a seasoned critic and had begun his play-writing career, that Shaw became critic for the *Saturday Review*. From then until May 1898, week by week through ten months of each year, he wrote criticisms of plays being presented in or near London, and discussed theatre matters of all sorts. He composed his final piece in bed, to which he had been confined by a seriously injured foot — the prelude to a severe illness. Looking back over the years in which he had been "the slave of the theatre," he wrote:

> I can never justify to myself the spending of four years on dramatic criticism . . . The subject is exhausted, and so am I.[10]

Whatever he may have felt in that moment of lugubrious and un-Shavian self-appraisal, the comment itself was long ago

[9] Igor Stravinsky: *Chronicle of My Life* (London: Victor Gollancz Ltd., 1936), p. 68.

[10] *Our Theatres in the Nineties,* Vol. III, p. 386.

overruled. In 1906 the American James Huneker set to work and collected the *Saturday Review* pieces and published them in two volumes entitled *Dramatic Opinions and Essays*, Shaw relenting so far as to write a prefatory "Apology." Subsequently the pieces were published in the Standard Edition of Shaw's works, in 1932, in the three volumes called *Our Theatres in the Nineties*. Twenty years later a selection from the criticism, edited by Professor A. C. Ward, appeared in the World's Classics series, and still more recently a selection edited by Professor West has appeared in paperback format. Considering that these critical essays are in a field of journalism where transience is taken for granted, and that seven-tenths of the plays and nine-tenths of the actors mentioned have been quite properly forgotten, such a publishing history is astonishing. That the pieces continue to be read with edification and delight not only by Shavians but by everyone interested in the theatre argues a vitality that goes far beyond the ordinary critical application of standards of craftsmanship, with the addition of a comment or two on style and a little about the playwright's philosophy.

Not that Shaw was indifferent to these matters; on the contrary, his demands were exacting. But clarity and firmness in characterization; logic and movement — or, in more recent days, a meaningful absence of them; wit and lucidity in dialogue: these are fundamental in any play worth discussing at all. In demanding them Shaw does not differ from other competent critics, though he is often perceptive and stimulating in a way that is beyond the reach of his fellows, as when he makes such a remark as this:

> Half the explanations and contrivances with which melodramatists burden their pieces are superfluous attempts to

persuade the audience to accept, as reasonably brought about, situations which it is perfectly ready to accept without any bringing about whatever. The second-rate dramatist always begins at the beginning of his play; the first-rate one begins in the middle; and the genius . . . begins at the end.[11]

It is clear enough that if the theatre is to fulfill the role prescribed for it by Shaw, it must deal with life, and deal with it honestly. He had no patience with the conventions which, in the affairs of every day as well as those of the stage, enable us to pretend that human nature and human actions are something that they are not: that people driven by greed are motivated by patriotism, or Christian charity, or a magnanimous sense of responsibility to society; that poverty is ennobling rather than degrading; that sexual love is the most important of the emotions; and so on. It is the first requirement of a play that it concede nothing to these conventions, but instead deal uncompromisingly with truth. The point is well illustrated by some remarks that Shaw made in reviewing a Boucicault play. The passage deals with the stage Irishman; and readers of *John Bull's Other Island*, to say nothing of the plays of O'Casey and Synge, would do well to have it before them:

To an Irishman who has any sort of social conscience, the conception of Ireland as a romantic picture, in which the background is formed by the lakes of Killarney by moonlight, and a round tower or so, whilst every male figure is "a broth of a bhoy," and every female one a colleen in a crimson Connemara cloak, is as exasperating as the conception of Italy as a huge garden and art museum, inhabited by picturesque artists' models, is to a sensible Italian . . . The occupation of the Irish peasant is mainly agricultural; and I advise the

[11] *Ibid.*, Vol. 2, p. 83.

reader to make it a fixed rule never to allow himself to believe in the alleged Arcadian virtues of the half-starved drudges who are sacrificed to the degrading, brutalizing, and, as far as I can ascertain, entirely unnecessary pursuit of unscientific farming. The virtues of the Irish peasant are the intense melancholy, the surliness of manner, the incapacity for happiness and self-respect that are the tokens of his natural unfitness for a life of wretchedness. His vices are the arts by which he accommodates himself to his slavery — the flattery on his lips which hides the curse in his heart; his pleasant readiness to settle disputes by "leaving it all to your honour," in order to make something out of your generosity in addition to exacting the utmost of his legal due from you; his instinctive perception that by pleasing you he can make you serve him; his mendacity and mendicity; his love of a stolen advantage; the superstitious fear of his priest and his Church which does not prevent him from trying to cheat both in the temporal transactions between them; and the parasitism which makes him, in domestic service, that occasionally convenient but on the whole demoralizing human barnacle, the irremoveable old retainer of the family. Of all the tricks which the Irish nation played on the slow-witted Saxon, the most outrageous is the palming off on him of the imaginary Irishman of romance.[12]

If the people in a play must be "real," what they do must also be in some sense real. Shaw therefore had nothing but scorn for the "poor old well-made play," with its patterned plot and contrived situations, that was the stock-in-trade of the Victorian theatre. On the other hand, it must not be supposed that he wanted only Zolaesque "naturalism." Given truth of character, he was prepared to accept any amount of incon-

[12] *Ibid.*, Vol. 2, p. 29.

gruity and exaggeration of circumstance and event. The aim is truth, not verisimilitude.

When Shaw felt that an author had a "grip on the realities of life," he was prepared to concede much to him, even though the point of view expressed might differ entirely from his own. Early in his *Saturday Review* career he defended Henry James on this ground.

> There is no reason why life as we find it in Mr. James's novels — life, that is, in which passion is subordinate to intellect and to fastidious artistic taste — should not be presented on the stage . . . As it happens, I am not in Mr. James's camp: in all the life that has energy enough to be interesting to me, subjective volition, passion, will, make intellect the merest tool. But there is in the centre of that cyclone a certain calm spot where cultivated ladies and gentlemen live on independent incomes or by pleasant artistic occupations. It is there that Mr. James's art touches life . . .[13]

Still, it was not enough for the Creative Evolutionist that a play deal with life. It must deal with it purposefully; and the purpose must — as we have seen — be didactic.

> Drama [he wrote in 1902] is no mere setting up of the camera to nature: it is the presentation in parable of the conflict between Man's will and his environment: in a word, of problem.[14]

Now the problem of the conflict between Man's will and his environment, from Shaw's point of view at least, is the problem of morality. For him, the purpose of the universe is the evolu-

[13] *Ibid.*, Vol. 1, p. 6.

[14] *Mrs. Warren's Profession*, "The Author's Apology," p. xxii.

tion of force and matter into intelligence and spirit. Man is the highest point yet reached in that evolution — he represents the beginning of self-consciousness. But man's function is not to rest on the Life Force's laurels: it is to strive for further progress towards the goal. The condition of this progress is the achievement of a society in which the Life Force can operate most fully: that is, the unflagging pursuit of morality — individual, political, financial, sexual, or whatever else.

One function of art, therefore — and specifically of dramatic art — is to prompt man to examine the morality that he accepts and practises; to show him how it is deficient and how it may be improved; and to exhort him to achieve the improvement. It follows that the true artist is always a rebel against society; he belongs by nature among the genuinely unconventional people — not after the fashion of that self-styled "disciple of Bernard Shaw," the rascally Louis Dubedat; but rather in that of Major Barbara, who comes to perceive that the real vices of society are not drunkenness and war, but poverty and inequality. When Shaw appeared before a parliamentary committee on censorship in 1909, he insisted repeatedly — to the bafflement of his interrogators — that he was, as an artist, profoundly and deliberately immoral — "conscientiously immoral" — in so far as he, like Ibsen, was in determined revolt against conventional morality. A few years later he expressed the greatest misgivings about the new form of theatre, the cinema:

> The danger of the cinema is not the danger of immorality, but the danger of morality. The cinema must be not merely ordinarily and locally moral, but extraordinarily and internationally moral.[15]

[15] "The Cinema as Moral Leveller," *New Statesman* (June 27, 1914).

Because the cinema is under the control of international money-makers, it will simply be made to appeal to the widest possible audience, and therefore will necessarily work towards a dead level of morality.

> Now levelling, though excellent in income, is disastrous in morals. The moment you allow one man to receive a larger income than another you are on the road to ruin. But the moment you prevent one man from having a more advanced morality than another you are on the same road.

The situation is complicated by geography; and in a comment not much calculated to give comfort to Shavians who live in the hinterland he goes on:

> It is quite a mistake to suppose that conventional morality is all of one piece the world over. London cannot live on the morals of the Italian peasant or the Australian sheepfarmer. What is more, high civilization is not compatible with the romance of the pioneer communities of Canada.

Truth, to life, then, and moral purpose: these are the principal criteria in Shaw's criticism, and a dramatist's stature as an artist is directly proportionate to his achievement of them. Shakespeare had the first of them to a pre-eminent degree. He was, Shaw told the Heretics Club of Cambridge in 1911:

> a man of very great power and imagination . . . who produced a mass of plays in which he set forth his knowledge of humanity in a very wonderful way . . .

But he was also a man

> who evidently had no well-considered views of any kind . . . and practically left religion out of account.

The Bard sadly lacked moral purpose: only once or twice did he set out to write a problem play, and then with only a foggy idea of what he was about. Ibsen, on the other hand, had both truth to life and moral purpose — for the modern, he is the supreme dramatist. In British drama of the 1890's Shaw could find occasional glimpses of truth — as in Henry James, for example. But the vision of it that floods the stage with life was rare, and moral passion even rarer. Henry Arthur Jones approached greatness, especially in *Michael and His Lost Angel* — but he lost his nerve; Pinero was a pretentious trifler; Oscar Wilde was "in a certain sense . . . our only thorough playwright. He plays with everything . . ." [16] But he was "colossally lazy," and, except in *An Ideal Husband*, he spent his time in mere irresponsible rib-tickling.

The comments on Jones and Wilde draw attention to two other qualities that Shaw called for: courage and gaiety. The dramatist who is to offer a truthful presentation of life and to deal with it in terms of "conscientious immorality" must be prepared to face the risks involved — of public disfavour and critical vituperation. In Shavian terms, the failure of Jones — whose creative imagination and moral perception Shaw respected — was a failure of courage. Shaw had high praise for *Michael and His Lost Angel* — a play that dealt with a subject similar to that of Maugham's familiar short story *Rain:*

> When I respond to the appeal of Mr. Jones's art by throwing myself sympathetically into his characteristic attitude of mind, I am conscious of no shortcoming in Michael and his Lost Angel. It then seems to me to be a genuinely sincere and moving play, feelingly imagined, written with knowledge as to the man and insight as to the woman by an author equipped not only with the experience of an adept play-

[16] *Our Theatres in the Nineties,* Vol. 1, p. 9.

> wright, and a kindly and humorous observer's sense of contemporary manners, but with that knowledge of spiritual history in which Mr. Jones's nearest competitors seem so stupendously deficient. Its art is in vital contact with the most passionate religious movement of its century, as fully quickened art always has been. On comparing it with the ordinary personal sentiment of Mr. Grundy, and with those grotesque flounderings after some sort of respectably pious foothold which have led Mr. Pinero to his rescue of the burning Bible from Mrs. Ebbsmith's stove, and his redemption of Mrs. Fraser by the social patronage of the Bishop's wife, I unhesitatingly class Mr. Jones as first, and eminently first, among the surviving fittest of his own generation of playwrights.[17]

Jones's clergyman, however, having contravened conventional morality, is permitted by the play neither to proclaim his triumphant sense of the rightness of what he has done and defy the moral world, nor to make the sickening discovery that he has been untrue to his own nature. In short, he becomes neither a hero of the Life Force nor a tragic hero

> in an emergency where a self-realization alone could save him from destruction; and if this failure were the subject of Mr. Jones's last three acts, then the play without a hero might be as tragic as Rosmersholm. But Mr. Jones does not set Michael's situation in that light: he shares his fatalism, accepting his remorse, confession, and disgrace as inevitable, with a monastery for the man and death for the woman as the only possible stage ending — surely not so much an ending as a slopping up of the remains of the two poor creatures.

Shaw wanted heroes, then; and it is easy to understand why he preferred comic heroes to tragic ones. Tragedy celebrates man in a hostile world that overwhelms him, mocks his ideals,

[17] *Ibid.*, Vol. 2, p. 15.

denies his hopes; in Arthur Miller's phrase, it documents his defeat. But the business of drama, as the Creative Evolutionist sees it, is not to document the defeat of man, but to proclaim his high destiny and urge him on to it. It needs not the melancholy cry of despair, but the gay laughter of courage.

Not — be it noted — the brainless laughter of forgetfulness, nor even what Constance Rourke has called[18] "the tender laughter of reconciliation." These are only the complement of the tears of tragedy; they are the other side of the coin of despair. Shaw was as susceptible as anyone else to such laughter, and many a time he came from the theatre with his sides aching — only to find that his real discomfort was not physical at all.

> Unless comedy touches me as well as amuses me, it leaves me with a sense of having wasted my evening. I go to the theatre to be moved to laughter, not to be tickled or bustled into it; that is why, though I laugh as much as anybody at a farcical comedy, I am out of spirits before the end of the second act, and out of temper before the end of the third, my miserable mechanical laughter intensifying these symptoms at every outburst. If the public ever becomes intelligent enough to know when it is really enjoying itself and when it is not, there will be an end of farcical comedy.[19]

That he did not mean the last comment literally is obvious; most of his own plays would never have been written if he had. As we have seen, in a letter to Florence Farr, in 1892, he had argued that farce was by no means to be scorned; but clearly he would add that farce must be instrumental. There is no value in the laughter by which man merely disguises

[18] In *American Humor.*
[19] *Our Theatres,* Vol. 1, p. 42.

from himself his sense of life's futility and his own pettiness; but the laughter that affirms his freedom and hope and faith in his high destiny is beyond price:

> By laughter only can you destroy evil without malice, and affirm good fellowship without mawkishness.[20]

Discussing Meredith's *Essay on Comedy*, he asserted:

> The function of comedy . . . is nothing less than the destruction of old-established morals. Unfortunately, today such iconoclasm can be tolerated by our playgoing citizens only as a counsel of despair and pessimism. They can find a dreadful joy in it when it is done seriously, or even grimly and terribly as they understand Ibsen to be doing it; but that it should be done with levity, with silvery laughter like the crackling of thorns under a pot, is too scandalously wicked, too cynical, too heartlessly shocking to be born. Consequently our plays must either be exploitations of old-established morals or tragic challenges of the old order of Nature.[21]

It follows that the idea that a play must please the public is the height of irresponsible nonsense. The transformation of the art of acting into the art of pleasing is shameless prostitution. The job, for writer and actor alike, is *not* to please the public — for the public is moral, and the theatre's function is to shake it out of its morality.

> People don't go to the theatre to be pleased: there are a hundred cheaper, less troublesome, more effective pleasures than

[20] *Ibid.*, Vol. 1, "The Author's Apology," p. vi.
[21] *Ibid.*, Vol. 3, p. 87.

> an uncomfortable gallery can offer. We are led there by our appetite for drama, which is no more to be satisfied by sweet-meats than our appetite for dinner is to be satisfied with meringues and raspberry vinegar.[22]

To Pope's remark that

> The drama's laws the drama's patrons give;
> And those who live to please must please to live —

Shaw replies:

> But you cannot get out of an argument by simply telling a lie in a heroic couplet.[23]

His criticism of the production of a play paralleled his criticism of the play itself. If a theatre is a temple, then those who work in it constitute a priesthood. To engage in a ritual act of "metaphysical self-realization" is a sacred responsibility, and the participants are entitled to something better than simple respect from the public. In an age when "being on the stage" was commonly eyed askance as a form of profligacy, Shaw never tired of proclaiming the right of the actor to be treated as an artist, a man of high and noble calling. He was as pleased as anyone else when Henry Irving — whose genius Shaw respected as fully as he derided his judgment — was knighted.

For his part, the actor must accept his responsibility to his calling by measuring up to its demands, which are high indeed. They begin, not with mere technical competence, but with technical excellence:

> I am strongly of the opinion that nothing but superlative excellence in art can excuse a man or woman for being an artist

[22] *Our Theatres,* Vol. 3, p. 246.
[23] *Ibid.,* Vol. 1, p. 228.

> at all . . . I have a large charity for loose morals; they are often more virtuous than strait-laced ones. But for loose art I have no charity at all.[24]

So Shaw wrote in 1918. One does not read far into *Our Theatres in the Nineties* before finding how blunt and devastating he could be in dealing with second-rate acting, and also how quick he was to applaud skill. What he required of the actor is spelled out in a discussion that precedes a review of *Henry IV, Part One*:

> I plead, then, that acting is potentially an artistic profession, and that by training and practice a person can qualify himself or herself to come to a manager or author and say, "Within the limits imposed by my age and sex, I can do all the ordinary work of the stage with perfect certainty. I know my vowels and consonants as a phonetic expert, and can speak so as to arrest the attention of an audience whenever I open my mouth, forcibly, delicately, roughly, smoothly, prettily, harshly, authoritatively, submissively, but always artistically, just as you want it. I can sit, stand, fall, get up, walk, dance, and otherwise use my body with the complete command of it that marks the physical artist." An actor might know all this, and yet, for want of the power to interpret an author's text and invent the appropriate physical expression for it, never, without coaching, get beyond Rosencrantz or Seyton. It is, therefore, only the minimum qualification of a skilled stage hand; and if an actor is not that, then he is merely a stage-struck unskilled laborer or handy man, and his "conceptions" of Ibsen or Shakespeare are mere impertinences.[25]

Technical excellence, then is not enough. There must be intelligence; for "it is not perfect articulation, but perfect intelli-

[24] "Scratch Opera," *The Nation* (June 22, 1918).
[25] *Our Theatres,* Vol. 2, p. 127.

gence, that finds the nail in every phrase and hits it on the head unerringly."[26] And there must be imagination also; for only through imagination and intelligence together can the actor discover the humanity that is the essence of every good play and bring his technical skills to bear on it appropriately.

Even the presence of these three qualities — imagination, intelligence, and technical excellence — does not guarantee a first-rate production, for there is a further and imponderable difficulty. A play is initially the expression of a single mind, the projection of a single view of humanity. A performance, on the contrary, is the composite product of many minds, not one of which may necessarily share the dramatist's view of things. When Shaw discussed the publishing of his first volume of plays, in the preface to *Plays Unpleasant,* he made a rueful admission which disdainers of play-reading, as compared with playgoing, would do well to consider:

> The more unquestioned a playwright's authority is on the stage, and the more friendly and willing the co-operation of the manager and company, the more completely does he get convinced of the impossibility of achieving an authentic representation of his piece as well as an effective and successful one. It is quite possible for a piece to enjoy the most sensational success on the basis of a complete misunderstanding of its philosophy: indeed, it is not too much to say that it is only by a capacity for succeeding in spite of its philosophy that a dramatic work of serious poetic import can become popular . . . Not even when a drama is performed without omission or alteration by actors who are enthusiastic disciples of the author does it escape transfiguration.

In a letter to Henry Arthur Jones in 1902, Shaw wrote:

26 "The Dying Tongue of Great Elizabeth," *Saturday Review* (February 11, 1905).

> As for me, the theatre only exasperates me when I care about the play. I have almost come to the conclusion that actual performance is only advisable as the last resource of a thoroughly undramatic bungle. After all, one can't help planning the effect for people who know worse than if the author had written like a child for children.

They are lonely comments; and perhaps the experience that underlay them led to the writing of one of the most moving phrases in all Shaw's works. For if the dramatist finds his intentions misunderstood and his purposes frustrated as the products of his imagination come to embodiment on the stage, what of the millennial frustrations and cosmic defeats of the Creative Power itself?

> You have told me I am alone [says Joan]. France is alone; and God is alone. And what is my loneliness beside the loneliness of my country and my God?

Nevertheless, though in a way Shaw is saying that the unacted play is better than the acted one, his is not the loneliness of romantic agony, contemplating with haunted delight the sweetness of the unheard melody. Life remains — and life changes; there is the high challenge to seek out and support its purposes at every moment; and the theatre is an instrument — sometimes exasperatingly crude, it is true — for helping man to rise to that challenge. In Shaw's view everyone concerned in the presentation of a play, from the playwright to the lowliest bit-part actor, is the servant of a high and holy purpose.

Even the critic may have his value, as Shaw knew well. Looked at in one way his own criticism, with its gaily ferocious attacks on everything second rate or irresponsible, and its exuberant affirmation of high aims, was the scourge by which he drove money-changers from the temple. Looked at in another, it was a zestful and imaginative but systematic crusade for the acceptance of his own plays. Looked at in either way it is first-rate criticism — penetrating, lucid, witty, uncompromising. That it has limitations is to be expected: Shaw did not profess to represent the culmination of the Life Force's efforts. But the limitations are of the sort that inevitably arise when a man establishes a clear hypothesis about life and holds to it with consistency. Like the hypothesis, they are on the grand scale. Few would disagree with a comment made about drama in the Preface to *Androcles and the Lion*:

> We must not forget that the best dramatic art is the operation of a divinatory instinct for truth.

But the moment someone asked Pilate's question, we should all be at loggerheads. John Keats in one corner would argue that truth is beauty; and in another (except that he would not remain in a corner) Bernard Shaw would contend that it is morality. Keats, pointing to Shakespeare, would maintain that the secret of his power over truth is Negative Capability —

> that is, when a man is capable of being in uncertainties, mysteries, doubts, without any irritable reaching after fact and reason.

To which Shaw would gaily reply that the point about Shakespeare is not his Negative Capability at all, but his Positive Incapability. But his treatment of his Elizabethan rival deserves a separate chapter.

# 9
# *Superman versus Man: G.B.S. on Shakespeare*

THE REVIEW of *The Merchant of Venice* that Shaw sent to John Morley in 1880 was by no means the first review that he wrote, for he had then been reviewing plays for the Manchester *Guardian* for some time. It was nevertheless prophetic, for it was a thoughtful discussion of the work of the most renowned actor-manager of the day: Henry Irving. Irving was then in the third year of his long reign at the Lyceum, where he and Ellen Terry were to dispense Shakespeare in the spectacular Irving style, to enraptured Victorians, for more than two decades. As a lad in Dublin, Shaw had seen Irving act and been greatly impressed by his power, and he tells us that he had believed he saw the promise of a renewal of life in the theatre as Irving's art matured. What he witnessed at the Lyceum, therefore, not only disappointed but profoundly disquieted him. He began his review in this way:

> During a phase of taste to suit which all intelligible fictions are obscured by farfetched interpretations, a theory representing Shakespeare as a morbid creator of sombre and preposterous figures has been offered to the public by Mr. Henry Irving, a man of singular appearance and full of that love of the mysterious and grotesque with which students of the picturesque become seized before they have advanced to a conception of the indifferent familiarity with the external machinery of effect which the adept master feels.[1]

[1] British Museum, Shaw Mss. 50690.

At this point the reader may well be disposed to agree with Morley, who had decided that Shaw had no knack for journalism. To read on, however, is to find that in fact the piece prefigures much that Shaw was to write a few years later about contemporary treatment of Shakespeare. He praises the play itself, acknowledging that it is "unusually perfect" although poetry, which the Elizabethans understandably looked for at the playhouse because books and readers were scarce, is not really wanted by a modern audience, who can find it in libraries. He discusses the characters of the play with perception and good sense. But as to the production, while he acknowledges its power, he attacks it squarely on two points: Irving's complete distortion of the character of Shylock, and his cutting of the play to suit his portrayal of that role.

> Mr. Irving calls his arrangement of the "Merchant" an "acting version." What *does* he call the original?

So the essay ends.

It was fifteen years after he wrote this piece that Shaw became drama critic for the *Saturday Review*. Irving was still in charge of the Lyceum and Shakespeare — but Shaw had undergone the development in thought and experience which the preceding chapters have described. We may see how that development affected his criticism by turning from his *Merchant* essay to a review of *Cymbeline* that he wrote in September 1896. Irving produced the latter play and took the part of Iachimo, the villainous Italian who wagers that he can seduce the wife of his friend Posthumus, then devises evidence to show that he has won the bet. The part of Imogen, the innocent victim of Iachimo's villainy and consequently of Posthumus's jealousy, was played by Ellen Terry. Shaw began his account of the play[2] thus:

[2] *Our Theatres in the Nineties*, Vol. 2, pp. 195–202.

. . . It is for the most part stagey trash of the lowest melodramatic order, in parts abominably written, throughout intellectually vulgar, and, judged in point of thought by modern intellectual standards, vulgar, foolish, offensive, indecent, and exasperating beyond all tolerance. There are moments when one asks despairingly why our stage should ever have been cursed with this "immortal" pilferer of other men's stories and ideas, with his monstrous rhetorical fustian, his unbearable platitudes, his pretentious reduction of the subtlest problems of life to commonplaces against which a Polytechnic debating club would revolt, his incredible unsuggestiveness, his sententious combination of ready reflection with complete intellectual sterility, and his consequent incapacity for getting out of the depth of even the most ignorant audience, except when he says something so transcendently platitudinous that his more humble-minded hearers cannot bring themselves to believe that so great a man really meant to talk like their grandmothers. With the single exception of Homer, there is no eminent writer, not even Sir Walter Scott, whom I can despise so entirely as I despise Shakespeare when I measure my mind against his. The intensity of my impatience with him occasionally reaches such a pitch, that it would positively be a relief to me to dig him up and throw stones at him, knowing as I do how incapable he and his worshippers are of understanding any less obvious form of indignity.

Shaw is writing here in the role in which, so far as his Shakespearian criticism is concerned, he is best known. Since he wrote the *Merchant* review, his prose has become swift, rhythmical, and athletic, his mind more deft, resourceful, and urbane; and he has discovered the joy of creative destruction, having perhaps read in Bakunin[3] of

[3] In a famous article published first in 1842. See *The Political Philosophy of Bakunin*, ed. G. P. Maximoff (Glencoe, Illinois: The Free Press, 1953), p. 34.

> . . . the eternal spirit which destroys and annihilates only because it is the unfathomable and eternally creative source of life. The urge of destruction is at the same time a creative urge.

Iconoclasm, Shaw was to comment, is

> perhaps the one pursuit that is as useful as it is amusing.[4]

The object of his iconoclasm here is that Shakespeare-worship which he called Bardolatry. In the early years of the nineteenth century the Romantics — especially the enthusiastic Hazlitt — had given tremendous impetus to Bardolatry, impetus that the Victorians more than sustained. Carlyle, in 1840, could in the space of a single page describe Shakespeare as a Prophet, a Seer, a Priest, a kind of universal Psalmist, and a blessed heaven-sent Bringer of Light — all complete with the capital letters that are not ordinarily used in writing of mortal men. And though in the closing decades of the century historical and textual studies were leading some academic critics in the direction of a more sober judgment, their work was as yet obscured by the treatment of Shakespeare in the theatre itself — especially Irving's. The generation addressed by Shaw had been brought up to revere the name of Shakespeare as they revered the Deity and the pound sterling; and against all such worship Shaw continually rebels, just as he rebelled against the worshippers of Marx. Whenever he has to deal with the conventional attitude to Shakespeare he either rages, as in the Cymbeline piece, or becomes flippant or ironical, calling Shakespeare by his first name or likening him to the author of the advertisements for Cassell's *Popular Educator*. Yet, like

[4] *Saturday Review*, May 13, 1899. "Giving the Devil his Due."

any earnest iconoclast, he is not destructive simply for the sake of destruction. The early review of *The Merchant of Venice* made clear that he profoundly admired Shakespeare as a playwright; and the admiration had not decreased. His desire to dash the image in pieces arose out of a deeper desire that the worshippers should see beyond the image to the subject itself. Bardolatry is a curse to those who commit it, for the blind worship of Shakespeare makes development beyond him impossible; and it is unjust to its object in making of him an unearthly being, destroying his real vitality and even his interest, and obscuring the quite searching questions that he sometimes asks.

It was partly to supply a credible human figure in place of the gilded image that Shaw was to write in 1910 *The Dark Lady of the Sonnets.* There he showed Shakespeare as a bold young gallant, vain of his success in the London theatre, wittily resourceful, self-reliant to the point of impudence. The play is, as William Irvine says, a "brilliant little tour de force." [5]

Yet even after so many years of Shavian war on Bardolatry, the London public was not ready for Shakespeare the Man. In 1914, concluding the Preface to the published version of the play, Shaw recorded ruefully:

> I . . . unfortunately represented Shakespeare as treasuring and using (as I do myself) the jewels of unconsciously musical speech which common people utter and throw away every day; and this was taken as a disparagement of Shakespeare's "Originality." Why was I born with such contemporaries? Why is Shakespeare made ridiculous by such a posterity?

[5] William Irvine: *The Universe of G.B.S.* (New York: Whittlesey House, 1949), p. 283.

Incidentally, earlier in the Preface Shaw defended Shakespeare stoutly against two charges that were being whispered against him by one section of his ridiculous posterity: that he was a sycophant and that he was sexually perverted. Shaw hated these sneers as much as he hated Bardolatry itself.

But to return to the *Cymbeline* review. Having castigated Shakespeare, Shaw makes some amends before proceeding to deal with other enemies:

> But I am bound to add that I pity the man who cannot enjoy Shakespeare. He has outlasted thousands of abler thinkers, and will outlast a thousand more. His gift of telling a story (provided someone else told it to him first); his enormous power over language, as conspicuous in his senseless and silly abuse of it as in his miracles of expression; his humor; his sense of idiosyncratic character; and his prodigious fund of that vital energy which is, it seems, the true differentiating property behind the faculties, good, bad, or indifferent, of the man of genius, enable him to entertain us so effectively that the imaginary scenes and people he has created become more real to us than our actual life — at least, until our knowledge and grip of actual life begins to deepen and glow beyond the common. When I was twenty I knew everybody in Shakespeare, from Hamlet to Abhorson, much more intimately than I knew my living contemporaries.

Shakespeare, then, has genius — that fact at least Shaw never questions. And he is perfectly clear as to the source of that genius — it is simply a fund of vital energy so far beyond the ordinary as to be "prodigious." Shaw's own genius, he averred, was of the same kind. When Shakespeare succeeded in pouring some of his vital energy into his characters they became more real than those of actual life — that is why his plays continue to hold audiences through the centuries. Looking at *Cymbeline*, Shaw cannot find the vital energy save in two minor persons and one major one — the calumniated Imogen. Contemplation of Imogen leads him into a piece of sharp analysis:

> Do, please, remember that there are two Imogens. One is a solemn and elaborate example of what, in Shakespeare's opinion, a real lady ought to be. With this unspeakable person virtuous indignation is chronic. Her object in life is to vindicate her own propriety and to suspect everybody else's, especially her husband's . . . Her fertility and spontaneity in nasty ideas is not to be described: there is hardly a speech in her part that you can read without wincing. But this Imogen has another one tied to her with ropes of blank verse (which can fortunately be cut) — the Imogen of Shakespeare's genius, an enchanting person of the most delicate sensitiveness, full of sudden transitions from ecstasies of tenderness to transports of childish rage, and reckless of consequences in both, instantly hurt and instantly appeased, and of the highest breeding and courage. But for this Imogen, Cymbeline would stand about as much chance of being revived now as Titus Andronicus.

These remarks about Imogen did not come suddenly to Shaw's pen as he reviewed the production. They were the result of a searching study of Imogen's role. Almost a month before the play was to open, he had written Ellen Terry a chaffing letter about her part: "It is downright maddening to think of your slaving over Imogen. Of course you can't remember it: who could? . . . To learn Imogen requires a Bishop's wife, not *you!*"[6] A week later she wrote him an

[6] Christopher St. John (ed.): *Ellen Terry and Bernard Shaw, A Correspondence* (Toronto: The Macmillan Company of Canada Ltd., 1931), p. 42.

unhappy note about the difficulties she was having, and in three days he sent off a reply headed "The Intelligent Actress's Guide to Cymbeline," [7] in which he not only set forth his theory of the two Imogens, but proceeded with five pages of discussion and advice about the playing of the part: what to cut and what to retain, and why; the feelings and actions and effect of Imogen at this point and that. In later letters he made further suggestions, and Ellen responded with warm gratitude.

The things that impress one in this "Guide" are its author's perceptiveness, his concern for not merely salvaging but giving the fullest effect to that part of the role that he sees as the product of Shakespeare's genius, his equal concern that the imagination of the audience should be given full scope, and the boldness with which he cuts speeches to suit his purpose. This last requires further comment in view of some observations that he makes in the review, after discussing Imogen:

> For the purposes of the Lyceum . . . Cymbeline had to be cut, and cut liberally. Not that there was any reason to apprehend that the manager would flinch from the operation: quite the contrary. In a true republic of art Sir Henry Irving would ere this have expiated his acting versions on the scaffold. He does not merely cut plays: he disembowels them. In Cymbeline he has quite surpassed himself by extirpating the antiphonal third verse from the famous dirge. A man who would do that would do anything . . . The grotesque character tracery of Cloten's lines . . . is defaced with Cromwellian ruthlessness; and the patriotic scene, with the Queen's great speech about the natural bravery of our isle, magnificent in its Walkürenritt swing, is shorn away . . . And yet, long screeds of rubbish about "slander,

[7] *Ibid.*, pp. 46–51.

whose edge is sharper than the sword," and so on, are preserved with superstitious veneration.

There is an element of paradox in Shaw's violently condemning Irving's cutting of Shakespeare at the same time that he advised Ellen Terry on the cutting of her own role. But when Shaw cut the play, he was concerned with the production as a whole. What he wanted was the maximum of dramatic effect, the maximum of intellectual stimulation — and that meant convincing the audience that it was seeing a picture of real things happening to real people. What Irving wanted was to overpower his audience with pageantry, rhetoric — and Irving. Shaw's audience was to go out of the theatre awakened and alert; Irving's was to emerge stunned.

A similar difference marked their views on staging. Shaw regarded the scene of Imogen's awakening in the gloomy mountain gorge as sadly marred not only by the "utter deficiency" of certain of Ellen Terry's fellow actors, but also by the "inappropriate prettiness and sunniness of the landscape scenery," which lacked "nothing but a trellised porch, a bamboo bicycle, and a nice little bed of standard roses, to complete its absurdity." These comments are part of Shaw's long campaign for the intelligent, appropriate use of stage settings. His argument — which does not concern Shakespearian plays only — is the simple one that some plays require scenery and therefore should have it and some plays do not require scenery and therefore should not have it. "The poetry of 'The Tempest,' he wrote in 1897, "is so magical that it would make the scenery of a modern theatre ridiculous . . . If Sir Henry Irving were to put the play on at the Lyceum next season . . . what could he do but multiply the expenditure enormously and spoil the illusion?" He goes on with a statement of his case that shows how well he knows the tricks of imagination:

> A superstitious person left to himself will see a ghost in every ray of moonlight on the wall and every old coat hanging on a nail; but make up a really careful, elaborate, plausible, picturesque, blood-curdling ghost for him, and his cunning grin will proclaim that he sees through it at a glance. The reason is, not that a man can *always* imagine things more vividly than art can present them to him, but that it takes an altogether extraordinary degree of art to compete with the pictures which the imagination makes when it is stimulated by such potent forces as the maternal instinct, superstitious awe, or the poetry of Shakespeare . . . You can do best without scenery in The Tempest and A Midsummer Night's Dream, because the best scenery you can get will only destroy the illusion created by the poetry; but it does not at all follow that scenery will not improve a representation of Othello.[8]

In the main such critical pieces as the *Cymbeline* review are concerned with rescuing Shakespeare, not destroying him — rescuing him from the Bardolaters who blind themselves and smother him, from the bad actors and producers who distort or dismember him, and from his own faults of rhetorical bombast, triteness, and sometimes ineffective characterization. Shaw himself thought of his criticism as aimed at "restoring Shakespeare's integrity."

How successful he was it is of course impossible to say. How does one assess the role of an individual in bringing about a change of popular taste? For years he was scoffed at and vilified for his comments on Shakespeare — by theatre managers, dramatic critics, and the public. Some of those whom he alienated were people whose esteem he would have

[8] *Our Theatres in the Nineties,* Vol. 3, p. 241.

prized. On January 2, 1897, Samuel Butler — one of the men whose thought influenced Shaw most — picked up his pen and wrote irritably in his notebook:

G. Bernard Shaw

I have long been repelled by this man though at the same time attracted by his coruscating power. Emery Walker once brought him up to see me, on the score that he was a great lover of Handel. He did nothing but cry down Handel and cry up Wagner. I did not like him and am sure that neither did he like me . . .

The dislike — no this is too strong a word — the dissatisfaction with which he impressed me has been increased by his articles in the *Saturday Review* since it has been under Frank Harris's management — brilliant, amusing, and often sound though many of them have been. His cult of Ibsen disgusts me, and my displeasure has been roused to such a pitch as to have led me to this note, by his article "Better than Shakespeare" in this morning's *Saturday Review.* Of course Bunyan is better than Shakespeare in some respects, so is Bernard Shaw himself, so am I, so is everybody. Of course also Bunyan is one of our very foremost classics — but I cannot forgive Bernard Shaw for sneering at Shakespeare as he has done this morning. If he means it, there is no trusting his judgment — if he does not mean it, I have no time to waste on such trifling. If Shaw embeds his plums in such a cake as this, they must stay there. I cannot trouble to pick them out.[9]

Still, Shaw persisted in his campaign; and certain venturesome spirits among his contemporaries began to listen to him. Of these the most important, so far as the theatre is concerned,

[9] *The Notebooks of Samuel Butler,* ed. Geoffrey Keynes and Brian Hill (London: Jonathan Cape, 1951), p. 45.

were William Poel (who indeed had begun a campaign of his own, before Shaw), Johnston Forbes-Robertson, and Harley Granville-Barker. They especially carried forward the movement to produce Shakespeare in Shakespearian fashion. Writing his "Valedictory" for the *Saturday Review*, Shaw, although he was still being made the victim of journalistic abuse, felt that his four years of iconoclasm had begun to show results:

> When I began to write [he commented], William was a divinity and a bore. Now he is a fellow-creature; and his plays have reached an unprecedented pitch of popularity. And yet his worshippers overwhelm my name with insult.[10]

It must be recognized, however, that Shaw's iconoclastic attacks were prompted by something deeper than mere hatred of Bardolatry and theatrical distortion. They were prompted — after 1890, at least — by his clear conviction that Shakespeare, even in his restored integrity, could not satisfy the spiritual and intellectual needs of a genuinely modern person: great as he is, he is not good enough.

The conviction stems from Shaw's belief that the theatre is a place of worship, a church. Like the church, it has its apostles; and in its apostolic succession Shakespeare has his place. In the Preface to *Heartbreak House* Shaw was to list him, along with Euripides and Aristophanes and others, as the occupant of one of the "everlasting seats." And in his iconoclastic assaults — especially the *Saturday Review* pieces — he was mainly concerned with dissipating error and distortion in the treatment of him and reaffirming the truth about him. Yet a succession is a succession, and Shakespeare must not be

10 *Our Theatres*, Vol. 3, p. 385.

thought of as the final apostle, any more than Shaw: he must be seen in relation to the long story of the slow evolution of the mind and character of man. Looked upon so, he diminishes, Shaw argued: often his laughter is coarse; his characters hollow; his themes trite; his treatment of sex sensual, romantic, and immoral; his politics execrable.

Shaw's rejection of Shakespearian comedy is not surprising. He himself held in the main, as we have seen, a Meredithian view of comedy as a social corrective that was to purge mankind of vice and folly. Indeed, he regarded Meredith's handling of the subject as far too dainty. Meredith's comic artist is a social physician who treats his patient with oil of peppermint; Shaw's prepares for an appendectomy. If the theatre is to be a "factory of thought" and a "prompter of conscience," it cannot spend its energies in celebrating the joys of mere animal life.

His dislike of Shakespeare's romantic treatment of sexual love is part of the same pattern. As a biological device for continuing the race, sex has its important place. That it should be a source of pleasure is merely incidental, not worth a mature person's consideration. But to treat it, in the theatre or anywhere else, as giving rise to the "most irresistible of all the passions," and allow it to settle the fates of societies and empires, while at the same time refusing to discuss it openly, is to practise not just irresponsibility, but the most outrageous fraud. Not that Shakespeare idealized sex quite in the way that many Victorians were to do, in effect almost denying that it has a physical component. Even when he treats it romantically, he contrives constantly to remind us of its physical basis. Rosalind and Orlando may romanticize, but Touchstone will break in from time to time to remind us of what they are about. And though he may treat marriage romantically when he looks at it through the eyes of unmarried lovers, there is not much idealization in his treatment of marriage and family relationships themselves — one thinks of *Othello, Lear,* and *Cymbeline.* Nevertheless, in this matter Shakespeare could not conceivably have Shaw's approval. For though his romanticism may be tempered, he accepts fully the two assumptions on which the conventional treatment of sex had for centuries been based (and on which it continues largely to be based, in spite of Shaw). These assumptions are that woman exists chiefly for the pleasure of man, and that she is the property of man. When *King Lear* opens, Cordelia is to be handed over as a chattel, and her sole duty is to please whatever man receives her. Brabantio and Capulet and Shylock and all such Shakespearian fathers are as enraged when their daughters slip through their fingers as when their ducats do so; and except for Jessica (whose father, for the Elizabethans, did not count since he was a Jew), those daughters are invariably punished.

It is not easy to answer this objection to the conventional attitude to women revealed in Shakespeare. Shaw is willing to allow that Shakespeare may have partly seen through the convention, as he saw through many others, and concedes that in some moments of insight — as when he depicts woman as the pursuer of man — he has moved quite beyond his age. He was even willing, late in life, to admit that if *As You Like It* actually represents a somewhat cynical compromise with public taste, so does *Arms and the Man.* But these are minor matters. The principal point is that Shakespeare in his treatment of women presents and adheres to an outmoded creed, a social pattern abhorrent to the modern mind. One may argue that he was not, like Shaw, a crusader; that he was an artist who was interested in treating life dramatically, not in changing it; that he could no more be expected to foresee the New

Woman than the Labour Party; that he had to work with life as he found it. But none of these arguments touches Shaw's main contention (which, of course, we may reject), that the drama's function is to celebrate and prepare for man as he ought to be and must become; that, whatever excuses we may make for him, the plain fact is that Shakespeare celebrates man as he ought not to be but is; and that he must therefore give way before the "iconographers of a new religion," as Shaw calls Ibsen and his followers.

As that phrase suggests, ultimately it is against the background of Shaw's religion that we must see his Shakespearian criticism. Our knowledge of that religion may not necessarily lead us to accept his Shakespearian criticism, but it does help us to understand it better. There is no doubt that it provided Shaw with some moments of richly suggestive insight. Perhaps the hint for the most notable of these came from Oscar Wilde, who in 1889 in his essay "The Decay of Lying" had caused his character Vivian to observe:

> "Schopenhauer has analysed the pessimism that characterizes modern thought, but Hamlet invented it. The world has become sad because a puppet was once melancholy."

It was eight years later that Shaw, having seen a Forbes-Robertson production of Shakespeare's tragedy, set down his conception of it and of its main character:

> Hamlet . . . is a man in whom the common personal passions are so superseded by wider and rarer interests, and so discouraged by a degree of critical self-consciousness which makes the practical efficiency of the instinctive man on the lower plane impossible to him, that he finds the duties dictated by conventional revenge and ambition as disagreeable a

burden as commerce is to a poet. Even his instinctive sexual impulses offend his intellect; so that when he meets the woman who excites them he invites her to join him in a bitter and scornful criticism of their joint absurdity, demanding "What should such fellows as I do crawling between heaven and earth?" "Why would'st thou be a breeder of sinners?" and so forth, all of which is so completely beyond the poor girl that she naturally thinks him mad. And, indeed, there is a sense in which Hamlet is insane; for he trips over the mistake which lies on the threshold of intellectual self-consciousness: that of bringing life to utilitarian or Hedonistic tests, thus treating it as a means instead of an end. Because Polonius is "a foolish prating knave," because Rosencrantz and Guildenstern are snobs, he kills them as remorselessly as he might kill a flea, showing that he has no real belief in the superstitious reason which he gives for not killing himself, and in fact anticipating exactly the whole course of the intellectual history of Western Europe until Schopenhauer found the clue that Shakespeare missed.[11]

The interesting implication is that Shakespeare himself did not really know what made *Hamlet* a tragedy, or why the Prince did not get down to business and kill his uncle. Shaw meant no slur on Shakespeare by the suggestion — he had already made a similar one about Ibsen, and in later years was quite content to accept the idea that he himself did not necessarily understand his own plays:

When I am writing a play [he wrote in 1944] I never invent a plot: I let the play write itself and shape itself, which it always does even when up to the last moment I do not foresee the way out. Sometimes I do not see what the play was driving at until quite a long time after I have finished it; and

[11] *Our Theatres in the Nineties*, Vol. III, p. 201.

> even then I may be wrong about it just as any critical third party may.[12]

Indeed, the inference is not that Shakespeare here fell short of an excellence that he ought to have attained, but that he was far ahead of his age, presenting a problem that neither he nor his age could understand or resolve.

As Shaw sees Hamlet, he is caught squarely in a conflict between convention and will. As a Renaissance prince, he has been trained in the conventions of his day — doubtless after the fashion of Castiglione's courtier. He is a scholar with a boundless — but conventional — admiration for the faculty of reason. He is a courtier who idealizes — in the conventional fashion — womanhood and family life. And he is a soldier, with a perfectly conventional belief in the sacredness of order and succession in the kingdom and the necessity of defending his own honor with his sword. In the play, Shakespeare places him in a situation where he is compelled to see that a whole series of the conventions that he has accepted simply do not square with the facts, and that moreover he is called on to act in conformity with a conventional morality — of revenge — which the will in him flatly rejects. Between these two powers, of will on the one hand and convention on the other, his intellect struggles — sometimes suggesting a way out through suicide, which the will rejects; sometimes lashing the will for failure to go through with the business of revenge; sometimes expressing the highest admiration for reason, even when he cannot so much as begin to reason his way out of his dilemma. Indeed Shakespeare has to end his problem eventually by a mere ruse, without solving it. If Hamlet had had any time left for reflection after he killed his uncle, he

[12] *Back to Methuselah,* "Postscript After Twenty-five Years," p. 257.

would have found himself as mystified about the problem of behavior as he was when he exclaimed in exasperation:

> I do not know
> Why yet I live to say "This thing's to do,"
> Sith I have cause, and will, and strength, and means
> To do 't.

Shaw takes the view, then, that Hamlet provides an image of the intellectual dilemma of Western Europe in the seventeenth and eighteenth centuries. In that period the impossibility of squaring with the steadily increasing body of known facts the ancient religious, political, and social conventions became more and more acute. In religion it resulted in Pyrrhonist struggles on the one hand and sectarianism on the other; in social life it resulted in Rakes' Progresses and Utopian experiments; in politics it resulted in the French Revolution. Schopenhauer's "clue" was what he called the Immanent Will — a surging force which, though blind, moves in and through all phenomena, always seeking a full realization of itself in a higher self-consciousness, and perfectly indifferent to any other end. Of course Hamlet must experience bitter conflict within himself. Representing a high point in the striving of the Immanent Will for perfect realization, he could not possibly be bound by convention: he could not kill his uncle in vengeance because the Will would not let him. As Irwin Edman has said, Schopenhauer was

> the first one . . . in the history of thought emphatically to insist on the primacy of will over intellect, on the instrumental character of mind in life and in philosophy.[13]

[13] Introduction to *The Philosophy of Schopenhauer* (New York: Random House, 1928), p. xiv.

His theory of the Immanent Will coloured the thought of many a nineteenth-century writer. But after Darwin had entered the scene with his biological evidence for the development of species and for what Shaw, at least, called the *ascent* of man, the Immanent Will could become the Life Force, which as we have seen seeks realization specifically through the development of ever higher species and particularly of a race of Supermen.

The ultimate reason for Shaw's dissatisfaction with Shakespeare is now clear. It was not merely because his treatment of sex is irresponsible, or his social creed obsolete. However great a genius he was, however vital his presentation of human life, we must not rest with him. Our business, and that of the modern dramatist, must not be with the past but with the future. We must concern ourselves not with Hamlet, who represents a stage of our development, but with the new man that is to come. In the Preface to *The Dark Lady of the Sonnets*, Shaw was to go far towards reconciliation with Shakespeare:

> It was not possible for a man of his power to observe the political and moral conduct of his contemporaries without perceiving that they were incapable of dealing with the problems raised by their own civilization, and that their attempts to carry out the codes of law and to practise the religions offered to them by great prophets and lawgivers were and still are so foolish that we now call for the Superman, virtually a new species, to rescue the world from mismanagement. This is the real sorrow of great men; and in the face of it, the notion that when a great man speaks bitterly or looks melancholy he must be troubled by a disappointment in love seems to me sentimental trifling.

Even this amounts to little more than saying that Shakespeare was a great man who did his best and who was (like other great men) ahead of his time — though he is not ahead of *our* time, and we must look for another.

It becomes clear that — regardless of whether one accepts the validity of the criteria of Creative Evolution in assessing Shakespeare — there is an irreconcilable difference between him and Shaw, and it concerns the essential attitudes that each holds to art, and the ranges of their respective imaginations. If we try to catch it within the bounds of a single phrase, we shall probably have to accept for the purpose some comment like that of Leonardo, that art has only two subjects: man and man's hopes. Shaw, as both critic and artist, is concerned with man's hopes: of physical and moral betterment through social and political change, and of spiritual growth through evolutionary development. Now Shakespeare the man may or may not have been offended by the cruel inequities of Elizabethan England. But it is certain that Shakespeare the artist found in man as he was — courageous and cowardly, modest and proud, humble and ambitious, puzzled and forthright and corrupt — the rich and exciting materials for a world of art that includes things at which Shaw, with his eye on the Superman, can only sniff in contempt. It has room for Pompey and Thersites and Mistress Overdone and Juliet's nurse and Sir John Falstaff, in all of whom Shakespeare delights — not necessarily in their coarseness itself (though perhaps he did), but in that special vitality of which coarseness is for them the natural expression. Shaw, recognizing the rich reality of Falstaff, rejected him with a shudder which the newly crowned Henry V would hardly have equalled. Among Shakespeare's characters, he says, there is

> only one man in them all who believes in life, enjoys life, thinks life worth living, and has a sincere, unrhetorical tear dropped over his deathbed, and that man — Falstaff!

He does not deny for a moment the richness and vitality of Shakespeare's art — its failure is not one of imagination and skill but of responsibility; for in celebrating man, rather than man's hopes, Shakespeare is in effect subscribing to

> the miserable doctrine that life is a mess and that there is no way out of it.

His pairs of lovers are only glamorizing sensuality and degradation; his tragic heroes merely poetize brutality and death; and all of them demonstrate endlessly that as flies to wanton boys are we to the gods: they kill us — or marry us off — for their sport.

Still, it is interesting to note that at least as regards Shakespeare's politics Shaw did a curious about-face. He began by loathing them. His references to them in the *Saturday Review* articles are contemptuous: Shakespeare's politics are detestable, his social views not worthy of the faintest interest of any educated or capable modern person. The attack culminates in a review of *Julius Caesar*,[14] where that play is described as "the most splendidly written political melodrama that we possess," but one in which we see the contemptible

> travestying of a great man as a silly braggart, whilst the pitiful gang of mischief-makers who destroy him are lauded as statesmen and patriots.

Caesar, of course, was one of Shaw's heroes; and when, in 1900, he wrote the preface to his own play about him, he again attacked Shakespeare's portrayal. Which playwright offers the truer picture of a dictator in action, the twentieth century should be able to judge.

At all events, Shaw's opinion of Shakespeare as a political thinker had changed completely by 1910, when he came to

[14] *Our Theatres*, Vol. 3, pp. 297–303.

write the Preface to *The Dark Lady of the Sonnets.* There he fell just short of making his Elizabethan rival an honorary member of the Fabian Society. He rationalized away Shakespeare's supposed contempt for the commonalty by saying that the lines in which it is supposedly revealed are not political sentiments but "merely a record of observed fact." And he defended Shakespeare against the charge that he was a flatterer of the nobility:

> Whoever will read *Lear* and *Measure for Measure* will find stamped on his mind such an appalled sense of the danger of dressing man in a little brief authority, such a merciless stripping of the purple from the "poor, bare forked animal" that calls itself a king and fancies itself a god, that one wonders what was the real nature of the mysterious restraint that kept "Eliza and our James" from teaching Shakespeare to be civil to crowned heads . . . Surely a more mercilessly exposed string of scoundrels never crossed the stage.

We cannot measure the effect of Shaw's Shakespeare criticism — any more than the effect of any other critic's work. It is certain that he was one of the most vigorous and outspoken champions of the movement to rescue the Bard from the Bardolaters and return him to humanity; and that, if he alienated many readers, he stimulated many others to look freshly at Shakespeare — not necessarily with Shavian eyes, but at least with their own. Probably we are his beneficiaries in more ways than we know: how much did the Shavian campaigning of the 1890's contribute to the twentieth century's discovery of *Troilus and Cressida*, which — observes Kenneth Muir —

> from one point of view, in its exposure of "idealism," might be regarded as the quintessence of Ibsenism as interpreted by Shaw?[15]

[15] Kenneth Muir: "Troilus and Cressida," in *Shakespeare Survey 8* (Cambridge University Press, 1955), p. 38.

Like other first-rate criticism, Shaw's is not always right; but it is perceptive, forceful, suggestive, eminently lively and readable, the purposeful expression of a well-informed, honest, enormously energetic mind. And at its core it is religious. There is a divinity in the plays of Shakespeare — a majestic, all-powerful Being, who moves in strange ways, shaping the lives of men sometimes through the stars that govern our condition, sometimes as a providence who watches over the fall of a sparrow. Always he is awesome and mysterious. But this Shakespearian divinity was not satisfactory for the theatre of Shaw; he must have one who inspired not awe and mystery, but confidence and purpose. And he found it in the Life Force. One can fancy him rebuking Shakespeare in New Testament language: "You worship you know not what. I know what I worship." Whether it follows that salvation is of the Shavians is of course another matter.

# 10
# *End and Beginning*

WHEN IN 1889 he gave his lecture on acting "by one who does not believe in it," Shaw was acknowledging a paradox which was closing in on him: that while illusions are in a sense falsehoods, they are also the way to truth. Eventually he was to recognize that men live by their illusions, and his concern became the replacing of prescientific Christian myths with post-Darwinian biological ones. Long before he wrote *Back to Methuselah*, however, or even *Man and Superman*, he had perceived the importance of the arts in modifying our conduct by modifying our illusions, and had become a master of the art which, perhaps more than any other, deals in illusion.

It is surprising that G. K. Chesterton, for whom a paradox was only slightly less important than the Pope, should have failed to notice this paradox in Shaw; even more so, since he began his book about Shaw by discussing him as an Irishman. Chesterton knew well enough how much the English theatre owed to the Irish, especially for comedy: Farquhar, Congreve (not born in Ireland, but brought up there), Goldsmith, Sheridan, Wilde, Shaw, Synge — without them what would English comedy after Shakespeare amount to? Yet why in this particular branch of this particular art have Irishmen shone so splendidly? Beaumarchais, who of all the Continental writers of comedy is nearest to these in spirit, said that he laughed in order not to weep. Perhaps they too, sons of a country whose history was hunger and persecution, created a stage world of laughter because their real world was of tears.

But how real is the real world? When Joseph Conrad, through his spokesman Marlow, observed that "we live, as we dream — alone," he was affirming that every person has his own intuition of reality, that it exists for himself only, and that it is in the long run incommunicable. It was not a new idea, of course. Shakespeare's Prospero, reflecting that we are such stuff as dreams are made on, was stating it too, complicating it by making the dreamer part of his own dream. All the same the individual dreamer, unless he is insane, knows which of his dreams is the one he lives in daily, the one he calls reality, however inconsistent, paradoxical, and incommunicable it may be. Out of all the data that experience proffers to him at any given moment he selects some, imposes on them a more or less satisfying organization, and so makes of them his reality — the dream by which he chooses daily to live. The unselected data he may refuse to contemplate — as a Jehovah's Witness might refuse to read a book on evolution — for fear of his dream being turned into a nightmare; or, if those data sometimes impinge insistently on his consciousness, he finds ways of accommodating them to his dream. How differently, someone has remarked, how differently the same flowers bloom for a gardener, a bride, and an undertaker.

The ordinary man builds and inhabits his dream with little conscious reflection on the process or its significance; he shrugs off its uncertainties, inconsistencies, and paradoxes as best he can; he declines to worry about its incommunicability. There are those, however, who are driven to struggle with their intuitions of reality, to extend and deepen their perceptions, to find in their dream some clue of coherence in which they may be wholly involved. Among them is the artist, who is impelled moreover by a passion to give his dream expression, to communicate it even though it is incommunicable. It is tempting to apply to him Matthew Arnold's phrase about seeing life steadily and seeing it whole. In this fragmented age we are only too well aware that no one ever saw life whole: "God does not allow the whole truth to be told," says Joan, exposing once and for all the silliness of judicial oaths; nor does He allow it to be seen. Yet the artist's concern is with wholeness — as much wholeness as is possible to him — and with coherence, which is perhaps what Arnold meant by steadiness.

It is only as his intuition of reality takes on meaningful coherence that it approaches being communicable. In *Art and Reality* Joyce Cary describes how Tolstoy

> sat impatiently trying to find out exactly what his feeling, his intuition, was.
>
> So all great artists are preoccupied, as if by nature, with reality. They assume, from the beginning, that it is their task to reveal a truth about some permanent and fundamental real.[1]

The meaning that the artist perceives and feels, then, is what gives his intuition vitality and shapes his art. It is Cary's perception of life as a pilgrimage offering the possibility of what he calls grace — that loyalty to the secret inner nature which can redeem the individual, from destruction by custom and official morality as from immorality — which makes possible his gallery of portraits, from Mister Johnson to Thomas Wilcher. As the artist's readers, hearers, or viewers, we may reject the meaning that he has perceived; but the fact is that

[1] Joyce Cary: *Art and Reality* (Cambridge University Press, 1958), p. 85.

without it the work of art would not exist. We may, for example, reject in whole or part Thomas Hardy's intuition of a reality in which Crass Casualty obstructs the sun and moon, and Time plays at dice with men's hopes. We may smile at the sometimes crude devices — all those undelivered letters and just-missed engagements — by which he demonstrates the haplessness of man under the working of chance. All the same, without that intuition he could not have given us the grandeur of Egdon Heath, the unconscious humour of the Cantles, the heroism of Tess, or the silent flight of the dewfall hawk. These are the product of his intuition of reality, an intuition that is moreover not merely an intellectual perception, but a felt one — so profoundly felt that in almost every line of Hardy we sense his peculiar compassionate recognition of the simultaneous dignity and pitifulness of man.

Further, it is primarily the nature of the artist's intuitions that determines his style. If he is a writer, it determines his choice of words and his way of using them. "A man that is born falls into a dream like a man who falls into the sea," says Stein in *Lord Jim;* and Conrad's perception of life as a solitary dream, in which nevertheless the dreamer is impelled to pursue the practical, to act responsibly with his fellows, to observe and judge, is what gives to his prose its characteristic quality of restlessness in repose. No amount of counting his adjectives or analysing his connectives will provide the slightest clue, except in the light of his intuition about life.

It is clear that Shaw came to recognize all this as he worked through his long apprenticeship in letters. He began a projected essay called "From Dickens to Ibsen," in 1889, with the comments that

> the greatest man is the completest man, he whose eyes are as good as his ears, and his head as his hands . . . [and] the

> greatest work is not so much the greatest artistic feat as the greatest lesson, revelation, illuminant . . .[2]

The account that I have given of his critical writings about music and the theatre shows how essential to great art, in his view, was the artist's intuition of reality, and how — given, of course, the technical mastery without which the art is not in any case worth discussing — style is the product of that intuition. "A true original style is never achieved for its own sake," he was to comment in the "Epistle Dedicatory" of *Man and Superman:*

> Effectiveness of assertion is the Alpha and Omega of style. He who has nothing to assert has no style and can have none . . . Your Royal Academician thinks he can get the style of Giotto without Giotto's beliefs, and correct his perspective into the bargain. Your man of letters thinks he can get Bunyan's or Shakespeare's style without Bunyan's conviction or Shakespeare's apprehension, especially if he takes care not to split his infinitives.

In the foregoing chapters I have been trying to show, however, not merely how Shaw came to perceive these matters from the outside, as it were, and to apply them to music and the theatre: that much might have made him a critic, but only a critic. I have tried to show also that if we are to understand and do justice to him as an artist of the theatre, we must take account of the shaping of his dream — his development of an intuition of reality that was not only an intellectually perceived meaning but a profoundly felt one, felt in the blood and felt along the heart. Through his "devil of a childhood" and his impoverished struggle in London, his painstaking study of music and economics, his untiring fight for so-

[2] British Museum, Shaw Ms. 50690, No. 7.

cialism and his compulsive philandering, he came gradually to a coherent hypothesis in which every phase of his experience was meaningfully included. He came to comprehend that individual lives are only aspects of a more mystical *Life*, which is a vast and ageless process of growth in the direction of mind, a pilgrim's progress from matter to spirit, requiring for its accomplishment the greatest freedom; in which the residues of the past continually impede the coming of what is to be, and the commoner human passions are powerful but vestigial nuisances; which offers man the opportunity either to make his own life significant by giving himself courageously to its cause, or to fall to shameful destruction by rejecting it.

The secret of Chesterton's superiority to most other critics of Shaw is simply in the fact that he was the first, and remains one of the few, to see this truth about Shaw and take it seriously: that he had experienced conversion.

> It was just about this time that he began to create not only a pulpit of his own, but a church of his own. It is a very vast and universal religion; and it is not his fault that he is the only member of it—

Chesterton wrote; and again:

> In his latest work, especially in *Man and Superman*, Shaw has become a complete and colossal mystic.[3]

I do not mean to suggest that every artist's intuition of reality comes to him through an essentially religious experience. I do mean that Shaw felt the experience as a religious one. Chesterton's error is in dating it so late—at the time of

[3] G. K. Chesterton: *George Bernard Shaw* (New York: Hill and Wang, 1956), p. 128.

*Caesar and Cleopatra* (1899). All the evidence, as I have been trying to show, suggests that, slow though it was, it was completed when Shaw wrote *Candida* in 1894.

He had at that time written four other plays. The second of these, *The Philanderer*, I have already discussed. It reflects the author's interest in Ibsen, his growing dislike of chicanery, and his concern with his own philandering. The first and third, *Widowers' Houses* and *Mrs. Warren's Profession*, reflect mainly aspects of his socialism. *Widowers' Houses* presents a relentless and hateful picture of the practices of slum landlordism in London and their effects — not on the tenants but on the landlords. It is all the more hateful because recent events have made it clear that the practices it depicted have not, seventy years later, ceased to exist. *Mrs. Warren's Profession* deals with the evils of prostitution — again, not in its effects on those who are usually called its victims, but on the capitalist-managerial class who get rich by it. The fourth play, *Arms and the Man*, gave Shaw his first stage success, though its first production ran at a loss. It is a swift farcical satire on romantic notions about war and love, and on class distinction. "Oh, war! war!" cries the inadvertent hero of the Bulgarian cavalry, near the end of the play, "the dream of patriots and heroes! A fraud, a hollow sham, just like love."

In writing these plays Shaw was of course trying his hand in a medium which hitherto — disregarding his "Passion Play" — he had explored only by way of criticism. He was learning the techniques of the art for himself, which is a different thing from criticizing their practice by others. Nevertheless, although *The Philanderer* is a weak play, the other three certainly are not: they take up significant themes and deal with them through narratives and situations that are lively and for the most part dexterously handled; they have, too, as has *The*

*Philanderer*, unquestionable strength of characterization. Oscar Wilde, at the height of his popularity, wrote to thank Shaw for a copy of *Widower's Houses* and express his admiration for the "horrible flesh and blood of your creatures"; William Archer disliked the plays, yet understood their merits and importance and called the publication of *Plays Unpleasant* "an event, literary and theatrical, of the first magnitude"; Yeats's dismayed recognition of the power of *Arms and the Man* I have already referred to. Further, various subjects that were to be treated in the later plays are adumbrated here; not only such general themes as socialism, but more specific psychological and moral ones. Vivie Warren is faced with the question whether the benevolent use of money that has been iniquitously gained mitigates the initial evil — which Major Barbara was also to wrestle with. In *Arms and the Man* Major Saranoff, coming gradually to self-awareness from his earlier Byronism, foreshadows many a Shavian hero. All four of the plays exhibit that quality of Shaw on which W. H. Auden has commented:[4] the shrewdness of his insight into the relation between character and occupation.

What essentially distinguishes *Candida* and the great plays that follow it from these four is not simply the perfecting of technique or the clarification of themes. It is that in the earlier plays the socialism, anti-romanticism, Ibsenism, and so on exist for themselves alone, are disparate and in a sense constricting. In *Candida* and after, these themes have come under the control of a vision that is large enough to contain them, and can see them from without even when it is presenting them from within. That vision is Shaw's intuition of reality, felt by him

[4] W. H. Auden: "The Fabian Figaro," *The Commonweal* (Oct. 23, 1942). Reprinted in L. Kronenberger, ed.: *George Bernard Shaw: A Critical Survey* (New York: World Publishing Company, 1953).

as coextensive with his experience, fully coherent within the framework of a hypothesis by which he is entirely resolved to stand or fall. In *Candida*, in short, we have entered the world of the mature artist, as distinctive and coherent as the artist's self, with a degree of communicability that is commensurate with his mastery of his medium.

What then are the characteristics of this Shavian world? I suggest that the most important fact about it is that it is a world not of being but of becoming. Its people are not called into existence for the sake of what they are and what they do, but for what they may and ought to be and do. Their actions raise questions of morality, but those actions are not contained within an unchanging moral order that commends the poisoned chalice to the poisoner's own lips and causes rebellion ever to find rebuke. They are creatures of time and destiny, but they are not caught in a Sophoclean cycle where

> Time is awake, the Wheel is turning,
> Lifting up and overthrowing —

and that is all that can be said. They are often creatures of laughter, but what makes them comical is not their extravagant departure from some conventional norm, as in the plays of Molière or Jonson. Shaw's comic figures themselves contain the criteria by which we judge them; indeed, they judge themselves. His world is not permeated by divine unalterable order to which all must return, but by living change in which all must participate.

He is thus, surely, one of the first writers to exemplify fully the plight of modern man, for whom every fact turns out to be a question, and especially of the modern artist, facing the problem of imposing a meaningful permanence on what is constantly shifting. The mutability celebrated by Renaissance poets was yet contained within a cosmic order, and could be caught in controlling images of Fortune's wheel, the tuned spheres, and the like. It remained for the twentieth century to take to existentialism and develop the mobile. Not that Shaw would have had much patience with existentialism. It is perhaps his refusal to allow the grim fact of devouring Time to turn his gay courage into lugubrious stoicism that makes him so irritating to sad-eyed realists who prefer the sweet way to despair. For him, it is not endurance that matters, but challenge; his characteristic theme is not despair but conversion, conversion to fuller self-awareness, clearer perception of the potentialities of the individual's relation to the universe, and more courageous acceptance of the purposes of evolving life. It is true that the great heroes of tragedy, Sophoclean or Shakespearian, also come to self-awareness. Oedipus, Hamlet, Othello, Antony — all have poignant moments of such recognition. Those moments occur, however, as the hero comes in sight of his own destruction, and remembering his past he sees what he has become. The Shavian hero, on the contrary, looks forward. As A. R. Jones has observed in a recent essay,[5] Shaw's typical hero is just about to begin his life as the play ends. This is true even of the martyred Joan:

> WARWICK: I am informed that it is all over, Brother Martin.
> LADVENU (enigmatically): We do not know, my lord. It may have only just begun.

It follows also that the typical Shaw play ends in the major key of challenge and interrogation rather than the minor one of suffering and resignation: not with the agonized cry

[5] "George Bernard Shaw," *Contemporary Theatre* (London: Edward Arnold, 1962), pp. 57–75.

Thou 'lt come no more,
Never, never, never, never, never!

but the exultant call:

> Oh, did you think my courage would never come back? Did you believe that I was a deserter? that I, who have stood in the streets, and taken my people to my heart, and talked of the holiest and greatest things with them, could ever turn back and chatter foolishly to fashionable people in a drawing room? Never, never, never, never: Major Barbara will die with the colors . . . Glory Hallelujah!

If the contrast between Shakespearian tragedy and Shavian comedy seems inappropriate, we need only to turn to the ending of *Twelfth Night* or *The Tempest*, where the note of comic reassurance has such unmistakable overtones of gentle melancholy, to see that the difference between the two worlds remains.

Indeed, the feelings invoked in us by the Shaw world are those appropriate to it. Its creatures, like those of Shakespeare's world, know pain, anger, frustration, triumph, joy, love, hate, pity, envy, greed. But the treatment of them rests not in their creator's compassion, as with Shakespeare's world; for compassion, though it is the most inclusive of the emotions and can extend to Falstaff or Pompey Bum, is yet in a sense terminal: you can feel it for what *is*, but you cannot feel it for what *becomes*. Shaw, creating a world of becoming, fills it in every corner with the high-spirited, demanding note of challenge, and his question is not merely "What are you?" but "What ought you to be?"

He has given us, I suggest, a world that is the clear expression of his intuition of reality. The fact that the basis of the intuition was a Victorian one (tinged, for example, with Victorian ideas about progress) is irrelevant; it is as contemptible and idiotic to sneer at Shaw for being Victorian as to sneer at Shakespeare for being Elizabethan. Nor is the fact that we recognize some of its limitations or reject some of its pretensions greatly significant. Its science may prove to be false, its economics faulty, its sociology wrong — so are Shakespeare's. What matters is that the Shavian world *is* — an intuition of reality coherently perceived and deeply felt, communicated with superlative technical skill. The significant questions have to do with the extent to which the creatures that inhabit it are given meaningful life within it, and how they excite our minds and enlarge our experience by what they say and do.

*Candida* is the first play to present that world. Here is the Reverend James Morell, a vigorous, genial socialist clergyman, surrounded by his establishment — his wife, his secretary, his assistant, his father-in-law. Not one of them sees himself or his world clearly except his wife, Candida, who has the quick, almost intuitive sense of reality that Shaw's best women characters often display. The group almost constitutes a miniature of the Victorian middle class as seen by Shaw. Also, it constitutes a sample of the stuff with which the Life Force is working. Into its midst has come the young Eugene Marchbanks, whom Shaw calls a poet — though surely the label is only an excuse for making him eccentric, wilful, intense, at once intellectually courageous and graceful and physically timid and gauche. He is in a disturbed state, partly because he has been brought up as a protected son of the nobility and has no knowledge of the world into which he has entered, but much more because he has fallen in love with Candida, though she is fifteen years older than he. Morell, stung with jealousy, compels Candida to choose between him and his young rival. As she makes her choice — to remain with her husband — there comes to Marchbanks the sudden moment of recognition. It is a moment of pain — but at once it becomes also one of triumph. The life of the Morell establishment that he has observed — Morell himself, utterly self-satisfied in his readiness to call all men his brothers, his well-meant socialism, his everlasting preaching; the father-in-law, boisterously greedy, wily, suspicious; the secretary, with her self-enslavement and pathetic sexual hero-worship; Morell's assistant, fatuous and ineffectual — is this what is called happiness? "Out, then, into the night with me!" cries Marchbanks, and again, in the ringing voice of the man that he has just become:

> I know the hour when it strikes. I am impatient to do what must be done . . . I no longer desire happiness: life is nobler than that.

The first of many Shavian heroes to do so, he has found himself.

As with many of the other heroes, too, the discovery has been brought about through a woman. Candida is in command of the situation throughout the play, not because of her principles (Shaw once called her "that very immoral female") but because of her freedom from illusions. She gives herself to Morell because she loves him, knowing that because she loves him she must minister to his weakness. She turns away Marchbanks because she does not love him, knowing too that he is strong enough to find his way, though she cannot discern where it leads. Just so the Life Force reaches forward through higher states of individual consciousness to purposes of which it is itself unaware.

Candida, the woman without illusions, can of course exist only in an illusion: the fictional world of comedy.

> And what is all this Life but a kind of comedy [wrote Erasmus], wherein men walk up and down in one another's Disguises, and Act their respective Parts, till the property-man brings 'em back to the Tyring House . . . Thus are all things represented by Counterfeit, and yet without this there were no living.[6]

Shaw had been perfecting his control over a world of illusion in order to convey reality; he had been doing so in another sense as well. More than once he complained of the triteness of Shakespeare's passage about the seven ages of man's acts, in his view a sentimental and superfluous expansion of the view that Erasmus (and many before him) had expressed. Perhaps Shaw found more satisfaction in contemplating a remark of Oscar Wilde's, in a letter to the *Daily Telegraph:*

> For anybody can act. Most people in England do nothing else. To be conventional is to be a comedian. To act a particular part, however, is a very different thing, and a very difficult thing as well.

For he had, a little before he wrote *Candida*, brought to perfection a particular part that he was to play before the world with unfailing skill for fifty years.

A good deal has been said about the figure called "G.B.S.," not a little of it by Shaw himself, for he was well aware of himself as a man on stage, an actor with a mask. Near the end of his life he commented:

> There are many portraits of my reputation, and so few of my real self that without them I should doubt, like Peer Gynt when he peeled the onion, whether I have any real self.[7]

[6] *The Praise of Folly* (trans. H. W. Van Loon).

[7] Sydney Olivier: *Letters and Selected Writings,* Introduction by Shaw (London: George Allen & Unwin, 1948).

In the same place he told how his wife remarked, about one of the portraits of what he took to be his "real self":

> It's not a bit like you: you're always acting.

Had he worn the mask so habitually that he had grown into it? Marcel Marceau, that incomparable mime, has in his repertoire a piece in which he plays the part of a mask-maker who tries on a number of faces that he has designed — sad, merry, thoughtful, bewildered — one after another. As he removes each one, his own face reappears. At last he tries on a mask of comedy, wears it a little too long — and finds that it has stuck. Then behind its fixed smile the body of Marceau describes in silence how at first casually, then urgently, and at last with the fierceness of despair, the mask-maker struggles vainly to find himself again. Oscar Wilde, in the tortured effort at self-appraisal which he composed in Reading Gaol, remarked:

> a man whose desire is to be something separate from himself, to be a Member of Parliament, or a successful grocer, or a prominent solicitor, or a judge, or something equally tedious, invariably succeeds in being what he wants to be. That is his punishment. Those who want a mask have to wear it.[8]

Shaw was at least partly conscious of the dilemma as early as 1901 when he wrote, in answer to the question "What is your honest opinion of G.B.S.?"

> Oh, one of the most successful of my fictions, but getting a bit tiresome, I should think. G.B.S. bores me except when he is saying something that needs saying and can best be said in the G.B.S. manner. G.B.S. is a humbug.[9]

[8] *The Letters of Oscar Wilde*, ed. Rupert Hart-Davis (London: Rupert Hart-Davis, 1962), p. 487.
[9] *Sixteen Self-Sketches*, p. 54.

Throughout the catechism of which that question and answer are only a small part, the G.B.S. voice and manner are constantly present. Shaw had been wearing the mask for fifteen years or more.

Every age is of course an age of public images; and every person wears a mask at least occasionally. Nevertheless, as the reference to Wilde reminds us, Shaw came to maturity as a writer in an age that had more than the usual number of conscious poseurs: one thinks at once of Wilde, Whistler, Beardsley, Lionel Johnson, Max Beerbohm. Discussing this phenomenon with respect to Yeats, Richard Ellman suggests that a "subtle change in mental climate during the nineteenth century" seems to be involved. He contrasts the later posing with the Byronic pretensions of an earlier era and remarks that the Victorian esthetes were unlike the Byronists, who relished the idea of uncontrollable and destructive passion:

> To the esthetes all passion was repugnant. They set up as their hero the man of great sensitivity who was above passion.

Further:

> The implication of the esthetes' conception of the artistic personality is that a man is really two men. There is the insignificant man who is *given*, whether by God, by society, or simply by birth: there is the significant man who is *made* by the first.[10]

Shaw would have been aghast at the thought of being numbered among the esthetes, for whose arty posing and social irresponsibility he expressed his contempt more than once.

[10] Richard Ellman: *Yeats: The Man and the Masks* (New York: Macmillan, 1948), pp. 70–72.

Setting that consideration aside, however, what was the "significant man" who was made by him, the "something separate from himself," like? The development of that persona can be traced in the novels. I have discussed briefly the first four of them; in each, the central figure contains something of the author's developing projection of his wish-fulfilling self. By far the most interesting of these projections, however, is the one contained in the fifth and final novel, *An Unsocial Socialist* (1884). Sidney Trefusis, the hero of that book, is well born, highly intelligent, rich, widely read, unfailingly knowledgeable about the arts, attractive to women, outrageously unconventional yet perfectly self-possessed on every occasion, witty and fluent in speech, fond of a joke but quite above any meanness, highly sensitive but above passion and impervious to sentimentalism or romanticism or any sham, perfectly clear-headed and frightfully wise. He is, in short, very near to being Shaw's "significant" self. Shaw needed only to take Trefusis (minus his wealth, it is true, though even that came later) onto the public platform and play him for all he was worth, adding sparkle and gaiety and a most reckless brashness as his experience grew, to make of him the perfect persona, the perfect mask for himself.

If we ask why he should have done so — why he had to create the "G.B.S." role and play it — we shall find more than one reason. A mask is of course a device of concealment, of protection. For Shaw, the role of the man who was of great sensitivity but above passion could conceal the actor who had from childhood been repelled by the realities of our common flesh. The character who was too well bred to be bothered by questions of manners or class distinction could conceal the actor who was acutely aware of them. The character who spoke with the bold confidence of the expert on almost any subject whatever could conceal the actor who was often enough unsure and timid. The character who was always in the van of new movements in the arts could even sometimes rescue the actor when the latter had missed the boat — as in his treatment of the Impressionists, for example.

Still, a mask is something more than a device of concealment; it is also a device of affirmation. Because G.B.S. protected Shaw in the ways that I have just suggested, it also released him and provided him with a means by which he could express, unhampered by self-consciousness and with the most exuberant energy, his thoughts on any subject under the sun. Moreover, the device was doubly valuable for this purpose, since it caught the attention of the public as nothing else — nothing, at any rate, within Shaw's reach — could have done. Few if any would have listened to Bernard Shaw, but G.B.S. began to conquer audiences everywhere. As I have already remarked, the man who thought himself free of illusions had to turn to the devices of illusion in order to convey his truth.

His doing so through the role of G.B.S. has another aspect. I have spoken of the distinction that he drew between acting as "sham" and as "metaphysical self-realization." I think that unquestionably the latter process was involved in Shaw's playing G.B.S. The persona, the role, was not merely a means by which he could simultaneously protect himself and say what he wanted to say. Even more importantly, it was the means by which he could discover himself, explore his limitations, and eventually accept himself. That intuition of reality which found expression in the world of the Shavian plays — the world of growth and conversion, challenge and effort — would never have become coherent had Shaw not entered the G.B.S. role and so found out the qualities of his own being and pursued its potentialities.

> There is a relation between discipline and the theatrical sense [wrote Yeats, in *Autobiographies*]. If we cannot imagine ourselves as different from what we are and assume that second self, we cannot impose a discipline upon ourselves, though we may accept one from others. Active virtue as distinguished from the passive acceptance of a current code is therefore theatrical, consciously dramatic, the wearing of a mask.[11]

Nor is there any necessary contradiction between Yeats's remark and the one by Wilde which I have quoted; the mask provides simultaneously a limitation and an opportunity.

I have already suggested that as he went on playing the role, Shaw tended more and more to become G.B.S., so that eventually he could not agree even with his wife as to who was his "real" self. In later years the villagers of Ayot St. Lawrence were quite sure — as the neighbourly comments collected by Allan Chappelow indicate[12] — that they knew the "real" Shaw. Whether the gentle, kindly old villager that they describe so pleasantly was any more "real" than the man who contemplated with seeming equanimity Lenin's slaughter of Russian peasants and kept Lenin's photograph beside Gandhi's in his dining room, and assured a desperately worried woman that her husband was better off in one of Stalin's concentration camps than at home with her, is debatable. However, the question as to what is real, which must have been raised in caves that long preceded Plato's and which from start to finish of his career puzzled Shakespeare more than any other, is unlikely to be solved in the present stage of Creative Evolution, though an atomic age may of course put an end to it.

[11] W. B. Yeats: *Autobiographies* (London: Macmillan, 1955), p. 469.

[12] Allan Chappelow: *Shaw the Villager and Human Being* (London: Charles Skilton Ltd., 1961).

In any event, Shavolatry is as distressing as Bardolatry or Marxolatry, and Shaw would be the first to say so. If some of the less pleasing qualities of G.B.S. — the arrogance, the vanity, the egoism, and the callousness which is apt to accompany them — grew in Shaw as he played the role, and were aided by the cosmic sanctions of his religious belief and the more immediate ones of affluence and success, we can hardly be surprised. Our recognition of them is a small enough price to pay for what he gave the world when the genius whose maturing I have attempted to describe came at last to light. Perhaps they were necessary. George Orwell, in a delightful little essay, has listed what he takes to be the reasons why writers write, and the one that he names first is

> Sheer egoism. Desire to seem clever, to be talked about, to be remembered after death, to get your own back on grownups who snubbed you in childhood, etc., etc.[13]

Certainly Shaw never claimed to be perfect, nor was he one to cry over spilt carrot juice or sigh regretfully about unblotted lines. Besides, it is well to remember that his favourite character in fiction was not G.B.S., but Mr. Valiant-for-Truth.

13 "Why I Write," *Collected Essays* (London: Secker and Warburg, 1961), p. 437.

# *Index*